Charles Savage ✳ = Anne Eyres ✳
1696 – 1759 | 1711 – 1795

Anne ✳ | Susannah
1747 – 1794 | 1748 – 1829

Robert Eyres | Ellen ✳
1781 – 1869 | 1782 – 1838

✳ Elizabeth Sophia | ✳ Catherine Mary | Ellen | = Rev Rashleigh Duke
(Sophy) 1815 – 1889 | (Kitty) 1817 – 1892 | 1818 – 1891 | 1818 – 1908

Wilson = Caroline Staunton
?77

Caroline Elizabeth

2 Sons
& 1 Daughter

BURIED AT TACHBROOK

LANDOR

Jean Field

A BIOGRAPHY OF THE WRITER
WALTER SAVAGE LANDOR

PLUS A SELECTION OF HIS WORKS

BREWIN BOOKS

First published by Brewin Books Ltd
Studley, Warwickshire, B80 7LG
in September 2000

The view of St Mary's Church, Warwick which features
on the dust-jacket is taken from "Oken's Passage",
a water-colour by Pamela Colebourn.

ISBN 1 85858 167 2

Typeset in Baskerville by GCS, Leighton Buzzard, Bedfordshire, LU7 7AR
Printed in Great Britain by Alden Press, Osney Mead, Oxford, OX2 0EF

CONTENTS

iii

This book is dedicated to the memory of

Margaret Pamela Colebourn
(artist and writer)

The exceptionally gifted Pamela not only painted the beautiful miniature watercolours which appear on the dust-jacket and frontispiece, but she also gave much help and inspiration to me when this book and several others were in preparation. I will always remember with immense gratitude the sympathy, generosity and deep appreciation of beauty and nature which sprang so readily from her imaginative mind.

PREFACE

My aim in writing this book is to provide an introduction to the life of Landor and his numerous works, almost all of which are now out of print. Unfortunately space permits me to include only a brief selection of his works and those which have been chosen are not necessarily those considered his greatest. When making my selection I chose those pieces which seemed to indicate his humanity in the hope that Landor's sensitivity, his great sense of fun and his great command of style and language would gradually become apparent. Afterwards if any of my readers feel moved to discover more about this great man and his numerous works, then I feel I shall have succeeded in my task.

I HAVE TRIED TO MAKE THIS A BIOGRAPHY WITH A DIFFERENCE IN THAT IT IS NOT ARRANGED CHRONO-LOGICALLY. Apart from the summary of his life, which ideally should be read first, it matters little in which order the chapters are read. THIS IS A DIP-IN AND DIP-AGAIN BIOGRAPHY and readers must make up their own minds as to which aspect of his life they wish to investigate first.

When compiling this biography of Landor I was fortunate enough to have access to numerous documents, deposited in Warwickshire County Record Office in 1965 and 1979. Earlier biographers were given transcripts by members of the Landor family, but this is not at all the same as having free access to a professionally-catalogued, family collection.

An important point, which I would like to stress from the onset, is that in my opinion and in that of some other historians who have specially studied the matter, the name Landor should be pronounced *LARNDER.* Concerning this, I would like to quote from a Warwickshire local history book "The History of Knowle" (The Roundwood Press, Kineton 1972) by the late Eva Wootton. A footnote on page 70 reads,

"In December 1950 Mr E. Woodward Jeffcoat, an Extra-Mural lecturer from the University of Birmingham, gave a short course of lectures on "Some

Warwickshire Worthies," of whom Landor was one. In the course of his studies he visited some of Landor's relatives, then quite elderly, who told him their name was pronounced LARNder, and not LanDOR."

My own experience bears out the truth of this for when I was a child in Whitnash in Warwickshire during the 1940s, the cottages once owned by Landor's brother Henry were known as "Larner's Cottage", surely a corruption of "Larnders"? On old photographs these cottages are clearly titled "Landor's Cottages".

My thanks are due to a number of people who have been extremely helpful to me during my research. I would especially like to thank the Principal Archivist and all the staff at the Warwickshire County Record Office in Warwick and the Local History Librarians of Bath Central Library, Carmarthen Reference Library, Leamington Spa Library, Swansea Reference Library and Warwick Library. The archivists and staff of the National Portrait Gallery Archives in London, the Curator and staff of Tenby Museum, Abergavenny Museum and Swansea Museum, the staff of the Tourist Bureau in Abergavenny and the Chief Archivist and staff of Bath City Record Office and Bristol Record Office also deserve my thanks, as do many other officials, too numerous to list, who have taken great interest in my work. On a personal level I would like to thank family members and friends who have all been very patient. Ian Box, Ena Burton, Rhianna Chinn, Joan Greenwood, Margaret Lang, Margaret Leech, Shirley Reading, Pauline Molnar, Christine Short and Steven Wallsgrove all deserve special thanks, as does Lynn Barber of Whitnash who has acted as chief proof-reader.

David Higham Associates Ltd are to be thanked for permission to publish an extract from "Early Prose Writings" by Dylan Thomas (J.M. Dent 1971) and the Knowle Society for permission to publish a note from "The History of Knowle" by Eva Wootton (Roundwood Press, Kineton 1972). I would also like to thank The New York Public Library, The Henry W. and Albert A. Berg Collection of English and American Literature, Astor, Lenox and Tilden Foundations (for permisssion to include part of a letter by Elizabeth Barrett Browning which appears on page 173); Boston Public Library (for information concerning Kate Field); and Trinity College, Oxford (for information concerning Landor and Rev. George Somers Clarke).

I have made considerable efforts to contact other copyright holders, but any omissions drawn to my attention will be remedied in future editions.

ILLUSTRATION DETAILS AND ACKNOWLEDGEMENTS

Inset One

Landor's Birthplace at Warwick – By permission of Warwickshire County Record Office (C920 LAN Vol 1)

Warwick from the Banks of the Avon – By permission of Warwickshire County Record Office (PV WAR Gen 15)

W.S. Landor in 1804 by George Dance – By courtesy of Bath Central Library

W.S. Landor after Count D'Orsay 1839 – By courtesy of the National Portait Gallery, London

W.S. Landor by William Fisher – By courtesy of the National Portrait Gallery, London

W.S. Landor, a sketch by William Fisher – By courtesy of the National Portrait Gallery, London

W.S. Landor by William Faulkner – By courtesy of the National Portrait Gallery, London

W.S. Landor in 1855 – By courtesy of WCRO and the Landor Society of Warwick

W.S. Landor by Alinari – By courtesy of the National Portrait Gallery, London

Rugby School in 1809 – By permission of Warwickshire County Record Office (B RUG)

Ipsley Court – By permission of Warwickshire County Record Office (CR1908/ 206)

Old Studley Castle – By permission of Warwickshire County Record Office (PH132 /2)

Savage's House, Tachbrook – By permission of Warwickshire County Record Office (CR1908 /306)

Tenby from the North West by Charles Norris – By courtesy of Tenby Museum and Art Gallery

Cliffs at Monkstone – By courtesy of Tenby Museum and Art Gallery

Port and Bay of Swansea in 1792 by Thomas Rothwell – By courtesy
of Swansea Museum Service: Swansea Museum Collection

Briton Ferry and Vernon House by Thomas Rothwell – By courtesy
of the National Library of Wales, Aberystwyth

Laugharne – photographed by Jean Field in 1998

South Parade, Bath by W. Watts 1794 – By courtesy of Bath Central
Library

Drawing of Llanthony pre 1808 – By permission of Warwickshire
County Record Office (CR1908 / 247)

Ruins at Llanthony – photographed by Jean Field in 1997

Robert Southey by Edward Nash 1820 – By courtesy of the National
Portrait Gallery, London

Inset two

Landor's villa in Fiesole – By permission of Warwickshire County
Record Office (C920 Lan)

Gore House 1830 – By courtesy of the Royal Borough of Kensington
& Chelsea Libraries and Arts Service

The Countess of Blessington by Sir Thomas Lawrence –
Reproduced by kind permission of the Trustees of the Wallace
Collection

Shakespeare's Birthplace – By permission of Warwickshire County
Record Office (CR1908/350/1)

Guy's Cliffe House – By permission of Warwickshire County Record
Office (CR351/804)

Guy's Cliffe Chapel – By permission of Warwickshire County
Record Office (CR351/831)

Sydney Gardens, Bath by G. Wise 1820 – By courtesy of Bath
Central Library

Pulteney Bridge, Bath – photographed by Jean Field in 1998

St James Square, Bath by F. Curtis – By courtesy of Bath Central
Library

3 Rivers Street, Bath – photographed by Jean Field in 2000

Widcombe Church, Bath c1837 by J. Holloway – By courtesy of Bath
Central Library

The Whitnash Oak – photographed by Jean Field in 2000

Charles Dickens by Ary Scheffer 1855 – By courtesy of the National
Portrait Gallery, London

Eliza Lynn Linton, photograph by Barraud, c1890 – By courtesy of the National Portrait Gallery, London

A letter written by Landor in Bath – By courtesy of WCRO and the Landor Society of Warwick

Robert Browning by Michele Gordigiani 1858 – By courtesy of the National Portrait Gallery, London

Elizabeth Barrett Browning by Michele Gordigiani 1858 – By courtesy of the National Portrait Gallery, London

John Forster by C.H. Jeens – By courtesy of the National Portrait Gallery, London

Algernon C. Swinburne by the London Stereoscopic Co. – By courtesy of the National Portrait Gallery, London

Bishop's Tachbrook Church – By permission of Warwickshire County Record Office (PH 652/2/50)

Landor's Birthplace, Warwick by Francis Bedford – By courtesy of Birmingham Library Services

The Doorway of Landor's Birthplace on 30th Jan 2000 – by permission of Robert Francis Images

The Memorial to W.S. Landor in St Mary's Church Warwick – photographed by Jean Field in 2000

SUMMARY OF LANDOR'S LIFE

1775	30th Jan	Born in Warwick
1779–1782		Boarding School at Knowle
1783–1791		At Rugby School
1792		At Ashbourne, Derbyshire
1793		Trinity College, Oxford
	Summer	Probably visits Tenby
1794	June	Rusticated from Oxford
	Summer	In Tenby
1795		London, Tenby and Swansea
1796–1801		Mainly in South Wales, sometimes Warwick
1802	Summer	Visits Paris
1803–7		Mainly in Bath
1805	Nov.	Death of his father in Warwick. Inherits
1807	Summer	Visits the Lakes
1808		Sells Rugeley land, buys Llanthony Estate
	Aug–Nov.	Fights in Spain as a volunteer
1809–1810		Mainly in Bath
1811	May	Marries Julia Thuillier
	June	Living at Llanthony
1812		At Llanthony. Charles Betham arrives
1813		Quarrels with Betham. Financial trouble
	Oct.	Leaves Llanthony. At Swansea. Borrows money
1814	April	Sued for libel by Bethams
	Oct.	Arrives in Tours after a spell in Jersey
1815	Oct.	Leaves Tours with wife and brother Robert
1816–1818		In Como. Son Arnold born 1818
1819–1821		Mainly in Pisa. Daughter Julia born 1820
1821–1829		Living in Florence
1822		Son Walter born
1825		Son Charles born
1827		Visits Naples with Lord Blessington
1829		Buys a villa near Fiesole. Death of mother
1832		Visits England. Meets many poets

1833–5	At Villa Gherardesca near Fiesole
1835 April	Leaves wife and children. Then to England
1836	First stay at Gore House. Living in Clifton
1837–1849	Living in St James' Square, Bath
	Annual summer visits to Warwick, Colton etc
1849 March	Moves to 3 Rivers Street, Bath
1853 Aug.	Last visit to Warwick and the Midlands
1854	Sister Elizabeth dies. House in Warwick re–let
1855	Visits the Crystal Palace with Sir W. Napier
1857 Jan.	In court as witness for Yescombes
May	Exchange of letters with Mr Hooper
June	Publishes two pamphlets said to be libellous
July	Settles with the Yescombes
1858 Jan.	Poems "Dry Sticks" published (some libellous?)
March	Suffers a stroke
June	Yescombes issue writ for libel
July	Leaves Bath for the continent
Aug.	Convicted of libel. Returns to family villa
1859 May	Holyoake prints and circulates Landor's defence
July–Oct	At Siena and Florence. Helped by Browning
Nov.	Apartment in Florence with Wilson
1860–4	Living in Florence cared for by Wilson
1864 March	Visit of Swinburne
17th Sept.	Death in Florence

LANDOR'S PUBLICATIONS
(Separately Published Works)
The better known works are marked *

1836 * Pericles and Aspasia 2 vols (American Edition 1839)
Letters of a Conservative
A Satire on Satirists
Terry Hogan, An Eclogue
1837 * The Pentameron and Pentalogia
1839 * Andrea of Hungary and Giovanna of Naples
1840 * Fra Rupert
1846 * The Works of Walter Savage Landor (2 vols)
1847 Poemata et Inscriptiones
* The Hellenics of Walter Savage Landor (new edition, enlarged 1859)
1848 Imaginary Conversation of King Carlo-Alberta and the Duchess Belgioiosa, on the Affairs aand Prospects of Italy
* The Italics of Walter Savage Landor
Carmen ad Heroinam
Savagious Landor Lamartino
1849 Epistola ad Romanos
Epistola ad Pium 1X Pontificem
Statement of Occurrences at Llanbedr
Ad Cossuthum et Bemum
1851 Popery: British and Foreign
On Kossuth's Voyage to America
Tyrannicide
1853 * Imaginary Conversations of Greeks and Romans
* Last Fruit Off an Old Tree
1854 Letters of an American, mainly on Russia and Revolution
1856 Anthony and Octavius. Scenes for the Study
Letter from W.S. Landor to R.W. Emerson
1857 Walter Savage Landor and the Honourable Mrs Yescombe
Mr Landor Threatened (2nd edition 1857)
1858 * Dry Sticks Fagoted by Walter Savage Landor
1859 Mr Landor's Remarks on a Suit preferred against him
1860 Savonarola e Il Priore di San Marco
1862 Letters of a Canadian (no copy known)
1863 * Heroic Idyls
1876 After Landor's death, his works were collected by John Forster in 8 volumes "The Works and Life of Walter Savage Landor"
1891–3 Charles G. Crump published a 10 volume edition

1927–36 "The Complete Works of Walter Savage Landor" in 16 vols was published by Chapman and Hall. This was reprinted in the United States of America in 1969 by Barnes and Noble and in England by Methuen

PREVIOUS BOOKS BY JEAN FIELD

A TOUR OF ST MARGARET'S CHURCH, WHITNASH 1992
SHE DYED ABOUT MIDNIGHT (Warwick) 1992 Brewin Books
BENEATH THE GREAT ELMS (Whitnash) 1993 Brewin Books
KINGS OF WARWICK 1995 Brewin Books
ACORNS, OAKS AND SQUIRRELS 1996 Warwick Preparatory
   School
THE ASH GROVE (Whitnash) 1996 Sunken Bell Productions
THE ILEX AND THE MULBERRY TREE 1997 The King's High
   School for Girls, Warwick

*"LANDOR'S FAVOURITE FLOWERS" A WATERCOLOUR BY PAMELA
COLEBOURN, COMPLETED IN 1998.* Landor was extremely fond of flowers,
especially scented ones, and violets, cyclamen, lilac and mignonette are amongst those depicted
here.

1. FAMILY BACKGROUND
Details of Ancestors and Relatives
from Family Documents

In the reign of George the Third, a young woman was sitting reading a letter in the parlour of a house in High Street in Warwick. It was a fascinating letter, full of gossip and tiny details, so that its recipient read it over and over again, enjoying it afresh each time. The letter had been written by Miss H.G. Stanton in Bucknell, Oxfordshire on 18th June 1772 to Miss Elizabeth Savage, who was thanked for having entertained the writer on a recent visit to Warwick, which in those days was a thriving county town of around five thousand people. The centre of legal affairs and administration for Warwickshire, the town was always busy, although overshadowed by Warwick Castle and to all intents and purposes, ruled by the Earl of Warwick, who almost always managed to control local and parliamentary elections.

Although she was then living permanently in Warwick, Miss Elizabeth Savage's family home was the old manor house, appropriately always known as "Savage's House", in the nearby village of Bishop's Tachbrook, situated around three miles to the south of Warwick. Elizabeth and her three younger sisters had grown up in Tachbrook and, with no male heir, the girls were set to inherit the small estate between them, when their widowed mother died. In addition, their late father's will left provision for each daughter to have one thousand pounds when she married. Elizabeth's younger sister Mary was already married to William Bond of Northampton, but the other sisters had yet to secure suitable husbands. So it was that Elizabeth, at the age of twenty eight, was living in Warwick and "still looking" as the phrase went. H.G. Stanton knew this and in the letter described a suitable young man whom she knew.

"I was wishing the other day to Convey a Young Man to you or your sisters, he is exceedingly handsome, great sensibility and good Nature in his Countenance, very polite in his Manners and Worth fourteen hundred a year.

1

A fine object you Will say for Miss Landor to set her Cap at … his name is Harrison."

Miss Stanton goes on to ask Miss Savage not to talk too much about the young man in case word got back and he became vain!

"My Dear, they (men) *in general are pretty Well supply'd With that ingredient, I would Not for the world increase it."*

Apart from sending her love to Elizabeth's younger unmarried sisters Nancy (Ann aged 25) and Sukey (Susannah aged 24) the delightful letter went on to describe the lambs in the fields and the birds *"tuning their throats"*. The fact that this interesting letter has survived for over 225 years shows how amusing and special Elizabeth Savage found it.

However, perhaps the most interesting thing of all is that within two years of receiving the letter Elizabeth Savage was married, not to Mr Harrison who was described in the letter, but to Dr Walter Landor, the brother of the Miss Landor mentioned in the letter.

The Landors were an old Staffordshire family and as the eldest son Dr Walter Landor was set to inherit various properties near Rugeley which had belonged to the Landors for centuries. Starting as so many of the well-established landed gentry had done with tiny amounts of land, over the centuries advantageous marriage settlements with heiresses from well-endowed families had built up a sizable estate. The Landors had intermarried with the Taylors and the Nobles, and now there was a decent amount of property to be handed down to the eldest son. In addition, the Rectorship of Colton Parish near Rugeley had also come the way of the family and this was a good consolation prize to provide income for the second son. The right to collect the tithes of Colton Parish was usually leased out to the local squire for hundreds of pounds a year, so whoever was Rector had a secure and adequate income, plus a Rectory to live in.

Dr Landor had been well educated at Oxford University and elsewhere and he was much in demand as a physician to the landed gentry in the Warwick area. Although he knew that sooner or later he would inherit a large enough estate to provide a good living he helped swell the family finances until that time came by following a lucrative profession. Many of the Landors had been lawyers and one of his cousins remained in charge of the family law firm in Rugeley.

Dr Landor had arrived in Warwick in 1760, when at the conclusion of his medical training, at the age of twenty seven, he had married Mary Wright, the only surviving daughter of Richard Wright, for long an attorney in the town. Mary was sole heiress to a large amount of land and money which had been amassed by her father and grandfather and prospects for the couple must have seemed excellent. Dr Landor and his wife moved into a sizable house in Sheep Street, (now Northgate Street) close to St Mary's Church in Warwick, but fate was not kind to the couple. In the course of the next eight years five daughters were born, but only the middle daughter, Maria, born in 1764, survived infancy. Mary born in 1761 died in 1764; Charlotte born in 1762 lived only a few months; Martha born in 1765 died in 1766 and Louisa born in 1768, died the day she was born. In September 1769 Mary Wright Landor also died at the age of 38 and was buried in the same vault in St Mary's Church as her four infant daughters. (A commemorative slab can still be seen on the floor, near the far wall of the Regimental Chapel.)

By this time, Dr Landor as a widower with a five year old daughter to bring up, was in need of help and it would appear from the letter sent to Elizabeth Savage in 1772 that it was Mary, his unmarried sister, a year younger than himself, who came to the rescue. In those times, the unmarried females in a family were expected to render domestic help to others in the extended family who were in need. Although their estates were relatively small, the Landors were firmly middle class, landed gentry, and it would have been natural for Dr Landor's sister to come to live in Warwick to help instruct Maria as a young gentlewoman, instead of leaving her education and care to the servants or strangers. That Miss Stanton jokes about the thirty seven year old Miss Landor to Elizabeth Savage suggests that they all knew one another socially and it may well have been that Dr Landor was first introduced to his second wife by his sister.

It was nearly five years after the death of his first wife, that Dr Walter Landor married Elizabeth Savage, on 17th May 1774. Dr Landor's sister Mary died seven months later in December 1774 and one cannot help speculating that perhaps Dr Landor's decision to marry again was precipitated by an illness suffered by his sister. Whatever the reason, this second marriage, solemnised in St Nicholas, the smaller of the two churches in the town, was to prove a marvellous move for Dr Landor whose finances and property, not to mention his family-life, were to have an enormous boost.

The newly-wed Landors were able to move into Eastgate (now Landor) House, a most desirable residence in Smith Street, which had become vacant some time previously and was available to rent from Ann Johnson's Charity. Within 41 weeks of their marriage, on 30th January 1775, Elizabeth provided her husband with a healthy son and heir and as was the custom, the baby was named WALTER, after his father and SAVAGE after his mother's family.

That same year 1775 also saw the births of several other remarkable people including the writer Charles Lamb on 10th February, William Mallord Turner the painter on 23rd April and Jane Austen the novelist on 16th December. Far away, across the Atlantic Ocean, the War of American Independence began, but change was in the air in England too.

At first glance, it seems an odd thing for Dr Landor to rent a house in Warwick when he could have asked his father for a loan to buy some property, but Eastgate House was a truly beautiful property in a prime position. Dr Landor was a trustee of Ann Johnson's Charity which owned the house but far from abusing his position, he spent much of his own money in caring for the place. For the next eighty years there was to be a Landor residing in Eastgate House and all the Landor tenants, first Dr Landor, then his widow, then his eldest daughter loved the house and garden as if they actually did own the property. For around eighty years, the house remained one of the most desirable town houses in Warwick.

Between 1776 and 1782 another three boys and three girls were born to Dr Landor and his wife and all seemed healthy children. As the number of children increased, so also did the family fortunes for in 1781 Dr Landor inherited his father's estates in Staffordshire and in 1786 he inherited Ipsley Court in Warwickshire and later a share in Hughendon Manor in Buckinghamshire. Ipsley Court and the share of Hughendon Manor came his way because John Norris, a wealthy second cousin of Mrs Landor, had no legitimate heirs. Whilst his illegitimate children could inherit money, the estates were entailed and so Dr Landor accepted gratefully.

Both Dr Landor and his wife enjoyed visiting Ipsley Court in West Warwickshire immensely and during the summer they stayed there for long periods. The Jacobean house had been demolished in the 1730s but the two side wings remained and provided good accommodation.

Being an excellent physician, Dr Landor was much in demand and he was often called upon to attend many of the local families of landed gentry. His patients included George Lucy, owner of Charlecote House who regularly "*over loaded his stomach and bowels*" according to one document. Like many others in the late 18th century this bachelor gentleman had to have emetics administered from time to time.

Dr Landor continued to practise medicine until around 1790, when Dr William Lambe arrived in Warwick to take over the practice. Lambe was a very talented doctor with advanced views and although he left Warwick for London early in the nineteenth century, he remained friendly with the Landor family, especially Walter Savage Landor, for the rest of his life.

Although a great scholar and local magistrate, Dr Landor loved his fun and he was a member of "The Rump and Dozen Society" along with his brother-in-law and several other members of the local gentry. Meeting at the "Three Tuns" in Warwick (now the Lord Leycester Hotel) one member would bet a rump of beef to a dozen bottles of port wine with another member that a certain fact was true. On more than one occasion Dr Landor won the wine!

It must have come as no surprise to members of the Landor family that as he grew older, Walter Savage showed signs of independent thought. As a child he might not have known it, but he came from a family with a long and spirited history and many of his ancestors had shown rebellious streaks in their character.

One Walter Landor in the seventeenth century attacked a neighbour who had impounded his cattle. When taken to court, he admitted the offence, but said he struck the plaintiff only once and with good reason!

A previous Robert Landor, young Walter Savage's great-grandfather, had broken his neck in a hunting accident near Rugeley in 1711 and his widow, fearing that the same fate might befall her only son, tried to warn him off all dangerous sports. Happily Robert Landor, Walter Savage's grandfather, grew up gentle and studious and became a lawyer, being admitted to the Middle Temple in 1726 at the age of eighteen. As so often happens with a quiet man, he married a very spirited woman, Mary Noble, who was a member of another old Staffordshire family. Not only did she live to be ninety five years of age, she kept almost all of her own teeth and remained *"mischievous to the last"* according to one of her grandsons! The alliance of the Landors and the Nobles was amusingly described by Elizabeth Landor (Walter Savage's Aunt Betty) many years later. *"It mended the blood but marred the manners"* Aunt Betty said – surely a tribute to the lively antics of Mary Noble.

Mary Noble Landor lived on until Walter Savage was around the age of twenty, but although her husband, the seemingly quiet Robert, died when Walter was six, he too must have had a great influence on his grandson.

Robert Landor was a keen supporter of the Jacobite cause as were several other members of the family, including his cousin Rev. John Taylor who (following his father and grandfather of the same name) was Rector of Colton near Rugeley. After the failure of the Jacobite rebellion in 1746, many trials took place and in 1751 Rev. John Taylor was found guilty at Stafford Assizes of publishing a seditious libel against King George the Second. He spent a couple of years in Stafford Gaol, afterwards complaining that his health suffered for want of exercise whilst in prison.

Obviously Rev. John Taylor and Landor's grandfather Robert, being of a similar age and persuasion, were in constant touch with each other. Both men had been in their thirties in 1745 and both had done much to publicise the Jacobite cause after the defeat in 1746. Amongst the numerous Landor family documents now preserved in Warwickshire County Record Office are verses, some delightfully witty and scurrilous, in support of the Jacobite cause. Many of these verses were said to be in the handwriting of Robert Landor and were almost certainly composed by him. The Hanoverian kings, the Whig party and anti-papists in general were mocked and anyone reading these verses today would wonder no longer why Robert's grandson, young Walter Savage Landor, nearly half a century later was asked to leave Rugby School after writing similarly outspoken verses.

Robert Landor wrote an epigram to be annexed to his Ode for Sept 23rd 1747 about Lords Bagot and Gower who he believed had betrayed their former friends. The epigram ended,

Who then played ye old Farce,
of showing his A- - -
and hiding his damn ugly face.

All Walter Savage Landor did in 1791 when he was sixteen was write typical schoolboy verses about posteriors and the goddess of sewers in impeccable Latin!

Whether or not his grandson ever saw any of Robert's verses, it is remarkable that some of the Jacobite writings were in the form of imaginary dialogues. Many decades later, Walter Savage Landor first achieved worldwide fame for writing a whole series of

"Imaginary Conversations" which may have been originally conceived after hearing about, if not reading, those written by his grandfather. Walter Savage Landor wrote the first three of his Imaginary Conversations in 1797 when he was only twenty two, and this was only sixteen years after the death of his grandfather.

Dr Walter Landor was not exempt from this independent streak running through his family for in 1774, the year of his second marriage, he led an Independent party in Warwick which had sought to break the stranglehold which the Earl of Warwick had on Parliamentary elections in the town. At that time the county town returned two M.P's and, as had been customary, the Earl of Warwick sought to nominate his two brothers. Having very strong Whig (or reforming) principles Dr Landor and his followers actually managed to force an election and they were partially successful in that one of their nominees, Robert Ladbroke, was elected. Critics today may scoff and retort that all sides in eighteenth century elections resorted to bribery and that anyway only the more privileged men were able to vote, but in 1774 there is no doubt that Dr Landor did a brave thing.

Thus it would seem that, in many respects, Walter Savage Landor was following family tradition when he made political criticisms in his early poems and prose works. With the remarkable intellect that he possessed, it was natural that he should use his abilities to comment on all aspects of life as he saw it, whilst still a teenager.

Much has been made by previous biographers of the incident around 1791, which occurred at a time when a French invasion of England following the French Revolution seemed likely. In front of his younger brothers and sisters Walter, then around the age of sixteen, suddenly burst out

"I wish the French would invade England and assist us in hanging George the Third between two such thieves as the Archbishops of Canterbury and York!"

By way of reply his educated and spirited mother promptly went over and boxed her eldest son's ears before walking briskly away. Years later this spirited exchange was still recalled vividly by the younger children who had been quite scared at the time. The Landor family seems to have been anything but dull! When this incident is viewed in context, it might have been that his mother felt that her eldest son was going the way of his ancestors and might land himself in a libel action or even gaol.

With the libellous words which Rev. Taylor published prior to his imprisonment still vivid in the memory because of the consequences, various members of the Landor and Taylor family were extremely worried when young Walter Savage Landor began to publish his poems. Thinly veiled criticism of the establishment and monarchy appeared in various early books of poetry, not to mention a number of personal remarks about clearly recognisable people, such as some Oxford Dons. Exact names may not have been used, but Landor's intention was perfectly obvious.

For the whole of his writing career it seemed that Landor sailed close to the wind and that this became entirely natural to him. It could be said that such satire was in his genes. Maybe this was why many members of his own family despaired of his behaviour from an early age and when he was prosecuted for libel several times in the course of his life, they were not unduly suprised.

In fact he was not the only member of the family to risk imprisonment. Although he was a clergyman, Landor's youngest brother Robert at one stage published savage anonymous letters in daily newspapers. Another brother, Henry, offered to go to gaol in Robert's place should the identity of the writer ever be discovered.

A fascinating glimpse of the life led by the Landors in the 1780s can be gained from a description which Walter wrote much later in his life. One morning in 1786 Sir Robert Lawley and Dr Landor entered the stable block at Canwell Hall, in Staffordshire. Sir Robert Lawley, 5th Baronet, was the owner of the Canwell Hall estate, situated on the site of an ancient priory between Tamworth and Sutton Coldfield, and he and Dr Landor had been friends for many years. They both supported the Whig party and five years previously Sir Robert had stood as godfather to Landor's youngest son Robert. As it was, on this bright morning in 1786, Dr Landor, then aged fifty three and of a florid complexion, was accompanied by his two eldest sons, Walter aged eleven and Charles aged nine, both of whom had ponies of their own lodged in the stables. All four seemed in a good humour and were looking forward to an exciting session of coursing.

"*Landor, how many bottles of port have we drunk together just about here?*" said Lawley pointing to a favoured spot inside the stables. "*Oh, better talk of dozens Sir Robert*" replied Dr Landor with a smile.

"*My father used to say that Robert Landor was AN HONEST DOG FOR A JACOBITE*" and even as he spoke Sir Robert Lawley roared with laughter at some private family joke which had been perpetuated for many years.

Perhaps it was not surprising that with his great liking for port, Dr Landor suffered a great deal from gout in his later years and he died from cancer at the age of 72. His wife Elizabeth Landor, small in stature, but with great spirit, lived to be almost 86 and, so her daughters claimed, could read without the aid of glasses at the age of 84. Walter Savage's maternal grandmother, Ann Savage who was one his sponsors at his baptism, had lived to be 84 and it was said that from her Walter inherited his leonine looks later in life.

In fact few of the females in Walter's family seemed to be meek and mild characters, although in those times women were not allowed to own property in their own right. As a young man Walter was a crack shot with a pistol – the only thing was that his eldest sister Elizabeth was even better than he was! It is said that they used to practise shooting at a piece of tin in the garden of the family house in Warwick. Elizabeth and her younger sisters, Ellen and Mary Ann, were clever women having been well educated, and later in life they endowed an infant school near their home.

As for Walter Savage Landor's three younger brothers, the second son Charles grew up to be one of the three handsomest men in Staffordshire – or so his cousins claimed. He inherited the family living of Colton, near Rugeley, and he was a much-loved Rector there for several decades. Like three of his brothers, Charles was an excellent scholar at Rugby School and Oxford University, but his main interests were said to be hunting shooting and coursing. Yet he was loved by his parishioners for his kindness and respected by all for his high sense of honour and integrity. Charles died at the age of seventy two, but his widow Catherine Wilson Landor had the company of her two unmarried daughters Sophy (Sophia) and Kitty (Catherine) besides her married daughter Ellen and her family. The only son, Charles Wilson Landor, became Rector of a parish in Worcestershire. In later life, these nephews and nieces, especially Sophy and Kitty were very supportive to Walter Savage Landor when he lived alone in Bath.

Walter's next brother, Henry Eyres Landor, was the only son of Dr Landor not to attend Oxford University, perhaps because such education was so expensive, especially with four sons in the family. However Henry seemed happy to become a law clerk, first at the age of fifteen in the family law firm in Rugeley and later in London. In time he became a highly competent lawyer and the best-respected land agent in Warwickshire. He lived almost all of his life in Warwick and nearby Tachbrook and as he grew more wealthy, he bought back much property which had been inherited and sold by Walter or his mother. Dr Landor had always detested the huge feudal power still wielded by the Earl of Warwick in local matters and not long after his father's death in 1805 Henry had the immense satisfaction of turning down the Earl of Warwick who had asked him to be his land agent. Henry had a number of the nobility and landed gentry as his clients and it seems that many of these business contacts had been made whilst the Landor brothers were at Rugby School. A lifelong bachelor Henry eventually bought out other members of the family to own 'Savage's House', the original home of his mother and her ancestors at Tachbrook, and he spent the last decades of his life happily living there. He also became Lord of the Manor of Whitnash where many of his Eyres ancestors had lived.

Henry Eyres Landor died at the age of eighty six, but his youngest brother Robert Eyres lived to be eighty eight. Apart from Walter, Robert was perhaps the cleverest of the family and he won a scholarship from Bromsgrove School to Worcester College, Oxford. Robert was a fine classical scholar and after taking his degree, he became a Fellow of Worcester College. On taking a temporary appointment as Curate of Wyke Regis in Dorset in 1804, Robert had the sad task of burying the younger brother of the poet William Wordsworth when he was lost at sea off Portland Bill.

It was generally supposed to be family influence which had obtained the post of Vicar of St Michael's at Hughendon for Robert Landor and for a time he was also Court Chaplain to the Prince Regent. However he seemed to dislike court life and apparently soon resigned the latter post. Eventually his mother purchased for him the living of Birlingham in Worcestershire and, for the remaining forty years of his life Robert was Rector of the parish, living as Walter once said "*like a Prince bishop*".

Like Henry and especially Walter, Robert was a great art collector, the brothers adding many old masters to their picture collections throughout life. Robert was also a published writer of prose and poetry and many considered the work of the two Landor brothers to be similar in many respects.

As for Maria Landor, she lived with her father and her stepmother in Warwick and when the young Walter Savage was rude or naughty, as he often was in his childhood, she scolded him! In due course, she inherited nearly all her late grandfather's property and money and went to live in Bath. In 1788 Maria married Humphrey Arden, a descendant of the family of Shakespeare's mother, but the couple had no children and by 1809 both were dead.

In many ways the extended Landor family was a truly supportive and united one with the good name of the family being considered all important. On the whole they were a religious family, with duty being placed uppermost in importance. When she was widowed in 1805 at the age of 61, Elizabeth Landor saw to it that each of the younger children had sufficient income to live comfortably and even when her eldest son had made unwise decisions, she did her best to help him out of his difficulties.

The story of the long life of Walter Savage Landor is a fascinating one, not only from his own point of view, but from the viewpoint of members of his family. Obviously he was endowed with healthy genes for a number of his immediate family lived well into their eighties and nineties, but he also seemed to inherit a certain independence of thought. How much was promised to this young Landor heir and what high expectations his parents and grandparents must have had. Had material matters been uppermost in his mind, with his inherited wealth and leadership qualities he might have secured a peerage for the Landor family and have been admired by many. However, as things turned out, the fact that he possessed his paternal grandfather's love of verse and extreme hatred of the Hanoverian kings, his father's early reforming views on politics, his mother's volcanic temper and a tremendous intellect capable of the highest classical scholarship and deepest philosphical thought made him a formidable person and excellent writer. Yet deep down, Walter Savage Landor was an extremely vulnerable character and his spiritual loneliness, great generosity and extreme sensitivity helped to make him a most fascinating figure in English literature.

2. THE EAGERLY-AWAITED HEIR
Landor's first Seventeen Years were Spent
Mainly in Warwickshire

When Walter Savage Landor was born in Eastgate (now Landor) House in Smith Street, Warwick around 3 o'clock in the afternoon of 30th January 1775, never was a healthy baby boy greeted with greater enthusiasm! For decades the Landor and the Savage families had been dreaming of such a moment. Dr Landor took no chances and present at the birth was a fellow physician, Dr Holyoake and Miss Pearson and Mrs Cockbill, probably both experienced midwives.

Walter Savage Landor was privately baptised on the day of his birth, as was the custom at that time in many middle class families. Dr Landor's previous child, Louisa, the last daughter of his first marriage, had died the day she was born in 1768, so a clergyman from the nearby St Nicholas' Church probably visited the house later that same January day to perform the short but important ceremony for the new baby.

Not quite eight weeks later, on March 23rd (according to the next entry in the register of baptisms in St Nicholas Church) Walter Savage Landor was formally *"received into the church"*. A family document states that this public ceremony took place on Sunday February 26th, but whatever the true date, his sponsors were his maternal grandmother Ann Savage and also Dr Landor's old friends John Lloyd and General Powell, who had retired to Warwick after war-service in America.

Without any doubt, the Landor son and heir had been born in a most beautiful house, near to the old East Gate of Warwick. From the brick facade fronting Smith Street, to the stables and other utility rooms adjoining Chapel Street to the side, the L-shaped house was well designed and well appointed. Being over eighty years old and incorporating the remnants of previous dwellings on the site, the whole house was full of character and had innumerable ancient nooks and crannies. Besides eight main bedrooms, a large stone-flagged hall, an imposing staircase and several reception rooms with fine oak panelling, there was an old brewhouse, a dairy, a hen house and a pigsty besides plenty of spare rooms in which to house servants and child-nurseries. In short the house had what estate agents would call "considerable charm and flexible accommodation".

From 1692 when Eastgate House had been partially rebuilt, the dwelling had almost always been the residence of one of the leading physicians in Warwick. This pleased Dr Landor, who felt this fact might enhance his medical practice.

However the age of the house and the fact that it belonged to Ann Johnson's Charity meant that quite a lot of work needed to be done to smarten the place up and modernise it. The same charity owned two fifteenth-century cottages which adjoined the house, but these were let independently to much poorer families. Although Dr Landor was a trustee of the Charity for many years (when he took up residence in Eastgate House he was Secretary) it seems that over the years, he paid for many repairs himself and only asked the charity to contribute perhaps half the amount. Originally set up in 1733 to benefit the poor and needy of Warwick, in the forty years of its existence, the charity had been of great assistance to many people. However its income was limited to the rents of the few properties it owned, so the scale of the help it could provide was very limited.

One thing Elizabeth Landor was delighted about was that the garden of the house was large and like the house, had much potential. Over decades, the garden had been enlarged until it occupied around one and a half acres and a variety of large trees, including elms, cedars and chestnuts provided a scenic frame for the tower of St Mary's Church not far away. Near the house there were a number of established mulberry trees, fig trees and vines and an old summer house was tucked away in a secluded corner. Nightingales could often be heard in the garden, besides a whole host of other birds including robins and blackbirds.

A small and energetic woman, herself brought up in the nearby village of Bishop's Tachbrook, Elizabeth Landor soon set about her task of organising the house. She was intelligent and very kind, but even she was pushed almost to breaking point when babies arrived almost every year.

After the first year or so, the young and capable Mary Perry was engaged as a live-in children's nurse. With four other servants to help with the meals and general housework, things were manageable, but it was still a very tiring life. By the summer of 1782 with six children under the age of eight and another on the way, Elizabeth Landor felt weary with the constant demands on her time and energy. Walter Savage Landor had been born on 30th January 1775, Elizabeth Savage on May 8th 1776, Charles Savage on May 7th 1777, Mary Anne on June 23rd 1778, Henry Eyres on January 23rd 1780 and Robert Eyres on May 10th 1781. All were thriving, healthy children and she was expecting another in mid-September.

In May 1782, an old friend of Mrs Landor's called at Eastgate House together with her own daughter aged six or seven. After looking at Warwick Castle, Mrs Butt and her daughter Mary arrived at Eastgate House where domestic affairs were not running too smoothly.

"*When we arrived at the Doctor's house, we were ushered into the parlour where Mrs Larnder received us very cordially; but before the fire – for there were fires all that summer – lay her eldest son Walter, a big boy with rough hair. He was stretched on the carpet and on his mother admonishing him to get up, he answered 'I won't' or 'I shan't'. She reproved him and he bade her hold her tongue. From that day this youth became the prototype in my mind of all that was vulgar and disobedient ... I saw also other specimens in this same family of a thoroughly undisciplined household. Walter had a sister about my age, and she was summoned to do the honours of her playroom to me. She took me upstairs, and whilst showing me her dolls she said 'I am glad you came today, for you have saved me from a good scolding, my mother is so much out of humour.' And in truth the poor lady, though exceedingly civil and hospitable was in such a perpetual fume, that her husband, a hearty, old-fashioned sort of man, a physician of the by-gone days, kept constantly saying to her at dinner, 'Come Betty, keep your temper; do, Betty, keep your temper'.*"

This account of the visit was written many years afterwards by Mary Butt, by then Mrs Sherwood and author of many moral tales for children. It is true that the picture painted of the Landor family is not a very flattering one and yet it is a very one-sided view. From the same book of her reminiscences, we learn that Mary Butt was the daughter of a very strict clergyman in Worcestershire and that from the age of six she was forced to learn her lessons strapped into a kind of iron collar, with backboards fixed over the shoulders. She was fed very plain food, in the main only dry bread and cold milk. Small wonder then that she found the more relaxed atmosphere of the Landor household undisciplined!

On that day in May 1782 Walter Landor was seven years of age and he was home on holiday from his boarding school. As soon as he was able to leave the nursery, he had been dressed as a young gentleman in breeches, waistcoat, jacket and frilled shirt and had been sent to a boarding school in the village of Knowle, around eight miles from Warwick. He was only four and half when thus banished from his home, except in the holidays.

In after years, Walter spoke little about this first school, but one incident concerning Mr Thomas Treherne, the schoolmaster, stood out clearly in his mind. Over 40 years later he wrote to his sister Ellen,

"I remember when I went to Knowle an old woman coming from Balsal-Temple to ... Treherne for a guinea, which he paid her yearly. She was one hundred and two when I was four and a half; so that it is in the range of possibility that she might have seen people who had seen not only Milton, but Shakespeare, Bacon, Spenser and Raleigh."

It will have become obvious from the description by Mary Butt that the Landor household was a place where hypocrisy did not flourish and the repression which was the order of the day in many other late eighteenth century households did not exist. In the late eighteenth century many women and children were forced to do as the male head of the houshold dictated, but a far more modern and open atmosphere seemed to pervade the Landor household. Although a typical man of his time and a very highly respected magistrate in Warwickshire, Dr Landor himself had been trying to modernise local government for decades and reforming politics were often given voice in his house. None of the children were harshly disciplined, indeed one might say that in many ways Walter and his siblings were indulged by their parents and other relatives. There was much talk of honour and duty, but the children, especially Walter, were left to absorb life as they saw it and were not afraid to speak their minds.

Mary Perry, the children's nurse, was a tower of strength and she was loved and respected by her charges, especially Walter and Robert. Like many other such substitute mothers, she kept in touch with the Landor children for the rest of her life.

Fond as he was of Eastgate House and his small, but snug bedroom with its old oak panelling and deep closet beside the fireplace, perhaps Landor's favourite place in the days of his childhood was his mother's old home in the nearby village of Tachbrook. Savage's House, as it had always been known, was a large, rambling, sixteenth century house not far from the church. With its front windows then overlooking a village street, the delightful house had a view over fields towards the picturesque Highdown Clump at the back. This ancient mound was topped with trees and there was always much local speculation as to its origins. The brook from which the village took its name was just a field away from Savage's House and in all probability it was there that young Landor learned the legendary fishing skills which were to last him a lifetime.

His grandmother, Ann Savage, who was one of his godparents, lived in this old Manor House together with her unmarried daughters Ann and Susannah until they both married in 1780 when Walter was aged five. One of his earliest and happiest memories was of walking in the garden of Savage's House at Tachbrook.

"Dear old Tachbrooke! … Well do I remember it from my third or fourth year; and the red filberts at the top of the garden, and the apricots from the barn wall and Aunt Nancy cracking the stones for me."

Around the time of his eighth birthday in January 1783, Landor was sent to Rugby School. It was not in his nature to submit to the teasing of older boys and when they laughed at him for being small and weak, he fought them! His first fight was against a bigger boy named Arthur Clifton, who had entered the school at the same time as he had. Arthur Clifton was the son of Sir Gervase Clifton of Clifton Hall near Nottingham and in later life he entered the army and went on to become a general. Unfortunately even on this occasion early in life, Clifton showed great fighting ability and Landor lost. He also lost when he fought a slightly older boy who entered Rugby in 1786 and who was the brother of one of the masters. On this occasion Landor had to admit that Walter Birch *"thrashed me well"* but as so often on occasions when two worthy opponents have fought hard, the two combatants then became life-long friends.

In the late 18th Century, such spontaneous, often lengthy fights amongst the juniors were not discouraged at Rugby and a few of the senior boys generally appointed themselves as organisers and referees. All the other eleven fights which Landor had were victories and because he commanded respect in this way, his rather odd views in other directions were tolerated by his fellow pupils.

His skill as a fisherman with a casting net was well-known and he had even caught pike in this way. Apart from fish which he often referred to in later life as *"the enemy,"* Landor loved all living creatures and plants and was one of the few boys in Rugby School who had never robbed a bird's nest. He once pulled a boy's ears for throwing stones at the rooks in the school close and he heartily disapproved of the usual bloodthirsty field sports, then beloved by the landed-gentry, including his father. At that time, most of the older boys at Rugby borrowed horses and regularly followed organised hunts, but Walter Landor did not.

He played cricket and football quite well and enjoyed fencing, but he was not keen on riding or dancing. This last was a most necessary skill for a gentleman, but he, being fond of long walks and more robust exercise, never did acquire much skill in that direction.

The headmaster, Dr James, was far from being liberal minded, and Landor was flogged at least once for falling asleep in a lesson. However Dr James stressed the idea of governing by principles of justice and what he called *"The Eternal Rule of Right and Wrong."* This sense of justice and fair play was to colour Landor's thinking for the rest of his life.

One of the books in the Junior Library was the recently published "Sandford and Merton" and this volume, which extolled the virtues of philanthropy and a simple way of living, made a big impression on Landor when he was a young pupil. He was always reading the book until teasing made him give it up, but a collection of readable stories such as 'Androcles and the Lion', with a linking moral narrative by Thomas Day, really fired his imagination.

As for Landor's own library, when still quite young he bought his very first books from the stall of an old woman in Rugby market. The books were Sir Richard Baker's "Chronicle of the Kings of England" and Michael Drayton's "Polyolbion", the most famous work of the Warwickshire poet. Later Landor bought a tiny edition of Catullus, Tibullus and Propertius.

As regards his studies, Landor had a fine brain but this was not always apparent in his early days at Rugby School. Well over seventy five years later Landor described his early school days in a letter to Robert Browning.

"He (Browning's son) *is quick at learning, I never was. Some idle thought always dropt in between me and my book, and I often had to learn*

again what I had learnt a few minutes before. Had it not been for my resolution to get beyond a cousin a year older, I should have been a dunce. I jockied him by learning in bed not only my lesson, but seven or eight words in the Dictionary. Before I was nine I had gained a remove, and before I was ten another, a third at thirteen."

The cousin a year older was William Venour, the son of Dr Landor's sister Catherine, who had married John Venour of Kingsmead, Wellesbourne in 1766. The Landors and the Venours saw much of each other and remained friendly all their lives.

From 1787 Landor's private tutor (for which his father had to pay extra) was Rev.Sleath, a man he respected and liked very much. Both Landor and a boy named Samuel Butler (the grandfather of the writer of "Erewon") were considered excellent classical scholars and on occasions Dr James would grant a half holiday to the entire school if either of them, or indeed any other boy, had completed an exercise worthy of such an honour. Several times Landor did in fact win a holiday for the other pupils by completing excellent Latin verses and his reputation at those times was enormous. Whilst at Rugby School Landor read the Port Royal Grammar twice and Ainsworth's Latin Dictionary once! In those days the education was almost all classical and prowess at Latin was the main requirement.

Two anecdotes about Landor's time at Rugby were related by Charles Reade, the father of the nineteenth century novelist. On both occasions it would appear that cheekiness and cleverness helped to manoeuvre Landor into a winning position against his headmaster.

" One day in full school, Master Landor had an apple of singular size and beauty. He had his Livy in one hand and this apple in the other and he read and read, and munched and munched, till the sound struck the Doctor. He espied the delinquent and ordered him to bring the apple to him. He put it on his desk ...and then, half relenting said "There, sir. Now if you want that again you had better sit down and make me a short line on the occasion. "Oh, I can do that and stand here" says Master Landor. "Do it then". The boy thought for a moment and soon obliged with a pentameter. 'Esuriens doctor dulcia poma rapit'. "Hum" said Doctor James "And pray sir what do you mean by E-sur-riens doctor?" "The gormandizing doctor". "Take it sir, you are too hard for me, you are too hard for me" said the Doctor delighted with his pupil."

On another occasion related by Charles Reade, the other boys asked Landor to try to win a half holiday from the headmaster by writing Latin verses. Landor duly obliged. In Rugby School at that time were seven boys named Hill and so Landor likened Rugby to the city of Rome reputedly built on seven hills. When the headmaster read the verses he said "*I don't ask you who wrote this for there is only one of you with the brains to do it. Half holiday? Yes.*"

However when he was in the upper school Landor incurred the displeasure of the headmaster several times, not least when as a praepostor or monitor he refused to call the sons of peers "Mister" when calling out the register. Feeling that the instruction, which had been copied from current practice at Eton School, was wrong, Landor refused point-blank to carry out the order. On several other occasions he made quick retorts and pert remarks to the headmaster, who began to recognise that a battle of wills was developing.

However, the younger, weaker boys were quick to realise that in Walter Landor they had a champion. In later life he recalled his treatment of the younger boys and he claimed to be the first to pay his fags.

"*Poor little Blacky Howard had three or four bottles of water to fill at the pump in a hard frost and was crying bitterly. I took pity on him and made him my fag at three pence a week I think. But this exempted him from obedience to others and I seldom exercised my vested rights.*"

At Rugby School at that time, a system of merit money was in operation and from time to time a shilling would be awarded for the best Latin verses. On one occasion when Landor was awarded a shilling he earned much admiration by calling "*Here Blacky*" and tossing the money to his fag. The headmaster then retorted that Landor had the pride of the devil and the impudence of he didn't know what!

By the time Walter Landor was a senior pupil his brothers Charles and Henry had followed him to Rugby School and Henry recalled many years later how Walter had threatened another boy who had ill-used him and also how he had given him his last shilling, leaving himself with no pocket money for a time. A slightly older boy, Fleetwood Parkhurst, of Ripple Court near Malvern, also had cause to thank Walter Landor and he became a firm friend.

In 1786 when Dr Landor inherited Ipsley Court in Warwickshire the lives of the Landor family must have been altered considerably for it meant that they had a large country retreat away from the County Town. In July 1786 Dr Landor had been sent a letter by

Thomas Douglas, one of the executors of the will of wealthy John Norris, a second cousin of Mrs Landor, inviting him to be present when the will was read after the funeral in London. The meeting was to be held at the house in Queen's Square, Bloomsbury, of Mr Keysell, another of the executors. Presumably it was from this meeting that contacts with the younger members of the Norris family began. Certainly in the years that followed, Charles Norris (1779–1858) who afterwards achieved fame as a painter in Tenby, became well known to the Landor family in Warwick as did his older sister Miss Elizabeth Norris. Elizabeth, John and Charles Norris were the illegitimate children of their wealthy father and although he was able to leave them his name and money, the estate at Ispley was entailed on a legitimate heir.

Walter's cousin, Sophia Venour, an older sister of William, had married John Shuckburgh of Bourton Hall in 1788 and she requested that Landor should write some verses for her. However fifteen year old Walter was not at all sure that the verses he had written for Sophy "To a Lady Lately Married" were appropriate and he asked Miss Norris then staying at Eastgate House to give her opinion. Being of a similar age to Sophy, Miss Norris would know whether or not they were suitable. Like many youths, Landor had a horror of being ridiculed and he preferred to check reaction beforehand.

Happily Miss Norris did like the verses which she thought "*exceedingly pretty*" and on 23rd September 1790 she wrote to him at Rugby School from his parents' house in Warwick. She began by wondering why he should hesitate for a moment to present the verses to Sophy and she passed on messages from his parents. Mrs Landor desired her love to him and hoped he had received her letter and some pigeons she had sent for him and his brothers. Dr Landor sent his respects.

Miss Norris then went on,

"*I cannot help admiring your way of employing your leisure … I think you are much in the right to make the most learned your friends and companions; but permit me to say, that though I think a proper spirit commendable and even necessary at times, yet, in my opinion, it is better to submit sometimes to those under whose authority we are, even when we think they are in fault, than to run the risk of being esteemed arrogant and self-sufficient.*"

What Miss Norris was referring to was Landor's attitude towards his headmaster Dr James. Everyone from his tutor Rev. Sleath to family and friends in in Warwick felt that Landor was wrong over the matter of refusing the order to call the sons of peers 'mister' but there were other things which he had done to anger his headmaster. Landor had sometimes felt slighted because he thought that the headmaster did not give him sufficient credit for his Latin verses and when he did give him credit, he singled out the worst ones for praise. There was a considerable amount of jealousy between Landor and Samuel Butler, with the latter on the whole gaining the greater credit, perhaps because he was quieter and less outspoken.

There can be no doubt that Landor was a most difficult boy to handle at school. He was extremely intelligent, but had few close friends. Walter Birch was about his closest friend and, like many such, was the exact opposite in temperament. Landor commented later "*At school Birch was named 'Sancty' from the sobriety of his manners; how different from mine*" but there is no doubt that Landor respected him a great deal.

On many occasions Landor and Birch would go for long country walks together and a favourite outing was to Bilton. Here they saw the estate once owned by Addison, where his only daughter, then quite old, lived still. Landor was already extremely fond of trees and on Addison's estate were some very fine and unusual trees. The row of Spanish oaks was reputed to be the first ever planted in England for Addison's friend Craggs had brought back the seed.

Long before he left Rugby Landor had written more verses and also had fallen in love for the first time! On a walk with Birch, Landor had been smitten with love for a girl he met purely by chance and for the first time he experienced palpitations of the heart, trembling knees and stammering tongue.

Henry Carey, later the well-known translator of Dante, was another school-friend of Landor and his home was at Sutton near Birmingham. When the time came for them to enter university, they both were students of the same college.

Fleetwood Parkhurst too remained a loyal friend and on many occasions Landor stayed at Ripple Court, near Malvern, in the holidays and Fleetwood's father, Parkhurst Senior, became very fond of Landor. In 1788 Maria Landor, Walter's half sister, married Humphrey Arden who had been a young ensign in the British Army, alongside the elder Parkhurst, in Canada during the War of American Independence a few years previously. When at Ripple Court, Landor became fond of Fleetwood Junior's sister Fanny, who, although still a child, would listen intently when he read stories and would chase about and climb gates with him.

The friendships and acquaintances made at public school provided very important contacts and later in life Landor's brother Henry, who became a lawyer and land agent was to act as agent for Lord Digby of Coleshill, a relative of whose was in Walter's year at school.

In after years Walter Landor was to look back on his childhood and teenage years with great nostalgia. Despite some disagreements, the Landor family was a united one and they often entertained the Venours, the Wades, the Welds and the Cliffords at Warwick and later at Ipsley Court. The family home of the Venours was at Kingsmead, Wellesbourne and in later years Landor was to remember Sophia, Mary Ann, and William Venour in particular as they were only a few years older than he was. Walter's aunt Susannah Savage had married Charles Gregory Wade in October 1780 at St Mary's Church, Warwick. Mrs Wade and her husband had two boys Charles and Arthur who were several years younger than Ellen, the youngest of the Landor children. The Wades lived on the South side of High Street and Mr Wade was Mayor of Warwick from 1786–7 and again from 1792–9. This last period of Wade's rule was highly controversial because elections for new Aldermen were suspended, thus ensuring a continuation of the High Tory regime.

Cousin Sophia and John Shuckburgh lived at Bourton Hall, in Bourton on Dunsmore and it is highly likely that the Landor family knew this house. A typical school holiday for Landor meant time spent with family and friends in several large houses and country estates. From Eastgate House in Warwick he might go to Ripple Court near Malvern to stay with the Parkhursts, or to Ipsley Court with his parents where he would visit friends at Studley Castle daily.

In 1791 Walter Birch left Rugby School and was matriculated at Magdalen College Oxford on 12th June. This left Landor with no restraining influence when he lost his temper, which he did quite frequently.

For some time in the latter part of 1791 the headmaster had felt that Walter was becoming impudent and things came to a head over an unlikely act. When Dr James asked Walter to copy some of his Latin verses into the official album, Walter added a line in faultless Latin that these were the worst of all the bad verses that Landor ever wrote. He followed this up on a later occasion with a couple of verses, again in faultless Latin, demonstrating typical school boy humour about the goddess of sewers and posteriors.

Many years later Walter explained the circumstances of his departure from Rugby School, which took place in December 1791.

"He (Dr James, the Headmaster) *certainly hated me for my squibs and had also threatened to expel me for never calling Will Hill 'Mister'; I having told him I would never call Hill or any other 'Mister' unless I might call the rest so. At last he wrote to my father that I was rebellious and incited others to rebellion and unless he took me away he should be obliged (much to his sorrow) to expel me. As I was within five of the head, and too young for Oxford, I was placed under a private tutor and matriculated at seventeen."*

The private tutor to whom Landor was sent was the Rev. William Langley, Rector of Fenny Bentley, near Ashbourne in Derbyshire. Landor took up residence early in 1792 and remained there for most of that year.

Amongst the Landor papers in Warwickshire County Record Office is a printed map of the area round Ashbourne which may date back to the time when Landor was resident there. From the map it could be observed that Fenny Bentley was a small village to the north of Ashbourne, surrounded by hills and woods. Since Landor loved country walking and beautiful trees, it could be assumed that this environment was much to his liking and that he often enjoyed the aspect of Bentley Wood, Basset Wood or Tissington Wood.

Proof if any were ever needed that Landor found his time at Ashbourne profitable came years later when he included Mr Langley in one of his "Imaginary Conversations"; that between Walton, Cotton and Oldways, published in 1829. In a footnote to this conversation Landor added,

"I pay this tribute to my worthy old tutor, Mr. Langley, of Ashbourne, under whose tuition I passed a year between Rugby and Oxford. He would take only one private pupil and never had but me. The kindness of him and his wife to me was parental. They died nearly together; about five and twenty years ago."

The Imaginary Conversation itself largely centres on fishing, a subject dear to Landor's heart, but one paragraph seems to describe typical Landor behaviour in Ashbourne. Mr Oldways gives a lengthy explanation to Isaac Walton in answer to his query as to why tulips and other flowers were growing out of the turf, and we obtain a delightful picture of "Leaping Landor" at this time!

"The garden was once divided by borders: a young gentleman, my private

pupil, was fond of leaping: his heels ruined my choicest flowers, ten or twenty at a time. I remonstrated: he patted me on the shoulder, and said, "My dear Mr Oldways, in these borders if you miss a flower you are uneasy; now if the whole garden were in turf, you would be delighted to discover one. Turf it then, and leave the flowers to grow or not to grow, as may happen." I mentioned it to my wife. "Suppose we do," said she. It was done; and the boy's remark, I have found by experience, is true."

Landor's studies seemed to progress extremely well in Ashbourne and the clergyman, who had once met Pope in Oxford, fired his pupil's enthusiasm for poetry and the classics.

In November 1792 Landor was matriculated at Trinity College Oxford when he and his father paid a short visit. On November 13th Landor was admitted as a commoner at Trinity and he paid his caution money of £20, then returning to Warwick for a month or so, until he took up residence in Oxford.

A poem, published many years later, paints an amusing picture of that Christmas of 1792, spent in Warwick. Even pre-Dickens and pre-greetings card, Christmas was still an important time for parties and for decorating the house with evergreens. The exuberant Walter Landor, did more leaping and tried to impress a girl in Eastgate House by reaching a sprig of holly for her from the ceiling. An early poem of his A HEAVY FALL (dated Christmas Day 1792) ends,

> I lept to snatch it from the ceiling;
> It hung too high … so tottering, reeling,
> A headlong fall I could not check,
> But fell outright upon her neck.

Lucinda, the young lady in question, had already slapped Landor's hand before his leap. What she thought of his fall was not recorded, but hardly surprisingly, the romance came to nothing!

3. STUDENT LIFE IN OXFORD
Resident 1793 to 1795.
Rustication for a Silly Prank

Although his eldest son was not entering Worcester, the college where he himself had been a student, Dr Walter Landor must have been delighted when his clever and outspoken heir had another chance to show his studious qualities. Having matriculated the previous November, Walter Savage Landor took up residence in Trinity College, Oxford at the end of January 1793, but he could hardly have chosen a more disturbed period in European history to begin his studies. On 21st January 1793 the Revolutionaries in France executed King Louis XV1 and almost all in Britain were extremely shocked when they learned of it. On 1st February, France declared war on Britain and the Netherlands, and public opinion in Britain turned very much against the Jacobins, as the extreme radicals were known in France.

However, many of the young, especially idealistic thinkers and writers, were still broadly in support of the French and Landor was amongst this number. Dr Landor had long since lost sympathy with the French Revolution and so had most of the former Whig supporters and politicians, but young Walter Savage was inclined to despise those who had turned against reform. In many countries of Europe, social, parliamentary and financial reforms were urgently needed, but the violence of the French Revolution scared those in other countries, who then became more repressive. This is what happened in England and William Pitt as Prime Minister embraced Tory ideas which he had previously denounced. Unlike many, Landor was never one to bend in the wind and throughout his time in Oxford he let it be known that he still embraced the ideas of the extreme revolutionaries.

From the onset Walter showed his individuality in Oxford. Although Rev. George Somers Clarke, one of the tutors at Trinity, was under the impression that Landor was going to lodge with him, in fact he took rooms in the college, probably above the Hall.

Rev. Clarke was quite sympathetic to Landor, but obviously the young man had far more freedom with rooms of his own.

Unlike every other student, Landor refused to wear his hair powdered, as was the custom of the time, preferring instead to have it in a small queue, tied back with a black ribbon. In actual fact shorter, unpowdered hair was the coming trend in London as the effects of the French Revolution were felt, but acceptance of this fashion was a few years away. Walter's tutor at Trinity, Dr Benwell, warned him that if he walked about Oxford with unpowdered hair, he was likely to be taken for a Republican, in favour of the French Revolution and as such stoned by a mob. Not only did Landor have the reputation of being a Jacobin, but he was deemed a 'mad Jacobin', because of his great enthusiasm for the revolutionary cause. The poet Robert Southey, who in after years became a great friend of Landor, did not seek his friendship in Oxford for this reason, although he shared many of his political ideas and became a student in the same year. Southey later wore his hair unpowdered and it was not long before other students copied their example.

There were many in Oxford at that time who thought that Landor was arrogant. Although some of his essays and Latin verses were excellent, he would never allow any of them to be entered for any of the prizes or competitions which were important in the University at that time. However such critics did not understand that many creative people find it difficult to accept failure and criticism of any sort and Landor was one of these people. If he did not enter, he could not lose, and so his faith in his own abilities could not be dented. Unless forced into things, people who are very unsure of themselves only fight battles they know they can win and Landor preferred not to have his poetic abilities put to the test.

Landor's special friend from Rugby School, Walter Birch, although a student at Magdalen, was often in Landor's company, as was Fleetwood Parkhurst, another friend who came to Trinity the following year. The two Walters, Landor and Birch, often walked together around Addison's Walk, near Magdalen College, or sculled together on the Isis. Despite there having been a swimming place on the river at Rugby School, Landor could not swim and sculling thus gave him a great sense of danger and excitement.

At Magdalen, Birch was a fellow student of John Norris, Landor's wealthy distant cousin, and no doubt Landor met Norris frequently. Not being able to travel abroad on account of the war with France, as young men had done in previous times, it is believed that Landor first visited Tenby in Pembrokeshire in Norris's company in the summer of 1793. Birch may have gone as well, for at that time Tenby had become very fashionable with the upper and middle classes.

All seemed to go well for Landor in Oxford during 1793 but 1794 proved to be a most difficult year. In early May came the news of the death of Aunt Nancy, his mother's sister of whom he had fond memories. She had been married to Godolphin Burslem in 1780 and although 47 year old Ann had died in Leicestershire, her body was brought back to Tachbrook for burial. Naturally his mother and grandmother and the rest of the family were greatly saddened, as was Landor when he heard the news.

Then, quite out of the blue, came the end of Landor's studies in Oxford. The episode in June 1794 which led to his rustication is best described in his own words. A few months afterwards, he wrote this account to Walter Birch.

"In the morning I had been (rabbit) shooting; in the evening I invited a party to wine. In the room opposite there lived a man universally laughed at and despised; but I must tell you why he was so – for we are naturally sorry for such people, and are careful not to increase their misfortunes. ...he was continually intruding himself where his company was not wanted; and hearing others talking of hunting and other diversions, always joined the conversation, and often mistook a laugh for an applause. For the very jokes that were passed on him gratified him highly, and puffed him up with an idea of his own consequence. ... (We called him Duke of Leeds.)

Well it unfortunately happened that he lived opposite to me and that he had a party on the same day consisting of servitors and raffs of every description. The weather was warm and the windows were open: the consequence was that those who were in my room began rowing those in his, who very soon retorted. All this time I was only a spectator; for I should have blushed to have had any conversation with them, particularly out of a window. But my gun was lying on another table in the room and I had in my back closet some little shot. I proposed, as they had closed the casements and as the shutters were on the outside, to fire a volley. It was thought a good trick and accordingly I went into my bedroom and fired. Soon the President sent up a servant to inform me that Mr Leeds had complained of a gun being fired from the room where I entertained my company, but he could not tell by whom; so that he insisted on knowing from me, and making me liable to the punishment."

Landor refused to confess but in the end was forced to admit the exact circumstances of what had ocurred. He was deeply ashamed and wrote to Walter Birch that the reason he had not confessed straight away was that he did not want to irritate his father "*with whom I was already on the most indifferent terms. I hardly doubted a moment . For tho my father had really shown me as much unkindness as was in his power, I was resolved if possible not to give him any further cause of complaint.*"

What Landor did not say in this letter to his friend was that politics may well have played some part in the row between the two groups. Leeds was a well known holder of Tory principles and Landor was one of the most radical students in Oxford. Also the friends whom Landor was entertaining that fateful evening were all likely to be young men in similar circumstances to himself. Many of the heirs of country landowners went to Trinity College, for example Fleetwood Parkhurst, but the other student, Mr Leeds, although wealthy, came from Hackney to the east of London. Landor very rarely went shooting, but on this occasion he appears to have wanted to impress his peers.

Thus ended Landor's career at Oxford in June 1794. He was rusticated for two terms, but the President said he hoped he would return after that, when the affair would be quite forgotten. His rooms were kept on and although the President had no option but to punish him, he said he trusted that father and son would be better reconciled in Warwick.

Landor said afterwards that his tutor, Dr Benwell, shed tears when the punishment was announced and there is no doubt that Walter had a great deal of respect for this learned man, ten years older than himself. Some of the other tutors however were not respected in the same way and came in for some unkind criticism in Landor's first book of poems.

The President of Trinity wrote a letter to Dr Landor, explaining the situation, but this was to no avail for Landor did not resume his studies when his period of suspension was up. By that time, Landor had had a serious quarrel with his father and had gone temporarily to live in London.

When his first book of poems was published in early 1795 some copies were sold in Oxford and although some unkind remarks had been made about him, the Rev. George Somers Clarke sent Landor a very friendly letter.

Of the unkind references, for example,

Alas chaotic is the dark,
Twixt C – and K –, and K – and C –

in the poem "To Dr Warton" Clarke wrote generously,

"But these little things promote the sale of the copies in the University, so that booksellers here are at present out of a supply."

The "K" reference which Landor made was to the Rev.Henry Kett, another of the Fellows at Trinity. Landor did not like or admire Kett and made a number of unkind references to him in the early poems.

Sadly despite Clarke's optimistic remark, few copies (perhaps less than fifty) were sold anywhere and the publishers lost money, as Landor could not afford to pay them the thirty five pounds which they had spent on printing costs. Eventually the bill was paid, but from that time forth, Landor was under no illusions that sales of his work would be easy to achieve. It may well have been that in Oxford some of the satire it contained was thought to be undeserved and in poor taste.

One might have expected that Landor would dislike Oxford after leaving Trinity in such circumstances, but in fact it was quite the reverse. In after years, he often visited his brothers Charles and Robert when they were students at Worcester College, and he continued to visit Robert when he became a Fellow of Worcester. On one of his visits Walter and Robert Landor worked together on some Latin poems and there seems little doubt that both brothers felt entirely at home in the academic atmosphere. From time to time in his later life, Landor passed through or paid brief visits to the city, but when he had sons of his own, they did not receive a formal school and university education. In fact when his eldest son was small, Landor joked to Southey in 1819,

"There are three places which my son shall never have my consent to enter: gaming-houses, brothels and colleges."

Perhaps Landor felt like getting his own back against an institution which had punished him! The other two venues were meant to be treated more seriously for he was known to dislike gambling and also brothels. In a letter to a friend, W.L. Bowles, in 1820, concerning Queen Caroline in Como, Landor wrote

"I and my friends habitually call her Di Grey – the name of the most celebrated strumpet of our Oxford days."

Today if one visits Trinity College, there are still some places Landor would have known and enjoyed, although many areas have been extensively renovated. The magnificent chapel, built in 1691–4, with its carvings by Grinling Gibbons and ceiling painting by Pierre Berchet, is recognised to be a masterpiece of English baroque and without realising it, Landor may well have been influenced by its classical beauty. Also it is possible to view the Hall and quadrangle across which nineteen year-old Walter Savage Landor once fired a fowling piece, as a prank to amuse his friends and in so doing, disturbed the evening prayers in the nearby chapel.

4. LATER VISITS TO THE MIDLANDS
Landor Maintained Contact with
Warwickshire all His Life

Walter Savage Landor was always very proud that he hailed from the same county as Shakespeare. Whether he realised it or not, the soft undulating countryside, the wooded views and the numerous willow-edged streams were to have a great effect on his outlook on life. In later life, one of his great sadnesses was that his children were not able to grow up amongst the beautiful trees and quiet fishing rivers he had known as a boy.

In Landor's time, 'Leafy Warwickshire', as it came to be known, was so well wooded that there was a tradition that a squirrel might cross the county without ever having to descend to ground level and a love of the majestic elms, oaks and other trees seems to be common to many writers in the county. As for Landor, the elms, chestnuts and cedars in the garden at Warwick and the numerous woods which he knew as a boy, gave him a love of trees which lasted all his life.

This early love of trees was aptly demonstrated by a letter he wrote to Robert Southey later in his life. Landor described a "*little privet I had planted when I was about six years old, and which I considered the next of kin to me after my mother and elder sister … whenever I returned from school or college, for the attachment was not stifled in that sink, I felt something like uneasiness till I had seen and measured it.*"

When Landor was born in Warwick in 1775 the old order of things still prevailed in the county town, much as it had done for centuries. However massive change was on the way and in 1779, the old church of St Nicholas, which was in a bad state of repair, was taken down and rebuilt (apart from the tower). This marked the beginning of a general refurbishment and rebuilding programme in South Warwick, round the family home. Nine years after the rebuilding of the church, Eastgate was recased in stone in 1788 and then in 1790 came a tremendous road and bridge building scheme, when a new bridge over the Avon was built, a widened road up Castle Hill was constructed and a new entrance to the Castle cut through opposite to

St Nicholas' Church. Much of the cost of the new bridge was borne by the Earl of Warwick who was then allowed to enlarge his park, taking in some areas previously in the town. The changes that were happening in Warwick were typical of those occurring in other places, yet in many ways the young, romantic Landor regretted the wind of change which blew in the Industrial Revolution and destroyed the picturesque countryside.

Once Landor had left Rugby School in the December of 1791, from then onwards he was only in Warwickshire for parts of the year. After Dr Landor inherited Ipsley Court near Redditch in 1786, some rebuilding took place there too. In a letter to John Forster in 1852, Landor described Ipsley Court, situated in West Warwickshire. (Ipsley is now part of the urban district of the modern Worcestershire town of Redditch).

"Ipsley Court was purchased by Samuel Savage early in the last century, with some farms and a park. He never resided there; and his steward, the rector of the parish, took down the noble old house, leaving only the two wings, one of which my father inhabited, adding a dining room of thirty feet or more. The whole length exceeds ninety. The opposite wing contains offices, stables, coach-houses etc. These wings were added in the time of Charles the Second. Nothing can be less architectural. The views are extensive, rich and beautiful."

Dr Landor and his family spent much time at Ipsley, especially during the summer months. One glance at the eighteenth century sketch of Ipsley Court on a document in the Landor collection in Warwickshire County Record Office will illustrate what Landor meant when he said the place had no architectural beauty. However today, heavily restored and rebuilt, Ipsley Court forms the attractive and unusual home of the Law Society and nearby Ipsley Church has undergone various refurbishment programmes to enable it to serve the needs of a modern parish. As to the extensive views which Landor and his family enjoyed, surprisingly some can still be seen today. If one crosses the road from Ipsley Court and enters Arrow Valley Park, lovely views to the south towards Studley and Alcester still exist and a walk beside the brook can still be enjoyed.

Each day if in residence at Ipsley Court with the family, Landor would walk out beside the brook in the direction of Studley. He described this scene very well in a short poem which remained unpublished until after his death.

I hope in vain to see again
Ipsley's peninsular domain.
In youth 'twas there I used to scare
A whirring bird or scampering hare,
And leave my book within a nook
Where alders lean above the brook,
To walk beyond the third mill-pond,
And meet a maiden fair and fond
Expecting me beneath a tree
Of shade for two but not for three.
Ah! my old yew, far out of view,
Why must I bid you both adieu.

The old yew may have been the one still standing close to Studley
Church and the girl he referred to may have been Dorothy Lyttelton.
Born in the same year as Landor, Dorothy lived with her uncles at
old Studley Castle, which was close to Studley Church. Landor later
recalled,
  "*It was soon 'Walter and Dorothea'; her uncles too called me Walter, and
liked me heartily ...*"
The timber-framed Studley Castle, built in Elizabethan times on
the site of a previous moated castle, is still almost as isolated and
beautiful as it was in Landor's time. Both Ipsley and Studley
were within a few miles of Ragley Hall, the seat of the Marquis of
Hertford and in the mid 1790s Lady Hertford said that Dorothy was
the most lovely and graceful creature she had ever known. Whilst it
was obvious that Walter liked Dorothy enormously as a friend, he
felt that he could not ask her to marry him. Years later Landor
said,
  "*I should have married this lovely girl if I had been independent. My future
property was equal to hers, my expectancies greater. But, having nothing, I
would not ask the hand of one to whom something would be given by her
uncle, who loved me heartily.*"
  At that time, Landor had no income except that which his father
allowed him and in any case Dorothy was destined to marry Francis
Holyoake, the wealthy landowner of the neighbouring estate at
Morton Bagot, who had banking interests in Wolverhampton. It is
said that all the Landor brothers loved Dorothy, but on her side, any
attachment seems to have been merely platonic.
  In late 1794, after spending a year and a half at Oxford University,

Landor returned to Warwick following his usual summer stay in South Wales. Shortly before Christmas, a terrible row broke out between Dr Landor and his eldest son, which resulted in the younger man banging out of the house "for ever". In mid 1794 Landor had been rusticated from Oxford University for two terms and the row may have been over this. Certainly the nineteen year old writer and his sixty year old father did not seem to understand each other at all.

Landor took lodgings in Beaumont Street, Portland Place, London and early in 1795 he approached the firm of Cadell and Davies to publish his first book "The Poems of Walter Savage Landor". Landor was unsettled and by April 1795 he had announced his intention of travelling to Italy.

It was at this stage that several of his Warwickshire friends decided to try to help. Dorothy Lyttelton wrote to him at some length trying to persuade him not to go abroad, for England was at war and travelling was unsafe. Dorothy was very friendly with Landor's eldest sister Elizabeth and in the early part of 1795 had been staying at Warwick with the Landors. Elizabeth was quite distraught over the family quarrel and Dorothy wrote and appealed to Landor not to ignore his favourite sister. Dorothy also said that her uncles were more than willing to act as intermediaries between Walter and his father, so keen were they to help the situation.

Several letters were exchanged in the first few months of 1795, but on 17th April Dorothy married Francis Holyoake who was, according to Landor "*the most vulgar man alive*". Perhaps Landor's hostility was on account of the man's wealth and, being a banker, his apparent preoccupation with money. One of the last things Landor ever sent to Dorothy was an advance copy of his collection of poems, plus some manuscript verses written especially for her. Dorothy actually wrote her last letter to Landor on the very eve of her marriage and she thanked him for the poems which she had sat up all night reading.

Landor kept Dorothy's letters all his life and in retrospect it was extremely sad that he had not been able to marry her for on the face of things they seemed made for each other. As things turned out, she had several children including Francis Lyttelton Holyoake, born in 1797 who went on to be M.P. for Stafford and High Sheriff of Warwickshire and was created a baronet. (Between 1834 and 1837 he had the building today known as Studley Castle constructed a short distance away from his mother's childhood home.) Sadly, Dorothy herself died in 1811 which was the very year that Landor eventually married a much younger, penniless woman.

In 1795, during that very difficult year, another very familiar Warwickshire person wrote to Landor to try to persuade him not to go abroad. His old nurse Mary (usually called Molly) Perry wrote to him in the August of 1795 sending her letter to the Pembrokeshire resort of Tenby, where he was spending the summer. Mrs Bird, as she then was, had been married not long before and Landor had sent her a wedding gift, as no doubt had the other family members. She wrote to thank Walter but began with a heart-rending request.

"*Honred Sir,*

May Health and Happiness attend you, and may I Live to see you at the Head of that Family who, next to a Husband, as my Best Affections. I hope the providence of God will direct you in Every thing, but O Sir, I hope you will Never go a Broad. My hart shuders at the thout of your Leaving England Lest I shud see you no more."

Like Dorothy's letters, this emotive note was kept by Landor for the rest of his life. As with some other long-established servants, the Landor family kept in touch with Mary Bird for the rest of her life and many years later, Landor's sister Elizabeth was still making regular visits to her old nurse.

Other friends also tried to help the Landor family during 1795. General Powell, Landor's godfather, had tried to interest him in accepting a commission in the army, either with the Warwickshire Militia or elsewhere. On hearing of the plan, it is said that other young commissioned officers in Warwick declared that if Walter Landor was given a commission, they would resign theirs! Landor's version of this story was that General Powell "*out of kindness to my father, an old friend, ... told him he would give me a commission in the army if I would abstain from sporting my republican opinions. My reply was 'No man shall ever tie my tongue; many thanks to the general'.*"

Quite what Landor and his father had quarrelled about will never be known, but with the large outgoings caused by the education of four sons, it was not inconceivable that Dr Landor had cash-flow problems. It would have been a considerable aid to the family finances had Landor accepted the commission, which may have been why it was later extended to Charles the second son, who also rejected it because he was destined to be the next Rector of the family living at Colton. Landor's reply was typical of his stance throughout his life.

Eventually, perhaps due to the intervention of Dorothy Lyttelton's uncles, after a period of some months, Landor gave up all thoughts of living abroad and he and his father were reconciled. It was agreed that the twenty year old writer could have one hundred and fifty pounds per year (his younger brothers one hundred pounds a year) so that he could live independently wherever he chose. When his money was gone, he was welcome to come back and live with the family in Warwick. The only proviso was that since he refused to earn his living by adopting a profession, when he inherited his estates he must make up to his younger brothers and sisters the amount of money by which he had depleted his parents' savings.

There was at this time in Warwickshire yet another person who offered Landor a place in his home, as he had done several times before, but his offer too was rejected. Dr Parr, the internationally-known scholar and Curate of Hatton, just four miles from Warwick, liked Landor very much and did all he could to encourage him.

Dr Samuel Parr, often nicknamed 'The Whig Dr Johnson', was a kindly man who had once taught at Harrow and had then been head of two other smaller schools. In 1786, when he was thirty nine and Landor aged eleven, he had settled in Hatton, having been given the living by Lady Trafford, the grateful mother of one of his former pupils. Whilst at Hatton Dr Parr took a few clever pupils as live-in students, but he was also an excellent parish priest, doing all he could to help his needy parishioners. A keen bell-ringer and habitual smoker of a long clay pipe, his lisp and pompous way of talking often detracted attention from his enormous classical knowledge and understanding of reforming Whig politics.

Perhaps Landor first met Dr Parr when he came to talk at Rugby School or perhaps Dr Landor and his wife invited him to dinner. Throughout his teens, Landor was often at Hatton where he sometimes dined. Dr Parr had two daughters, Sarah who was a couple of years older than Landor and Catherine who was seven years younger. Mrs Parr was a clever, shrewd woman but not always sympathetic to her husband, although in company the couple put on a brave face. Sarah was extremely clever and her father doted on her, but she saddened him greatly in 1797 by eloping at the age of twenty four to Gretna Green with John Wynne, an eighteen year pupil of her father's. However the marriage was not a success and more often than not in the next few years, Sarah Wynne was to be found at Hatton where her father paid her living expenses and those of her several children.

The Parr household was anything but boring and when Landor visited he never quite knew who would be dining there. Dr Parr was so famous in intellectual circles that many scholars and admirers of his radical politics went out of their way to call upon him and in the summer months he travelled around England, often dining on the high tables of various colleges at Oxford and Cambridge Universities.

Landor said of Parr,

"My first exercises in argument and eloquence were under his eye and guidance, corrected by his admonition anad animated by his applause. His house, his library, his heart were always open to me; and amongst my few friendships, of which indeed, partly by fortune, partly by choice, I have certainly had fewer than any man, I shall remember him to the last hour of existence with tender gratitude."

Whenever Landor did return to Warwickshire one of the first people he visited was Dr Parr who seemed to admire the younger man's rebellious independence. The two did not always agree, especially concerning poetry, but both respected the other's views. When questioned in later years, Robert Landor, who did not admire Parr and had once written an anonymous lampoon about him, thought that the two *"were kept from quarrels by mutual respect, by something like awe of each other's temper, and a knowledge that, if war began at all, it must be to the knife."*

In December 1797 Landor made sure that he was back in Warwickshire when the controversial matter of Income Tax was first dreamed up by William Pitt. In Warwick, as elsewhere, there were demonstrations against the proposals and naturally Landor and Parr were against, for they were both still in favour of the French Revolution and totally against the idea of the English fighting the French. Since the war with Napoleon (whom they both admired) was the reason for the tax, they both did all they could to help the opposition, many of whom were landowners who did not want their pockets to be hit. Landor prepared an address which he wanted to give to the meeting in Warwick, but the organisers felt that he was too much of a young hot-head and they would not allow it. So Landor published the address instead and *"To the Burgesses of Warwick"*, an eight-page pamphlet, remains as one of his rare political pieces.

It was not considered seemly for Dr Parr, as a cleric, to become too involved in politics and he was often forced to do his campaigning through others. It may well have been that he hoped Landor would take to a career in politics or become a political writer, thus giving voice to many of his ideas. However, once again, Landor decided against this and went his own way.

In the spring of 1798 Landor had his first long poem printed in Warwick by Henry Sharpe, the experienced local printer, book binder, bookseller and publisher who had sympathy with many of the Whig principles advocated by Parr. Whilst "Gebir" was being printed, Landor was staying at Ipsley and Sharpe had a terrible time trying to decipher papers sent piecemeal in almost illegible handwriting. Eventually the tiny book was published anonymously with plain grey covers and today it is a rare collectors' item. Dr Parr of course was delighted to receive a copy of the first edition of "Gebir". On his copy (now in the Bodleian Library) Parr wrote,

"By Walter Landor, my most ingenious friend, and the admirer of my dear daughter Sarah Wynne."

It was during this period in the last years of the 18th century that Landor's politics became a great embarrassment to his family in Warwick. His mother's sister Susannah was married to Charles Gregory Wade, a high Tory who held the office of Mayor of Warwick and controlled much of the local finance from 1792 to 1799. There were some at the time and very many later who believed that Wade's regime was corrupt and illegal and in the end it was the Earl of Warwick who threatened in 1799 to take Wade to the Court of Chancery if he did not stand down.

Throughout Landor's student days, there was another person on the Warwick scene who became very friendly with the aspiring writer and also Dr Parr. Dr William Lambe had come to Warwick in 1790 to take over the medical practice of Landor's father. In 1794 he had married a local girl, Harriet Welch, and Landor became very friendly with the couple.

William Lambe was an extremely clever young doctor, but many of his views were considered controversial. Having had early problems with his own health, he had devised unusual diets which he passed on to his patients. He was a vegetarian and drank only distilled water, thinking (correctly) that well and river water could potentially be a source of much illness.

It was on account of his preoccupation with water that Dr Lambe left a lasting impression on the history of Leamington. In 1797 he was one of the first people ever to analyse and publicise the properties of the mineral water which was found in certain springs in the Leamington area. In "The Transactions of the Philosophical Society of Manchester" Lambe outlined his findings which were that the presence of iron in the Leamington water might bring about curative effects similar to those at Cheltenham. The fact that Lambe was a well-qualified, well-known physician caused the Leamington Spa waters to increase dramatically in popularity.

It may well have been William Lambe's influence which persuaded young Landor to avoid tobacco and excess alcohol throughout his life. Most of the landed gentry at that time drank a great deal and many writers and intellectuals of the late 18th and early 19th centuries smoked or took opium, usually in the form of laudanum. The fact that Landor did none of these, although he sometimes enjoyed a few glasses of fine wine, is possibly down to family influence, re-inforced by the unusual ideas of William Lambe.

Landor mentioned in later life that he often thought of new poems whilst cleaning his teeth and these good habits, formed in his youth, bore fruit. Unusually for those times, like his paternal grandmother, he kept almost all of his strong white teeth until well into his old age. The fact that Landor was the eldest son of a well-qualified, practising physician seems to have given him a greater knowledge and interest in health matters throughout his life.

Although Landor himself apparently caught a mild version of smallpox when he was a baby, his brothers and sisters had been inoculated in 1782 by an early risky method. Infected pus from another smallpox victim was rubbed into a scratch on the child's arm and in theory at least, this brought on a mild form of the disease. Apart from himself, Ellen, the youngest of Landor's sisters, was the only one of the family to catch smallpox because she had not been inoculated at the same time as the others.

By the time Landor had his own children, a much better system of vaccination was possible – that pioneered by Edward Jenner. Landor developed strong views on the subject declaring in a letter to his sister Ellen in 1825, "*In my opinion every child ought to be inoculated with the vaccine at three months by order of the magistrates, and every parent who resists it to be imprisoned for a year ...*"

Perhaps Ellen had been scarred by smallpox herself? In 1853, just as he had advocated, smallpox vaccination was made compulsory in England. (How delighted Landor would have been in 1979 when world-wide mass vaccination eventually brought about the end of the smallpox scourge for ever.)

In 1803 William Lambe left Warwick and set up a practice in London. Sadly the following year his wife and baby daughter died suddenly of scarlet fever and Landor, being in Bath, first read the melancholy news in a newspaper. He was appalled to learn of the loss of his Warwick friend Harriet and immediately wrote to Dr Parr,

"Poor Lambe! Poor Lambe! Poor little Elizabeth and her mother, now indeed divine, what hours we have passed together ... Her image rises up everywhere before me. I sicken at the sight of beauty. Did she not treat me as a brother? Did she ever call me by more than one name? The sound of Walter was the sweetest of sounds. Pardon me, I will acknowledge it, she made me think myself a virtuous and great man. Certainly I never left her company, but what I was more happy and more deserving of happiness."

In later years, Lambe and Landor corresponded occasionally – Lambe treating both Shelley and Keats, besides many more influential people. He came to be remembered by many for telling John Keats to live abroad – in fact passing sentence of death upon him in 1820. In an age when the paths of many intellectual people seemed to cross, William Lambe touched the lives of many of Landor's friends and acquaintances. Like Landor, Lambe was a great walker and despite his original physical weaknesses which included extremely short sight, he lived to the age of 82, dying in 1847.

Lambe and Landor had often visited Dr Parr together, sometimes in the company of a barrister friend named Rough. Parr however welcomed Landor whether in other company or not and a delightful story is told of him when Landor arrived home unexpectedly.

On that occasion Dr Parr had a large number to dinner at Hatton and when one of the diners who had travelled a long distance related how Landor had suddenly arrived home (probably on the same coach) Parr said impatiently *"Eat your dinner, eat your dinner"*. As soon as the table cloth had been removed he said *"Drink your wine, my friends, drink your wine; I must go and see Walter Landor."* Parr then rushed out and immediately rode to Warwick, where he spent an hour with Landor, but he would not even take a cup of tea, for his own guests were waiting. In after years Landor used to laugh and boast that he was the only man who could have made Dr Parr ride half a dozen miles *"with his dinner in his mouth and his pipe out of it."*

Sometimes when Landor was home in Warwick, he visited

Leamington, which in 1801 was only a small village with a population of 315. This was less than many other villages in the near vicinity and thousands less than Warwick which had a population of over 5,550 in 1801. There was still a duckpond in High Sreet in Leamington and elm trees where the Parade now stands. Landor once wrote to Southey, explaining how he nearly inherited much of Leamington.

"I remember the time ... when Leamington had only two tenements that joined each other, and in the whole village only six or seven of any sort, besides the squire's, one Prew, who was the uncle of my grandmother. If her brother had lived, he would have had this vast property, at that time a small one. I cannot help smiling at the narrow escape I have had of three such encumbrances."

The fact that Landor was not often in Warwickshire in the first few years of the nineteenth century did not prevent him having sharp and often sad reminders of his home town. He was often in Bath or Clifton during the years 1802 to 1805, but in 1803 came news of the death of one of his cousins during the wars with Napoleon.

William Venour, the slightly older cousin from Wellesbourne, who had helped Landor through the first few difficult months at Rugby School in 1783, had taken up a career in the Royal Navy when he left school. He had been to the Naval Academy in Portsmouth and Dr Landor's old friend, Admiral Vincent, who often visited Eastgate House and dined with the family, had patronised him. William Venour had been made a lieutenant in the Navy at the age of sixteen and by the age of twenty five he had command of his own ship "The Calypso".

When he was an old man, Landor described William Venour's tragic death in a letter to a friend.

"The Admiral who commanded in the West Indies ordered him home with despatches. His friends say 'Venour you cannot. The crazy ship will founder.' He only replied 'I have orders'. He sailed the next day and went down, nobody knows in what part of the Atlantic. He was brave as a lion and gentle as a lamb."

The official verdict of the sinking was merely that the "Calypso" was lost with all hands off the coast of Jamaica.

Inevitably as Landor travelled to other places and lived there for periods of time, he saw less of Warwick and Warwickshire but he did pay quite a few visits after the death of his father in 1805. The death of Dr Landor was not unexpected as he had suffered from a painful

41

species of cancer for some time, but Landor was unable to attend his father's funeral because he was laid up at Clifton with a bad leg. Dr Landor was buried in a vault at Bishop's Tachbrook Church and later his eldest son assisted with the writing of a Latin epitaph. From an early age, Landor must have been familiar with the church at Bishop's Tachbrook, where many of his Savage ancestors were buried and he probably knew Whitnash Church too for many of his Eyres and Prew ancestors were buried in the churchyard in large chest tombs, situated immediately behind the East window of the chancel.

After 1805 when he had inherited his father's estate in Staffordshire, worth perhaps £800 a year, Landor made plans to sell and buy another larger estate elsewhere. He first tried to buy an estate at Wastwater in Cumbria, but this fell through and so he tried for Llanthony Abbey in Monmouthshire. Landor wanted his mother to sell her lands at Tachbrook (which would have come to him on her death) and instead invest the money in his new estate. This she agreed to do and after an Act of Parliament had given her the permission, the Earl of Warwick bought much of the property in 1808. The fact that Landor sold his paternal estates at Rugeley in Staffordshire too must have saddened his father's relations for much of the land had been owned by the Landors and Nobles since Elizabethan times.

Having sorted out his estate, Landor needed a wife and at last he married in 1811 in Bath. His bride was the seventeen year old Julia Thuillier, the eldest daughter of a bankrupt banker and straight after the honeymoon, he brought his bride to meet his mother and sisters in Warwick. Julia was very pretty with long, golden hair and it was this which had first attracted Landor. Her father who was of a good middle-class Huguenot family had only lost his money as a result of the wars with France because much of his business was based abroad. Landor also took Julia to visit Dr Parr who by this time had fallen on sad times. All Parr's family including first his younger daughter Catherine, then his wife and finally his beloved eldest daughter Sarah Wynne and her youngest child had died and he had been left alone, unable to gain permission to see his remaining two grandchildren in Wales. To ease his pain, Dr Parr had had a portrait of Sarah painted as she lay in her coffin and this gruesome reminder was on permanent display in the drawing room when the newly-wed Landors visited in 1811. Happily Dr Parr married again a few years later and the sad portrait of Sarah was removed from public gaze.

Dr Parr was very enthusiastic about church bells and Landor made a donation to the Hatton bell fund as did many other friends. Dr Parr never saw his young friend again for in 1814, Landor was forced to flee the country and then he and his wife went to live permanently abroad.

One interesting fact which may not have been known to Landor at the time, but which doubtless he had cause to ponder years later was that in August 1820 Dr Parr had met Marguerite, Countess of Blessington at a dinner in St James' Square, London. Parr it was who had dubbed her "*The gorgeous Lady Blessington*" by which name she has been remembered by posterity. Around seven years after Dr Parr had made the acquaintance of the Blessingtons, Landor was to become very friendly with them, both in Florence and elsewhere.

Warwickshire was never far from Landor's thoughts wherever he was living on the Continent. He wrote regularly to his mother and sisters as they did to him, and many of these letters give delightful indications of the character of the writers. By 1825, Landor had four children and many of the letters refer to Arnold, born in 1818, Julia Elizabeth born in 1820, Walter Savage born in 1822 and Charles born in 1825.

In 1822 Mrs Landor wrote saying how her daughters Elizabeth and Ellen met the young ladies of Studley Castle (the daughters of Dorothy Lyttelton, who had died some years before) but although they were handsome fine girls they were "*not like their mother in beauty and manners*". In January 1824 Landor's mother wrote lines that might be echoed by older people the world over.

"*I think sometimes it must be impossible that I should have lived to see you at this age.*" (wrongly she thought that he was fifty) "*Surely it is time I make room for others for I have passed my eighty-first year, have as many blessings as fall to the lot of mortals, and am very willing to go. Who would wish to outlive all their friends?*"

Mrs Landor's next letter in 1824 was a classic! She was far more interested in her eldest son's health than in his literary prowess. His first books of "Imaginary Conversations" had just been published and Landor must have been hoping for some praise.

"*I have heard you have a publication just come out. For God's sake do not hurt your eyes, nor rack your brains too much, to amuse the world by writing: but take care of your health, which will be of greater consequence to your family … I have heard your late publication highly spoken of by many, but as*

43

I am no judge, I shall say nothing relating to it. I wish you to take care of your eyes and your health and let the rest of the world go on as it has done."

Also in 1824 Mrs Landor first suggested that she should be responsible for educating young Arnold (then aged six) in England. Charles Wilson Landor (son of Landor's brother Charles) was then at Rugby School and it was suggested that young Arnold should join his cousin when he became old enough.

Mrs Landor remained disappointed. Not only did Landor fail to take up the offer of the English education for his eldest son, but he also remained unmoved by subtle hints of a visit to Warwickshire. He said that his wife wanted to remain in Italy and that he himself did not wish to leave his children. Each year of her life, it is said, old Mrs Landor repeated her offer to her eldest son, but her grandson Arnold was not allowed to take up the offer of an English education.

A letter from sister Ellen in 1824 told Landor that many were grieved that Dr Parr was not included in the first edition of "Imaginary Conversations" and that Charles Landor had been to see Parr. He had enquired

"How is Walter? I hope he is well. O, he has a mighty mind – a mighty mind."

Feeling somewhat guilty at causing his old friend any distress or disappointment, Landor at once wrote to Parr saying he would always be grateful and that he intended to include an expression of gratitude as a preface to the next volume of the "Imaginary Conversations". Sadly by the time the letter reached Hatton, Parr was already on his deathbed, but he may have been sensible of the contents.

When Mrs Landor next wrote in April 1825 it was to tell Landor of the death of Parr on 6th March. Her letter was another classic for she wondered how Dr Parr, in a world of which he complained so much, could have amassed so much money! Mrs Landor was amazed that he was able to leave his married granddaughter thirty thousand pounds and his other granddaughter ten thousand, whilst four thousand pounds plus three hundred a year went to his second wife. What Mrs Landor did not realise was that some of this money was only released by Parr's death and that much of the income had come from the estate of a cousin who had died in 1823.

In this same lovely letter Mrs Landor says that a Mrs Willoughby remembered Landor at school in Knowle and that the only shade in his character, even then, was a *"want of patience."*

In 1826 Ellen wrote a letter to her brother describing how Leamington Spa was enticing all the gentry away from Warwick and afterwards Mrs Landor had added a very amusing page of her own to Ellen's letter. She described how Dr John Johnson was going to write Dr Parr's biography and she thought it might have been better to have had someone else to write it "*who was accustomed to write something else besides prescriptions.*" Mrs Landor went on to say that she hoped Landor would settle his son in England but she wanted to see him at Ipsley or Staffordshire, rather than among the Welsh who made everything so uncomfortable!

The whole family, in particular Landor and his brothers Henry and Robert, were fond of collecting pictures and in Italy in the period following the Napoleonic wars, there were many bargains to be had. On several occasions Landor's mother and sisters were the talk of Warwick with the interesting works of art they had been sent. At that time, it was particularly difficult to ascribe older pictures to known artists, and with his natural enthusiasm, Landor often erred on the sensational side.

Landor sat for Gibson, the famous sculptor in 1828 and one of the resulting three busts was sent to his mother. Mr Middleton, an artist friend of the family in Warwick, visited Landor in Florence in 1828 and a drawing by him of young Arnold and young Julia was carried back to their paternal grandmother by Augustus Hare. It was said that old Mrs Landor doted on the drawing and touchingly during the last year or so of her life, according to John Forster, she "*used to salute the little faces and wish them good morning and good night.*"

It would thus appear that it was from his mother that Landor inherited many of his emotive traits concerning his children. Both he and his mother adored babies and small children and liked to see them as often as possible.

In October 1829, Landor's mother died, at the age of eighty five years and eleven months, and all of a sudden Landor was plunged into reminiscing about the country of his birth. Only a month or so before her death, Mrs Landor and Landor's two sisters had been entertaining Dorothy Lyttelton's daughters at Warwick and no doubt many forgotten memories had been rekindled. Landor recalled in a letter to his sisters all those family members he had long forgotten and as his nostalgia grew, plans to revisit Warwickshire began to form in his mind.

When eventually Landor left his wife and children in Italy and returned to England for a visit in 1832, he had been away for eighteen years. He might have been expected to rush straight to Warwick, but no – he saw many other friends before he showed his face at Warwick. Perhaps he felt ashamed that his mother had died without ever having seen her four grandchildren who had been born abroad or perhaps he was uncertain of his welcome. Landor's youngest brother, Robert, now the Rector of Birlingham, near Evesham in Worcestershire, a living his mother had bought him shortly before her death, was perhaps the greatest worry. Known to have been unsympathetic to Landor's political views in the past, Robert was now a High Tory, with completely opposing views to his eldest brother. Most like Landor in appearance and temper (although far taller at six feet two) Robert seemed to almost despise his eldest brother, whom he had opposed over Dr Parr's support for Queen Caroline and many other topics. Before Queen Caroline's death in 1821, Robert Landor had written a number of anonymous letters to the Times, condemning her in almost vitriolic terms and when several of his works had been published anonymously, they had been so good that they were credited as having been written by Walter Savage Landor himself. Landor had often had arguments with Robert in the past and he was wary of the reception he would receive when they met again.

Landor knew full well that his sisters and most of the rest of his family in England did not share his great enthusiam for the Great Reform Bill which eventually became law on June 4th 1832, after years of wrangling and political stalemate. The day many Whig supporters had planned for had arrived and Landor had no wish to miss the triumph which he and Dr Parr and many others had planned for years.

After initially visiting Ianthe (a close friend whom he had first met in Bath in 1803) and her family in Brighton and being part of the lively political scene in Sussex, Landor solved the visiting problem by opting out. He by-passed Warwick and went north to visit Southey and Wordsworth. This led to an outburst from Robert Landor when he found out later.

"Walter came from Italy – not to see his Brothers and Sisters – but to visit Wor(d)sworth."

It was the end of July before he arrived in Warwick, however when he did eventually arrive he so enjoyed himself that he found it difficult to tear himself away. Elizabeth and Ellen were delighted to see him, as was Henry who visited often. Landor stayed at least three weeks at the old house in Smith Street and was able to see for himself the huge increase in the size and importance of Leamington. His friend John Kenyon and his wife were visiting the spa town and no doubt too they were entertained in Eastgate House.

By this time, Landor was a reasonably well known writer in scholastic circles and his sisters enjoyed basking in his glory. Landor made the acquaintance of many new friends and the whole visit seems to have been an enormous success. Although he had not written to him much for the time he had been abroad, Landor seemed to get on well with brother Henry and from this time onwards, the two brothers corresponded regularly and warmly.

When Landor left Warwick, it was to travel to Bath and by sheer good fortune, his coach pulled into the yard of an inn at Evesham at the same time as his brother Robert was there. The two men had not had much to do with each other for a number of years but the impromptu meeting went well and Robert promised to visit his brother soon in Bath. Sadly gout prevented him from keeping this engagement but the ice was broken and on subsequent visits to Warwick, the two published authors met and discussed together.

Once the brief visit to England was over in the Autumn of 1832, Landor made plans for another visit. This was never to take place and eventually, after his matrimonial difficulties had intensified in 1835, he reluctantly left his wife and children in Italy and returned to England permanently, intending to live alone.

The previous year, in the Autumn of 1834, perhaps the most Warwickshire-inspired work of all had been published and Landor was greatly saddened when it proved not to be as popular as he had hoped. "The Citation and Examination of William Shakespeare" dealt with the alleged poaching incident when the young Shakespeare had been apprehended for deerstealing at Charlecote, the seat of the Lucy family, only a few miles from Warwick. In the work, Landor made good use of his local knowledge of roads and country ways, mentioning Wellesbourne and Walton Hill.

After Landor's arrival back in England in 1835, it appears to have been some time before he went to Warwick and long before then, trouble was brewing. In 1836 a cousin from Rugeley, Edward Wilson Landor, re-visited Landor's villa near Florence and fell in love with Landor's sixteen year old daughter Julia. They wished to marry, but feared (correctly) that there would be family opposition on both sides. A malicious letter from Arnold Landor to his father finished any hope of happiness for the two young lovers and Landor forbade the match. The Landor family members in Warwickshire were split, most of them backing Landor's refusal to allow Julia to marry Edward, because they thought she lacked the necessary social skills needed for a middle-class wife in England. Cholera was raging across most of the mainland of Europe and it was not easy to move anywhere, because of severe travel restrictions. In the end, Edward Wilson went abroad and young Julia Landor had to stay where she was and single.

Landor may have visited his sisters in the early part of 1837, but severely asthmatic, Ellen Landor died the following year in July 1838, possibly without having seen her eldest brother again. It was not until summer of 1839 that Landor visited Warwick again and by then family tempers had settled and Elizabeth was delighted to welcome her brother. Sophy Venour Shuckburgh, Landor's cousin, who was by then widowed and settled in Leamington, came to visit him and so did many other friends old and new. In that year of 1839 and in the following years, many of Walter's friends, such as Joseph Ablett visited Warwick and the Landor family enjoyed a kind of Indian summer. Landor accompanied Elizabeth on visits to other family members such as Charles in Colton and it became quite the custom for an annual summer visit to take place.

In 1840 Landor renewed an old friendship when he made the acquaintance of Anthony Rosenhagen, for this retired civil servant's second wife was none other than Frances, the little sister of Fleetwood Parkhurst with whom Landor had played so happily in his teens at Ripple Court, near Malvern. The Rosenhagens lived in Cheltenham and the couple were already old friends of Robert Landor whose Birlingham Rectory was not far away. Long before Landor himself had returned to the family scene, his sisters and nieces had been in the habit of staying with the Rosenhagens.

In December 1840 Landor and his brother Robert were properly reconciled when a copy of Landor's new work "Fra Rupert" was favourably looked upon by the younger brother. Although the eldest and youngest brother had met in recent years, their relationship had still been somewhat strained. Landor wrote to Lady Blessington,

"For a quarter of a century we have lived without any correspondence. Neither of us is good tempered – I am perhaps the worse of the two. However there is not, and never was a more honourable, upright, Christian gentleman

A NINETEENTH CENTURY ENGRAVING OF LANDOR'S BIRTHPLACE IN SMITH STREET, WARWICK   Eastgate House (renamed Landor House in 1892) is situated close to the Eastgate and not far from St Nicholas' Church.

THIS ENGRAVING "WARWICK FROM THE BANKS OF THE AVON" SHOWS THE SOUTH ASPECT OF THE TOWN AS IT WAS WHEN LANDOR WAS A STUDENT IN THE 1790s. St Nicholas' Church is on the right, St Mary's is in the centre and Warwick Castle can be seen on the left.

I

LANDOR AGED TWENTY-NINE. From the portrait by George Dance R.A., painted in 1804, the earliest known likeness of Landor.

II

LANDOR IN 1839 AFTER COUNT D'ORSAY.

III

THIS 1838 PORTRAIT BY WILLIAM FISHER SHOWS LANDOR AT THE AGE OF SIXTY-THREE. Originally owned by John Kenyon, the painting is now in the National Portait Gallery in London.

IV

THIS SKETCH OF LANDOR BY WILLIAM FISHER WAS COMPLETED ABOUT 1840. Despite the additional doodles, a stern-faced Landor is brought very much to life.

LANDOR ABOUT 1854 FROM A PASTEL PORTRAIT BY ROBERT FAULKNER. "I *wear it as an invalid,"* seventy-nine year old Landor said of the black velvet cap.

Walter Savage Landor
April 16. 55

LANDOR AGED EIGHTY. *This photograph, taken in Bath in 1855, is signed and dated by Landor on the mount. It is now owned by the Landor Society of Warwick and is currently deposited in Warwickshire County Record Office.*

VII

THIS PHOTOGRAPH OF LANDOR AGED EIGHTY-FIVE WAS TAKEN BY THE FRATELLI ALINARI IN FLORENCE IN LATE 1860. In the last few years of his life Landor grew a curly white beard in the winter. Kate Field took several copies of this photograph back to America with her in 1861.

IN HIS LAST YEARS LANDOR'S THOUGHTS OFTEN STRAYED BACK TO HIS TIME AT RUGBY SCHOOL. Time and time again Landor recalled the name of fifteen year old Spearman Wasey, who was admitted as a pupil in 1785 and died at school some months later. This view of Rugby School Buildings from the Close dates from 1809.

IPSLEY COURT FROM A DOCUMENT IN THE LANDOR COLLECTION IN WARWICKSHIRE COUNTY RECORD OFFICE. By the time the Landors inherited the estate in 1786 the main house had been demolished.

OLD STUDLEY CASTLE PHOTOGRAPHED IN THE MID-TWENTIETH CENTURY. Studley Church can be seen to the right.

SAVAGE'S HOUSE IN BISHOP'S TACHBROOK AS IT WAS IN THE MID-NINETEENTH CENTURY WHEN OWNED BY HENRY EYRES LANDOR.

THIS EARLY NINETEENTH CENTURY DRAWING OF TENBY IN SOUTH WALES
IS BY CHARLES NORRIS (1779-1858) WHO WAS A RELATION OF LANDOR.

CLIFFS AT MONKSTONE NEAR TENBY IN THE NINETEENTH CENTURY.
Landor and Nancy Jones used to walk together in such picturesque places. (See the poem on
page 174.)

THE PORT AND BAY OF SWANSEA IN 1792. Landor loved this area better than any and called it "The most beautiful coast in the universe".

ALMOST UNRECOGNISABLE TODAY, BRITON FERRY, NEAR SWANSEA, WAS AN UNSPOILT BEAUTY-SPOT IN THE 1790s WHEN LANDOR WALKED THERE WITH ROSE AYLMER.

*AS A YOUNG MAN LANDOR OFTEN VISITED LAUGHARNE IN
CARMARTHENSHIRE. This recent photograph taken from near Gosport House,
illustrates one of the beautiful views he enjoyed. In the 1790s a variety of fishing boats and
sailing ships would have been in evidence.*

*SOUTH PARADE IN BATH WHERE LANDOR OFTEN LODGED WHEN HE WAS
A YOUNG MAN.*

THIS DRAWING OF "LLANTHONY ABBEY NEAR ABERGAVENNY" WAS
COMPLETED BY MISS HOLDER AND SENT TO MARIA ARDEN, LANDOR'S
HALF-SISTER, AROUND 1808 WHEN HE BOUGHT THE LLANTHONY ESTATE
IN MONMOUTHSHIRE.

A RECENT VIEW OF PART OF THE RUINS OF LLANTHONY ABBEY (MORE
PROPERLY CALLED PRIORY).

ROBERT SOUTHEY PICTURED BY EDWARD NASH IN 1820. Southey and his first wife Edith stayed at Llanthony with the newly-wed Landors in 1811. Their accommodation was in one of the towers of the ruined abbey (now part of the Llanthony Hotel).

XVI

than my brother Robert ... His charities are large and judicious. He has a good library and some fine pictures and a large garden kept in excellent order."

Christmas in the year of 1841 was a very merry one for, at Landor's suggestion, Elizabeth hosted a large family party with all the brothers being invited and doubtless their families. Officially the party was to celebrate the youngest brother Robert having entered his 60th year and with Walter, Charles and Henry able to join Elizabeth in the wonderful old family home, there was reason for nostalgia.

It may well have been that over the Christmas and New Year period in 1841/1842 Landor attended a service in St Mary's Church, Warwick, for a poem published in "The Examiner" on January 8th 1842 concerned one of the memorials on the wall of the north aisle. Landor was reminiscing about Frances Verchild, a early friend of his who died aged six in August 1780 and the poem "On the Dead" began,

Thou in this wide cold church art laid,
Close to the wall, my little maid!
My little Fanny Verchild! thou
Sole idol of an infant vow!
My playmate in life's break of day,
When all we had to do was play!

The memorial to Frances Verchild can still be seen in St Mary's Church, close to the organ console, near the Regimental Chapel and many might consider it appropriate that four decades after Landor had written this poem, a memorial to him was placed on the opposite side of the nave, in a niche cut in the first pier on the south side.

When his children finally managed to come to England to visit him, Landor of course brought them to Warwick and took great delight in showing them familiar sights. In 1841 Landor's second son Walter had visited and in the summer of 1842 Landor's eldest son Arnold came to England. However he was soon on bad terms with his father and the two did not travel together round the relations. It was necessary for Arnold to visit Rugeley to discuss business matters with Walter Landor the lawyer and he probably visited Warwick also. It would appear that Arnold was very crafty and the Rugeley cousins were taken in by his plausible tales, thinking him hard-done-by. It was proposed that Landor's wife should receive five hundred pounds a year (an increase of one hundred pounds) and Landor would continue to receive four hundred a year. Any surplus money from the estates, after all mortgages, debts and repairs had been paid, (possibly two hundred a year) was to go into a fund for Landor's younger children.

In 1843 both young Walter and Julia arrived from Florence for a visit and Elizabeth urged her brother to bring them to Warwick for a month in June. Visits to Colton, Birlingham and Cheltenham took place later and Landor had a wonderful summer as he shared with his beloved daughter many of the places he loved, Julia and Walter left for Italy in October and once again Landor was miserable. He wrote to Rose Paynter,

"My dear Julia wished not only to be with me but alone with me as much as possible. We parted in unutterable grief, but youth and fresh scenes will soon assuage all hers. That is enough."

When Landor paid his usual summer visit to Warwick in 1844 he came by train, but he omitted to alight at Coventry to change trains for Milverton Station in Leamington. Landor was carried on to Birmingham where he passed the time by writing a letter to John Forster in a waiting room until he was able to catch a train back again.

In the summer of 1845 when Landor made his customary visit to Warwick he was able to write to Rose Paynter on June 18th,

"… The Percys, the only people I know well in this quarter of the world, returned on Saturday, and I dined with them at Guy's Cliffe on Tuesday. Lord Leigh, Mrs Clive, Mr Dugdale, were invited. But THE person was Mrs Somerville, the most wonderful woman the world ever saw …"

It was perhaps following this visit that Landor wrote his poem concerning the Chapel at Guy's Cliffe. Entitled "To Miss Isabella Percy" Landor's short poem referred to the legend of Guy of Warwick and was included in his "Collected Works" which appeared in 1846.

TO MISS ISABELLA PERCY
If that old hermit laid to rest
    Beneath your chapel-floor,
Could leave the regions of the blest
    And visit earth once more:
If human sympathies could warm
    His tranquil breast again,

Your innocence that breast could charm,
    Perhaps your beauty pain.

In 1847 Landor and his brothers paid their usual summer visit to Eastgate House in Warwick and Sophy Landor kept a diary of those delightful days. Her entry for 20th July ran,

"I was delighted to saunter up and down the the large grass plot with Uncles Walter and Robert, hearing them discuss various writings. Afterwards had a pleasant chat with Uncle R. alone and was confirmed in my old opinion of preferring his mind to Uncle W's, he does not display such brilliant flashes as Uncle W. but all that he utters is full of thought, his language, I think, the more elegant and various of the two, he never uses repetitions or hesitates for a word, but really has a stream of eloquence ..."

Perhaps Sophy forgot that Robert had been in the habit of giving church sermons for a number of years, so no wonder he had become eloquent! She went on to remark that on 22nd July, before Henry had to depart on business and Charles needed to return to Colton *"We drank to the health of our noble selves."*

After the other brothers had gone, Landor, who was not in any particular hurry to depart, suffered terrible earache and Sophy nursed him for several weeks. She wrote in her diary,

"It has been an inexpressible pleasure to me to attend on him. He is most patient and submissive, it is very delightful to see the strong attempts he makes to subdue his temper, I have seen bright gleams of deep feeling in his heart during this indisposition, which gives me much comfort."

In Southam, around eight miles east of Leamington there was an Eye and Ear Infirmary at that time and it was from this establishment that Dr Smith had prescribed the remedy for the earache. Later Landor was so delighted with his own recovery that he sent the remedy to his old friend Seymour Kirkup in Florence who was becoming profoundly deaf. Sadly, in this case the remedy was not so successful and Kirkup remained deaf till the end of his life.

In 1847 Mary Ann Venour died in Leamington and the following year her sister Sophy Venour Shuckburgh also died. In 1848 John Forster visited Warwick with Landor but a happy visit in 1849 was prevented by the sudden death of Charles at Colton. On July 12th Landor and his son Walter, on another visit to England, attended the funeral when Charles was buried in a vault in the chancel of Colton Church.

In 1850 Landor signed the register in Knowle Church at his niece's wedding. Charles' youngest daughter Ellen married Rev. Rashleigh Duke and the bride's brother, Rev. Charles Wilson Landor, newly ordained as a clergyman, conducted the service.

As usual Landor visited Warwick in the summer of 1851. In September 1852 Landor and his sister went to Knowle Lodge in Knowle, to visit brother Charles' widow.

Landor's very last visit to Warwick was in August 1853 when his niece Kitty was staying with Elizabeth. Eliabeth wrote to another niece,

"About bedtime Walter discovered there was no appearance of a box or bag – he had some keys – he was sure (I was not) that he started with a black trunk and saw it put in the train – we sent here and there and wrote to where he had changed trains, in vain. A nightcap I could furnish, but the under male garments were not resident here – we sent to Tachbrook and had some from thence. However the box did come on Weds afternoon uninjured."

On that last memorable visit, Landor went with Kitty to see Tachbrook once again, but most of the time was spent in Warwick. Whilst walking along the gravel paths in the garden at Warwick, Landor picked up the first few mulberries which had fallen and in a letter to John Forster, he recalled he had done exactly the same thing seventy five years previously.

Around this time, Landor wrote a particularly emotive poem on the subject of the old mulberry trees at Warwick – for about the first time in his life, at the age of seventy eight, he was feeling really old.

TO AN OLD MULBERRY TREE

Old mulberry! with all thy moss around,
Thy arms are shatter'd, but thy heart is sound:
So then remember one for whom of yore
Thy tenderest boughs the crimson berry bore;
Remember one who, trusting in thy strength,
Lay on the low and level branch full length.
No strength has he, alas! to climb it now,
Nor strength to bear him, if he had, hast thou.

This emotive feeling about the old mulberry tree was noted in one of the last letters which Julius Hare ever wrote to Landor. Noting how the ancient gods and heroes always had a favourite plant, Hare explained,

Twas SHAKESPEARE'S, MILTON'S, now 'tis LANDOR'S tree;
Precious to those who love the gifted three.

(In after years, this old mulberry tree became much loved. It survived until the 1940s and a scion of the tree flourishes still, close to the rear entrance of the King's High School for Girls. This school took over Eastgate House in 1879 and gradually utilised the garden to site new buildings. Generations of girls knew and loved both the mulberry tree and the ilex. This tree, which blew down in 1949, had also been well-known to Landor.)

That summer of 1853 was an extra-special time but none of the Landors guessed it would be the last. Only a few months later, Elizabeth Landor suffered a stroke and she died in February 1854, afterwards being buried at Tachbrook, like the rest of the family. Landor did not travel from Bath for the funeral for it was winter and there seemed little point.

During that sad summer of 1854, nieces Sophy and Kitty gradually emptied old Eastgate House of all its Landor trappings – the remaining pictures were sold and a whole era was ended. After eighty years, the house was to be let to other tenants.

Despite the fact that Landor paid no more visits to Warwickshire or the Midlands, he continued to write fairly frequently to his brothers Henry and Robert. Henry in particular did his best to persuade Landor to make plans to be buried at Tachbrook, but Widcombe churchyard near Bath remained part of the Landor's plans because it brought back memories of Ianthe.

Sadly when Landor was sued for libel in 1858 his brother Robert became very critical. "*Tomorrow I shall be ashamed of my name*" he wrote to a friend – a pity as his eldest brother could have done with more family support.

However, over a year later, as Landor (still officially the head of the family) was attempting to live independently in Florence and was in need of money, Robert and Henry Landor responded immediately to the request by John Forster. For the rest of Landor's life, two hundred pounds each year was sent by them to enable him to pay for rooms and service in the house of Wilson, Elizabeth Barrett Browning's ex-maid. To the very end, the Landor family were supportive of each other.

5. SOUTH WALES
Happiness in Tenby and Swansea,
but Misery in Llanthony

Walter Savage Landor adored South Wales! For around twenty-one years, from 1793 to 1814 he spent much time there, but in the end his hopes of making the place his permanent residence turned sour and he was forced to leave.

Whilst a young man of eighteen, in the summer of 1793, Landor took time off from his studies at Trinity College, Oxford to go for a vacation in the ultra-fashionable resort of Tenby. This was probably the first time he had visited Wales, but it was the beginning of a real love affair with the rugged western coast.

At that time Tenby was just beginning to change from a somewhat dilapidated, medieval, walled-town to a modern lively resort for visiting gentry. The old town and its small harbour occupied a gloriously sheltered position with high cliffs, interesting caves and numerous sandy beaches in the near vicinity. With a permanent population of well less than one thousand people (eight hundred and forty four in 1801) Tenby must have made a pleasant change for Landor from Oxford and Warwick both of which had far larger populations. Sea-bathing was just beginning to be fashionable and with an experienced and capable bathing woman in charge of the horse-drawn bathing machines in Tenby, many ladies felt reassured enough to take the plunge.

Furthermore the town was not then easily accessible, being around two hundred and sixty miles from London with coaches needing to pass through some sparsely populated countryside en-route. Public conveyances were few, and the journey from London took twenty nine hours. As the Revolution in France in 1789 and the resulting war between England and France had made it difficult and unsafe to travel on the Continent, many of the English gentry sought summer amusement in England or Wales. Tenby was ideally placed, being accessible by sea for the Irish gentry and by private coach for the English. However the awkward journey limited the number of visitors, so that it remained a resort for the select few.

The summer season lasted from May to October and plays, balls and assemblies were organised for amusements. With plenty of excellent excursions in the near vicinity to cliffs and castles, the visitor had the added pleasure of being able to walk on nearly deserted beaches at various places nearby.

All these factors combined to make Tenby a perfect holiday destination for eighteen year old Walter Landor. Not over-fond of large gatherings, the inwardly shy but outwardly confident young man adored walking amidst magnificent scenery. Coming from Warwickshire, which is as far from the sea as it is possible to be in England, he may not have visited any coastal resort previously for travel was expensive and his school holidays had mostly been spent visiting family and friends in the Midlands area.

However, much as Landor liked Tenby, the most important attraction was not quite so obvious. On his first visit in 1793 he met a girl called Nancy Jones and he began to write poetry to his 'Ione'.

It seems highly probable that Landor first visited Tenby in the company of John Norris, a distant cousin who was a year older. It was from John Norris's father that Dr Landor had inherited Ipsley Court in Warwickshire because John Norris, his sister Elizabeth and younger brother Charles were illegitimate. Although they could inherit their father's name and money, the strict laws of entail prevented them from inheriting the property. In 1793 young John Norris (rumoured to be the richest commoner in England) was studying at Magdalen College, Oxford in the same year as Landor's school friend Walter Birch and it is almost certain that the two cousins saw much of each other. Some years later Charles Norris went to live in Tenby, perhaps at the suggestion of his brother and Landor, and eventually he became one of the most famous painters of the area.

In the summer of 1794, after he had been rusticated from Oxford University in June, Landor made straight for South Wales again. Perhaps plans had already been made for the summer months before his abrupt departure from his studies or perhaps he fled to escape his father's wrath. Once again he was in the company of Nancy Jones, who, if Landor's poems can be relied upon to tell the story, was very keen on him indeed. "*One loved me at twenty*" and "*I only sinned but once*" he was afterwards to remark and there can be little doubt that the love affair with Nancy was very serious on both sides.

Landor had a liking for girls with golden hair and this Nancy possessed in abundance. Not tall (shorter than Landor who was of middle height) she has always been assumed to have been a local girl because of her local knowledge which Landor mentioned several times in his poems.

Once or twice it seems Landor had doubts about their relationship and sometime in 1794 he travelled to Swansea and from thence to the Gower port of Port Eynon. Landor took a boat from the enclosed harbour of Port Eynon, near the old Salthouse on the beach, to St Ives in Cornwall, where he stayed a few days with a friend. The journey must have taken a good few hours and whilst in St Ives Landor witnessed a deserter from the army being executed by a firing squad.

After leaving Tenby and Nancy in the autumn of 1794, Landor returned to Warwick, where after a huge row with his father late in the year, he abruptly left the family home and went to London, threatening to go to live in Italy for a time. Following the publication of his first volume of poetry in May 1795 however, Landor suddenly returned to Tenby in a hurry and remained there or in Swansea for the summer. This is all that is known officially, but after Landor's death, his younger brother Robert spitefully suggested (in a note in the margin of a book) that Landor had "*seduced a girl in Tinby the year before, with whom, he lived at Swansea till the birth of a Child.*"

Searches by R.H. Super, a particularly thorough biographer, revealed the burial in Swansea of a nine month old baby named Ann Jones on 9th May 1796 but there was no proof whatsoever that this was Landor's child. Also a twenty two year old woman named Ann Jones was buried on 15th November 1801, but the name was a common one in Wales and the circumstances were very vague. What is known is that Landor was in love with Nancy Jones and she with him, and that he carefully preserved a lock of her hair until his death.

For certain it is known that Nancy died young and that she was already dead in 1806 when Landor published an elegaic poem to her in 'Simonidea'. In this poem he mentions her "*briar-bound sod and upright stone*" and it sounds as if he had visited her somewhat deserted grave. In his last year of life Landor destroyed some old papers and it may well have been that some of those related to this love affair of long ago.

From around 1796 onwards Landor seems to have moved in a different circle of friends and the next seven years of Landor's life were some of his happiest ever. Most of the time was spent in Swansea with occasional visits to Laugharne, Tenby or St Clears. When the allowance of money which his father gave him (one hundred and fifty pounds a year, paid quarterly) ran out, he would return to Warwickshire.

When in Swansea Walter stayed in Rhyddings House, then fairly isolated and close to the sea. In 1795 Swansea was still largely unspoiled and the wonderful sweep of Swansea Bay, from the Mumbles to Porthcawl, was often compared with the Bay of Naples. The old coast road from Swansea to Mumbles passed through Oystermouth and Landor loved to take long walks in the area. On a clear day, the North Devon coast could be seen across the sea and from Townhill, mountains to the northeast were visible. In the 1790s Swansea was a growing city, with many of the old buildings being replaced to please the tourist trade. The place was later nicknamed "The Brighton of Wales" and pre-copper mines, pre-coal mines and pre-industrial docks, the place was exceptionally beautiful.

One area of Swansea where many of the fashionable people walked was on the Burrows, an undeveloped sandy area adjoining the sea. Between the bottom of Wind Street and St Helen's there were several walkways and it was whilst walking on the Burrows, not far from Rhyddings House, that Walter first met Rose Aylmer.

Rose was the sister of the 5th Lord Aylmer, whose lands were in Ireland and whose mother had married again after her first husband, the previous Lord Aylmer had died. Rose was sixteen years old, Landor and Lord Aylmer were both twenty one and Sophia Price, half sister to Rose was around six. The Aylmers seemed to be a tightly knit, supportive family and Landor was often invited to accompany them.

Nowadays the area of Briton Ferry is highly industrialised and a huge bridge carries a very busy road across the River Neath. However in the 1790s the walk from Swansea was an excursion into beautiful, unspoilt countryside. Landor captured this beauty in an early poem in which he describes a walk with Rose Aylmer. The poem called "ABERTAWY" began,

Along the seaboard sands there grows
The tiniest and the thorniest rose,
And Tawny snapdragons stand round,
Above it, on the level ground.

57

The fact that Rose Aylmer lent Landor a copy of a book she had taken from the circulating library in Swansea was to have great repercussions on Landor's poetry. "Progress of Romance" by Clara Reeve included "The History of Charoba, Queen of Eygpt" and Landor borrowed ideas from the plot of this to make a long poem "Gebir".

It was probably in the early Autumn of 1796 that Landor and his friends travelled to Bala on a grouse-shooting expedition. Already he had begun to write "Gebir" and along with his other luggage, the verses were carefully transported on the back of a Welsh pony. It was a long and difficult journey through the mountains to Bala and at the end of the break the precious verses were left behind. "*For many months they followed not*" recalled Walter in a poem written years later, but eventually the half-finished poem was re-united with its owner who was amusing himself shooting grouse nearer Swansea. When published anonymously in 1798, "Gebir" attracted the notice of at least one influential reviewer and from then on, Landor's reputation as a serious poet was assured.

Although most young men in that period indulged in grouse shooting and other such activities, Landor seemed to do so with reluctance and sometime not too long afterwards, he gave up shooting at birds altogether. Years later he described to Leigh Hunt how he had shot at a pheasant and many hours afterwards found it where it had fallen, not dead and in manifest torment. From then on, Landor did no more shooting.

At that time it seemed that at every available opportunity Landor returned to South Wales and more often than not he was in Swansea at Rhyddings House, not far from Brynmill. (The house still stands in Bernard Street, near Aylesbury Road, although it is much altered and has lost nearly all of its ground.) The Aylmer family had a house at Laugharne and often Landor would stay with them. This house was Gosport House, which presumably they leased from the Laugharne family, and the view from the terrace over the estuary was magnificent. Thick walls, delightfully cosy rooms, an interesting garden and a safe anchorage for boats below made this house almost idyllic.

In the autumn of 1799 the Honorable Rose Whitworth Aylmer, to give her her full title, then aged nineteen, went with her aunt and friends to Calcutta where the aunt's husband, Sir Henry Russell, had been appointed a judge. Rose became engaged to one of her cousins, but before the wedding could take place, she died of cholera on March 2nd 1800 aged 20.

Her family and friends were naturally devastated by the news and some time later Landor composed one of his most memorable poems in her memory. "Rose Aylmer", said to have been composed whilst he was cleaning his teeth before going to bed, was first published in 1806 and it was to become a great favourite of other poets so far apart as Charles Lamb in the nineteenth century and Dylan Thomas in the twentieth.

> Ah what avails the sceptred race,
> Ah what the form divine!
> What every virtue, every grace!
> Rose Aylmer, all were thine.
> Rose Aylmer, whom these wakeful eyes
> May weep, but never see,
> A night of memories and of sighs
> I consecrate to thee.

Strangely enough, Gosport House where Landor stayed with the Aylmers in the later 1790s is almost next door to the fisherman's cottage in Gosport Street, Laugharne where the young Dylan Thomas and his bride Caitlin set up house over 130 years later in 1938. The famous boat-house where Thomas spent his later years is directly across the bay. Dylan Thomas knew and loved the poetry of Landor for he included him in an early article for the "Herald of Wales" in 1932 ("Early Prose Writings, J.M. Dent and Sons Ltd, 1971) which concerned the poets of Swansea. Comparison of some early poems of Landor with some of Thomas's works makes it seem highly likely that on occasions both writers were describing similar scenes in the Swansea area. Of the poem on Rose Aylmer Thomas wrote, *"This is great poetry in every sense of the word; not a phrase, not a word, could be altered to its advantage; it is poetry in its strictest, most economical and concentrated form, full of that dignity and chastened splendour Landor instilled into everything he wrote."*

Landor and Thomas would no doubt have enjoyed discussing poetry together – it was a pity that 130 years separated them.

From around 1800 to 1804 Landor seems to have spent less and less time in Swansea and his other haunts in South Wales. Swansea was rapidly becoming more industrialized and its wonderful views were being marred. In 1804 the Mumbles Railway was built to carry limestone to Swansea in wagons pulled by horses. Landor detested the desecration of the beautiful scenery and he called the railway,

"That streak of black along the most beautiful coast in the universe"

Gradually Landor spent more and more time in Bath, but he was to remember all his life these happy years spent on the South Wales coast and in particular in the Swansea area. The happiness of the Twelfth Night party at Mrs Thomas' in Swansea in 1797 where he had proposed a lottery amongst the youths present to win the triangle of ribbon cut by Rose Aylmer from her bonnet ties, his country walks to beautiful places nearby such as Briton Ferry and his numerous tramps over deserted beaches were to live with him all his life. This period is best summed up in his own words,

"Never were my spirits better than in my twentieth year when I wrote 'Gebir' and did not exchange twelve sentences with men. I lived amongst woods which are now killed with copper works and took my walk over sandy sea-coast deserts , then covered with low roses and thousands of nameless flowers and plants, trodden by the naked feet of the Welsh peasantry, and trackless."

From hills near Swansea, on a clear day one could fancy one could see the Black Mountains some miles to the east. Landor was to recall this and a few years later he bought an estate in Monmouthshire.

Landor's father died in 1805 and he then inherited considerable estates in Rugeley in Staffordshire. Being of a romantic nature, Landor decided that he would prefer to own an estate amidst beautiful scenery so he sold his land in the Midlands and in 1808 bought a large estate which comprised the Manors of Cwmyoy and Llanthony in Monmouthshire, which included the site of Llanthony Abbey (more properly called Priory).

His mother was persuaded to sell her land in Bishop's Tachbrook in Warwickshire (which would have come to him on her death) and invest in the new estate. As his mother's property was entailed on him, it needed an Act of Parliament to allow the sale and for the entail to be transferred to Llanthony.

The property was glorious and it is very little changed today. It comprised over 3,000 acres of agricultural land, plus some spectacular mountain wasteland in the Vale of Ewyas, in Monmouthshire, not far from the border between England and Wales. The nearest town of any size was Abergavenny which was about twelve miles distant and the ruins of the Abbey lay well tucked away, seven miles along the winding road to Hay on Wye, which led off the main Abergavenny to Hereford Road. There can be few spots more remote or picturesque and Landor planned to build his new house around half a mile above the Abbey ruins on a spot overlooking some glorious scenery.

In order to service his new house and make welcome work for the local men, he planned to construct a new bridge over a nearby stream and also make a road to the next village of Longtown in Herefordshire. The undertaking involved an enormous amount of construction work which was always going to be awkward because of the difficulties of transport. An architect was engaged and the work began.

From the onset there seems to have been trouble with the local people and in June 1808 Landor's half sister Maria Arden wrote to his brother Robert,

"I think Walter a subject of great pity for he does not seem at all inclined to conciliate the peasantry about Lantony but on the contrary – therefore he must expect to be plagued". From the beginning of 1808 Maria Arden had been jokingly referring to Landor as "The Abbot of Llanthony" and a friend of hers had sent a pencil sketch of the abbey completed by Miss Holder some time earlier. (This sketch now forms an interesting item in the Landor Collection in Warwickshire County Record Office.) Maybe jealousy had a role to play, but in the Landor family, Maria Arden and her godson Robert Landor were always amongst Walter Savage Landor's severest critics. Wealthy Maria Arden died in Bath in late 1808 and her husband the following year. In her will she left five hundred pounds to each of her half-brothers and sisters with the exception of Robert Eyres Landor, her godson and youngest half-brother, and Walter Savage Landor, her eldest half brother. Robert was left four thousand pounds and Walter only one hundred pounds!

Although Landor had several comfortable rooms in one of the towers of the Abbey ruins which had been re-constructed as a shooting lodge by the former owner Colonel Wood, he was not in permanent residence and those he engaged to oversee the work proved inadequate. The new house was to have a drawing room and a library 18 feet square, a dining room 28 feet by 22 feet and 14 feet high besides six family bedrooms and another six for servants but, sadly, progress was very slow. Soon after purchasing the estate, Landor went to Spain to join the army for several months and in his absence little was completed.

In 1811 thirty six year old Landor married the seventeen year old Julia Thuillier and in the summer they came straight to Llanthony and took up residence in the tower rooms whilst the house was being finished. That hot summer of 1811 must have been idyllic for the newly-weds in their picturesque tower, for their first guests were Robert Southey and his first wife Edith, who spent three nights there in July.

Southey had visited the Abbey ruins once before thirteen years previously and he enquired if Landor had found St David's Cavern which Michael Drayton had mentioned in "Polyolbion", but which he had never managed to find. Bearing in mind that "Polyolbion" was one of the first books that Landor ever bought as a boy, he must have thought that it was kindly fate which had led him to purchase Llanthony.

Prior to Southey's visit Landor wrote,

"I now employ my mornings in cutting off the heads of thistles with my stick and hoeing my young chestnuts ... I have made a discovery, which is, that there are both nightingales and glowworms in my valley. I would give two or three thousand less for a place that was without them. I hardly know one flower from another, but it appears to me that here is an infinite variety.

Landor took his travelling carriage to met Southey and his wife. Ever health conscious, even at the age of thirty six, Landor said that as the guests intended to arrive late in the evening, he dare not sit outside on their coach as courtesy would dictate, for it would give him rheumatism. So it was arranged that he met the Southeys, and afterwards conveyed them to Hereford in his carriage.

That first evening must have been wonderful! With Landor excitedly pointing out glowworms, teenage Julia Landor nervously presiding over her first meal as hostess, and the nightingales making the Abbey ruins seem ethereal in the twilight, it must have been the ultimate in short breaks for the two couples.

Many years later, in 1850, Landor recaptured some of the magic of those happy days in a poem which he wrote for Southey's son Rev. Cuthbert Southey. One section of the poem described an evening at Llanthony in July 1811.

... Along Lantony's ruined ailes we walkt
  And woods then pathless, over verdant hill
  And ruddy mountain, and aside the stream
  Of sparkling Hondy. Just at close of day
  There by the comet's light we saw the fox

Rush from the alders, nor relax in speed
Until he trod the pathway of his sires
Under the hoary crag of Cymioy.
Then both were happy.

In fact the visit by the Southeys was such a success that other visits followed and during the next year, Landor's mother and sisters came and revelled in the scenery. Brother Henry had already visited the estate before purchase to assess the viability of such a venture, but it may well have been that the other members of the Landor family visited. Some of Julia's relations came and for many years afterwards, some guests, especially Landor's sisters, spoke of the happy summer walks they had had on the hills round Llanthony.

However, all was not well on the estate. From the onset in 1808, some of the tenants had not paid their rent and Charles Gabell, the solicitor in nearby Crickhowell whom Landor had engaged to conduct his business, seemed to make slow progress. Within five years, despite all Landor and his family could do, the romantic dream turned into major disaster.

What went wrong? The answer, as always, was a combination of things, the major being that Landor had bought at perhaps the worst time in history.

In almost every way, life was changing rapidly. Old systems of almost everything were being swept away and it was very difficult for businesses and estates to predict their annual income. In Wales and elsewhere in 1808, food prices soared as a series of bad harvests made it almost impossible for some tenants to pay their rents. Wholesale land enclosures by many large landowners were going on, in an effort to produce more food, and Landor hoped to have his fields enclosed too, but this required an Act of Parliament and his was rejected. The cost of the war with Napoleon was causing havoc with Britain's finances and so serious did this crisis become that in January 1811, around five months before Landor married Julia, the government was forced to introduce paper money as the economic crisis worsened. The seventy three year old King George III was declared insane and in February 1811, his son (the future King George IV) was appointed Prince Regent. The Industrial Revolution was gathering pace all over England as a rising population endeavoured to find work and food. It was a not a good time to plan a new venture.

It is easy to be critical afterwards but with hindsight, Llanthony, as Landor wanted it, was never going to work. He threw almost all of his money into a wonderful large estate, leaving little cash as back-up should things go wrong. He was attempting to achieve too much, too soon, people said in 1808 and 1809 when Landor bought thousands of fir cones in an effort to plant groves of cedars of Lebanon on his estate and imported merino sheep from Spain. House-building for himself, refurbishing other farm houses for tenants, bridge building, road building – all were enthusiastically set in motion, before the rents of the estate had been collected. When only a portion of the money actually materialised, Landor's cash flow problems began to reach crisis proportions.

The solicitor Gabell was sacked in favour of Baker-Gabb of Abergavenny, for Landor came to realise that the former had not investigated all the titles to the land which was purchased from Colonel Wood. Whichever way Landor turned he was frustrated. The Bishop of St David's was cool about his proposal to rebuild the church at Llanthony, Landor was turned down to be a local magistrate and several Welsh tenants began to be insolent to the man they perceived to be an English overlord.

Despite this in February 1812 Landor felt compassion for many of his sixty four tenants and their farm workers and he wrote to Southey,

"Three pounds of miserable bread costs two shillings in Abergavenny. The poor barbarous creatures in my parish have actually ceased to be mischievous, they are so miserable. We can find them employment at present and four-and-sixpence a day; yet nothing can solace them for their difficulty in procuring bread."

Typical of Landor's trouble at Llanthony was the affair with the farmer Tombes. He was a tenant recommended by Gabell the Crickhowell lawyer for one of the principal farms, but he paid no rent whatsoever. Landor sent a servant to demand rent from Tombes, but the man was assaulted and locked up. Landor then went himself to demand rent, but Tombes was out and his wife greeted the hated landlord with a torrent of abuse. Landor knocked on the door with his umbrella in one hand and his hat in the other, yet to his astonishment he was then taken to court for trying to gain access to the house by breaking the lock to the house in Tombes' absence.

Landor had already made an enemy of Price, the lawyer engaged by Tombes. Price was an Inspector of Taxes and as Landor had refused to "play the game" and invite him to dinner and send him small gifts of game, there was no love lost between the two men. It was praise-worthy and typical of Landor's high principles of not encouraging croneyism or dishonesty that he refused to comply with the usual niceties, but it marked him as a dangerous man to the other locals.

Landor of course lost the case as soon as the jury knew a local man was in trouble. No one in the area wanted to upset Price and Landor realised that he was bound to lose.

There were various other brushes with the law at this time and the experiences were to colour Landor's view of the justice system for the rest of his life. He may well have had right and honesty on his side, but with insufficient friends in high places, he was always bound to lose out.

John Thomas, the proprietor of the Queen's Head public house and the blacksmith's shop close to Llanthony, paid no rent either and he used as an excuse the idea that Landor possessed no title to the properties. Worse still Thomas was a poacher and he lent poaching tackle to others, so he was doubly dangerous. It reached Landor's ears that Thomas was given to bragging about his exploits in the inn and one night Landor followed him. Afterwards Landor described the events.

"*He broke down the fence of my wood, & was in no foot-path. He stood before me with his arms folded & told me I had better not touch him. I instantly took him by the arm and swung him thro the hedge. I know not whether this is an assault – but if I catch him in my woods again, there shall be no doubt about the matter …I trust I can punish the rascal for having a net.*"

Thomas tried to sue Landor for assault and Landor prosecuted him for poaching.

From January 1812 the tenant of the best farm was Charles Betham, with whom Landor was at first friendly and from whom he borrowed money. However Betham was an inexperienced farmer and once he and Landor had quarrelled, both men were as nasty and puerile to each other as they could be. There were arguments over the cutting down of trees, of Betham ploughing up beautiful flower meadows dear to Landor's heart, of uprooting trees and finally of Landor circulating a handbill concerning Betham's younger brother, who had come to live at the farm.

FELONY! Fifty Guineas Reward –

Whereas Frederick Betham, late an inferior mate in a merchant ship in the East India Company's service, did threaten, in the presence of several persons, at several times, that he would root up some fir trees in the plantation of W.S.Landor Esq.; and was seen, in the evening of Saturday the 15th of May, followed by a person with a spade or shovel; and the said trees were found about twenty minutes afterwards rooted up. whoever will give such evidence against this F. Betham as may lead to his conviction, shall receive 50 Guineas as reward from me,

W.S. Landor

Llanthony Abbey, May 28th 1813

These handbills were posted at various places in Usk at the time of the Quarter Sessions by Landor and a servant. More handbills were taken to Monmouth by Landor and his wife at the time of the Assizes. Landor was clearly very angry.

In July 1813 Landor wrote to Charles Betham, complaining bitterly about the conduct of Frederick Betham, his younger brother.

"No difference in respect to the tenure of the farm could authorise the rude and unmanly conduct of your brother, not only to me but to Mrs Landor, who has always treated him as if he were a gentleman. His education and rank in life do not permit me to chastise this insolence, but it is made known to those who will not suffer it to be forgotten."

Although some of his family in Warwick thought that things must be Landor's fault because his occasional bursts of bad temper had aways angered people, there can be few honest and principled people who did not sympathise with him at this time. A few of the local landowners sided with him, but Landor had made some powerful enemies and his tactics of trying to tackle vested interest, petty crime and general injustice with honesty and high principles alone, were never going to work in the short term.

Although things still looked bleak, he and Julia moved into the new house at Llanthony in the summer of 1813. Family portraits, some of the family wine, old master paintings bought by Landor in earlier days and new silver-plate and furnishings adorned the house, but Landor was not enjoying life. In August 1813 he wrote to Southey,

"This blessed day, to use an expression which people seldom use so

emphatically, my masons have left me, after a job of three years. I live in my house, merely to keep it dry, just as a man would live in a dog kennel to guard his house. I hate and detest the very features of the country, so much vexation have I experienced in it, I wish to God I could exchange it for a house in Bath, or anywhere."

Throughout the year of 1813 there had been a worsening financial crisis and in October, Landor and his wife suddenly left Llanthony forever. Tired of the strife, sick at heart because around £70,000 had gone into the purchase of the Llanthony Estate and yet he was left short of cash, trying to legally recover his rents from Betham, yet being sued for libel in return. – Landor was deeply troubled by the injustice of it all.

He and Julia went to the place he had loved most in the past and that was Swansea. Pursued by creditors, having almost next to no cash at all, Landor tried to raise money from money-lenders. For a few months, he and Julia lived quietly in a house on Mount Pleasant, owned by a Miss Rose. The glorious views of Swansea Bay must have soothed his soul, but Landor knew the storm clouds were gathering.

Frantic letters to Gabb, his lawyer in Abergavenny were frequent. In November 1813 Landor wrote,

"I am now so totally without money that even if a letter comes I have not enough to pay the Postage."

Gabb tried to sell the Llanthony and Cymyoy Church livings which belonged to Landor but they brought in only a fraction of what was expected. Landor had to borrow £400 from Rev James Burrow, his wife's uncle, to pay an outstanding debt to a silversmith and a massive loan of three thousand pounds was completed from the Swansea bankers. Still Charles Betham who had agreed to pay around £1,000 year rent for his various holdings had paid nothing since his arrival in Llanthony in 1812. In fact he claimed that Landor actually owed him money because he had spent money improving his farms!

The tale of Landor the highly-principled, idealistic gentleman landowner, versus the young and inexperienced farmers, the Betham brothers, came to a head in April 1814 when the libel case against Landor was tried at Monmouth Assizes. Clearly with blame assigned to both sides, Landor eventually had to pay one hundred pounds for the libel against Frederick Betham and a mere two pounds for the libel against Charles Betham. This might have been far worse, but by the time the case was heard, Landor had other more pressing things on his mind.

For some time, Landor had been unable to pay his mother the four hundred and fifty pounds annual income from the Llanthony estate which she was due and this gave her prior claim in the financial trouble. By mid-May 1814 Landor had decided to cut his losses and go abroad to escape his creditors, but first he planned on spending three weeks with his mother in Warwick. Sadly this last visit never materialized and he never saw his mother again.

On May 27th 1814 Landor wrote to Southey from Weymouth where he was spending his last night in England before sailing for France.

"Every hope of meeting you again in England has vanished ... The Court of Exchequer has decided in my favour; but B(etham) has been able to promise bail and replevy, so that the ends of justice are defeated. Nearly three years rent will be due before I can receive one farthing from him; and all my timber is spoiled. I shall be utterly ruined ... The laws of England are made entirely for the protection of guilt. A creditor could imprison me for twenty pounds while a man who owes me two thousand, and keeps me from the possession of two thousand more, can convert wealth and affluence into poverty and distress, – can in short drive me for ever from my native country, and riot with impunity on the ruins of my estate. I had promised my mother to visit her. I can never hope to see her again. She is seventy two, and her sorrow at my overwhelming and most unmerited misfortune will surely shorten her days. My wife, when she married, little thought that she should leave all her friends to live in obscurity and perhaps want ... Whoever comes near me is either unhappy or ungrateful ... I go tomorrow to St Malo. In what part of France I shall end my days I know not, but there I shall end them; and God grant that I may end them speedily, and so as to leave as little sorrow as possible to my friends ... I am alone here. My wife follows me when I have found a place fit for her reception. Adieu!"

When Landor fled abroad, the family in Warwickshire rallied round to help. After all, their fortunes were also heavily involved in Llanthony and because of the clause giving his mother prior claim to her annual sum of money, she was able to organise a rescue plan for the estate.

Eventually Landor himself signed away all control over the management of the Llanthony Estate which was legally his, and also the Ipsley Estate which would become his on the death of his mother. His mother granted him an annual sum of money of three hundred pounds on which to live abroad, but as this money came from the sum set aside for his younger brothers and sisters, he was supposed to repay it to them when he was able. (However, the arrangement went on for so many years that shortly before his mother's death in 1829, his brothers and sisters revoked all claim to any repayment.)

In 1814 Rev. Charles Landor, as the second son and therefore Landor's heir, was appointed as Trustee and the two lawyers, brother Henry and cousin Walter Landor of Rugeley, between them managed the estate. Landor's furnishings at Llanthony and Bath were sold, his brothers buying some of his paintings. Gabb, the lawyer from Abergavenny was paid, partly from his buying in some of Landor's wine and books but Gabell, the Crickhowell lawyer, remained unpaid for many years. Eventually all the creditors were paid but it took a very long time for this to happen and by then some of them were dead.

Landor himself suffered tremendously from the humiliation of his failures at Llanthony. From the time when he was born, he had always been educated into thinking that one day he would be a great landowner and he had determined to do his best for his tenants and his land. Unlike many of his contemporaries, he adored wild flowers, ancient meadows and most of all magnificent trees and he had looked forward to the time when his ideas concerning conservation and tree-planting could be put into operation. However in just six years, all his dreams had crumbled and he was left destitute; reliant on his mother for money on which to live.

Many years later, after the death of his older brothers, Landor's brother Robert was to confide to a friend,

"*I have here in my rectory a Titian valued at twelve hundred guineas which my brother Henry purchased at the (Llanthony) auction for ten pounds.*" It seemed in 1814 that Walter Savage Landor was destined never to enjoy his paintings or indeed anything else.

Although the Llanthony episode saddened Landor tremendously, he never lost his love for the Swansea area. During his exile abroad, time and time again he referred to the area and he was most interested when his mother wrote to tell him in 1826 of a visit his sisters had made to Swansea. In the autumn of 1829 when Landor moved into the Villa Gherardesca in Fiesole, he summarized his feelings about South Wales when he wrote to tell his sisters of his beautiful villa.

"*I never think of it* (Llanthony) *without thinking of the ruin to which it has brought me, leaving me one of the poorest Englishmen in Florence, instead of one of the richest. However they might not think me so badly off if they came to see my beautiful villa, my noble hall and staircase. Yet I would rather have had it near Swansea, the part of the world I liked better than any."*

6. TRAVELS IN EUROPE
Tours, Como, Pisa etc, then his own
villa near Florence

Like many other young gentlemen of his age, the first time Landor was able to go abroad was during the pause in the Napoleonic Wars in 1802, after the Peace of Amiens had temporarily stopped the fighting. Having long thought of Napoleon Bonaparte as a hero, Landor wanted to see France and Napoleon for himself. Despite a lack of cash, off he went, as did William Wordsworth and a good many more young people who could acquire money for the journey.

Landor left for Paris in July, but things did not go well to begin with. He was delayed for a day on the way to Paris and when he stopped at a hotel, he found there was no fire in any of the sixty bedrooms and he had to wear his shirt *"as damp as a newspaper from the press."* Landor was unused to hardships!

Once installed in Paris, Landor did as much sightseeing as possible. He enjoyed the Louvre for apart from the Royal Academy there were few places in London at that time where good pictures were displayed publicly. Landor visited the gallery on a good many days, spending much time learning about French and Italian art and this knowledge of pictures was to colour his own art collecting for the rest of his life.

He first saw Napoleon at a parade in the Tuileries and he wrote eagerly to Warwick to tell his sister Elizabeth all about it.

"His countenance is not of that fierce cast which you see in the prints, and which perhaps it may assume in battle. He seems melancholy and reserved but not morose or proud. His figure and complexion are nearly like those of Charles Norris. He rode a little white horse, about the size of my father's ... After I had seen Bonaparte canter by me at the distance of a dozen yards, I left my situation at the window and went down close to the gate of the palace. Presently came the chief consul and a half a score generals. The people made room through fear of the horses, which indeed were fierce enough, being covered with blue and red velvet, one half of which was hid with gold lace. Instead of going with the crowd, I pushed forward and got by the side of

Bonaparte's Mamelouk, in a place where there were none but soldiers. There was a very tall fellow just before me. I begged him to let me see Bonaparte, and observed that probably he had seen him often and shared his victories. The youth was delighted. "Ah! le voila, monsieur!" said he: and in a moment there was nothing between me and this terror of Europe but the backs of two horses, over which I could see him as distinctly as I see this paper."

Landor observed Napoleon again a few days later but he also noticed that the ordinary French people were no better off than they had been before the revolution because they still did not have their freedom. In the years that followed Landor turned more and more against his former hero and by 1805 just before the battle of Trafalgar, he was actually urging the downfall of Napoleon.

As for the remainder of the trip to Paris in 1802, Landor was lucky enough to acquire lodgings in the Petit Trianon at Versailles. Although sightseeing took up much of his time, he did manage to finish a Latin version of "Gebir" whilst he was there. ("Gebir" was Landor's first long poem and had been published in English in 1798.)

Things were not all sweetness and light however, one of the main troubles being his complaint *"My pocket begins to wax feeble"*. He wanted his brother Henry to ask his father to send him money from his next quarter's allowance or perhaps his mother would lend him a hundred pounds? It seems Landor had fallen in love and wanted to follow the girl and her family to Switzerland.

However, the peace of 1802 did not last and after around a month, Landor like many other English people had to return home. Landor then hoped that this holiday romance would blossom and he waited in vain in Warwick for a letter. When nothing came, secretly he blamed his mother for intercepting his mail!

The war was resumed later in 1802 and all further travel abroad being out of the question, Landor spent his time mainly in Bath. However in 1808, shortly after purchasing the Llanthony Abbey Estate in Monmouthshire , Landor suddenly surprised almost all his friends by rushing to Spain to fight as a volunteer against Napoleon's army. Napoleon planned to make his brother King of Spain, but suddenly there sprang up huge organised resistance from the Spanish and volunteers from all over Europe joined in.

Whilst many in England applauded and encouraged the Spanish resistance, Landor and two Irish friends whom he had met in Brighton decided to give practical help and in August 1808 they set sail from Falmouth bound for Corunna. Landor and his friends, wanting to join the army of General Blake, proceeded to Lugo. By then, like many sympathetic foreigners, Landor had made a donation to help the war cause by giving around one hundred and ten pounds for the relief of the town of Venturada, destroyed because it was loyal and stuck out against the French. Landor was in charge of a group of volunteers to whom he gave as he had offered,

"a daily allowance of full pay to every soldier I am leading to the armies, together with some occasional gratuities to keep up their spirits on the march."

Landor and his troop proceeded to Villa Franca and from thence to Astorga where Blake's army had its headquarters. Soon afterwards Blake moved southwards but Landor and many other divisions were sent elsewhere. He saw little, if any, direct action but at Bilbao at least he felt himself to have done something useful. Landor later told Southey,

"I had the satisfaction of serving three launches with powder and muskets and of carrying on my shoulders six or seven miles a child too heavy for its exhausted mother. These are things without difficulty and without danger; yet they please, independently of gratitude or applause. I was near to being taken the following day."

However, by early October 1808 Landor was on his way home, full of disgust at the way in which the Convention of Cintra had been signed, with the English giving the French armies the opportunity to withdraw. He sailed for home but the Peninsular War had many more twists and turns before Napoleon was frustrated in his attempts to conquer Spain and Portugal. In later life Landor became very friendly with General Sir William Napier who had been in charge of a regiment under Sir John Moore in Spain. Napier wrote a history of the Peninsular War for which he received much acclaim.

If Landor the idealist fought in Spain, the next time he went abroad it was as a fugitive from creditors. Just six years later, after some miserable times at Llanthony, Landor set sail from Weymouth bound for St Malo. From St Malo he sailed for Jersey and there his wife Julia and Laura, one of her sisters, joined him. They spent a month in Jersey, but on the day before they were due to travel to France, Landor and his wife had a row so severe that he imagined it would be the end of their marriage.

Landor had decided to leave Jersey and as usual once he had made up his mind, he wanted no inquest about it. However Julia did not want to go and in the end she taunted her husband saying such things as it was her own fault for marrying so old a man. Laura was so upset by the things which the twenty year old Mrs Landor said that she burst into tears. Julia told Laura not to be such a fool as to cry and if she herself cried it certainly would not be about her husband! (In after years Laura married Colonel Stopford and the couple remained staunch friends with Landor.)

Of the quarrel Landor wrote,

"I endured all this a full hour and a half without a syllable of reply; but every kind and tender sentiment was rooted up from my heart for ever … No woman could or ought to live with a man by whom such language was merited; nor could any man support life with a woman from whom it fell undeserved. ..I am resolved to see her no more … I have neither wife nor family, nor house nor home, nor pursuit nor occupation."

Poor Landor realised the basis of the trouble was that his wife seemed to enjoy rowing with him. She could not leave him alone. He went on,

"A thousand times have I implored her not to drive me to distraction; to be contented if I acknowledged myself in the wrong; to permit me to be at once of her opinion, and not to think a conversation complete without a quarrel. The usual reply was, 'A pleasant sort of thing truly, that you are never to be contradicted!"

That night in 1814, Landor was very troubled and he rose at dawn and walked to the other side of the island and boarded an oyster boat for France. He landed at Granville and took a pony to the town of Tours where he decided to settle alone.

However, after an interval of some months, Landor had a letter from his wife's sister. Julia had been very ill but now she was a little better and she desired to join him. So in February 1815 Landor travelled to Dieppe to meet his young wife, then only twenty one, and bring her and her English maid to the house in Tours which he had rented.

It was probably a courteous rather than a passionate reunion. Julia was no doubt resigned to her fate of living abroad without the support of her family around her and Landor, for all that he welcomed the reunion, had lost all love for her when she treated him so unkindly in Jersey. Julia never again returned to England and she chose to spend the remainder of her long life in France and Italy.

It was just at this time in the spring of 1815 that Napoleon escaped from Elba and there was renewed fighting between the French and

English, resulting in the defeat of Napoleon and the French at the decisive Battle of Waterloo, near Brussels, in June 1815. Although there were numerous English families in Tours at the start of 1815, most had left by the early summer, but Landor had elected to remain.

One evening soon after the Battle of Waterloo, Landor was out walking on the Esplanade in Tours when he saw a muffled horseman ride up to the Prefect's house. Having had a close look at the French Emperor some years previously, he remained convinced that it was Napoleon himself whom he saw on that night, as he was fleeing to La Rochelle.

When Landor fled from Llanthony his business affairs were in a mess but his mother, his brother Henry Eyres Landor and the family law firm in Rugeley worked out a rescue plan leaving the Llanthony Estate in the hands of trustees. The creditors were to be paid as and when it became possible and once the documents had been drawn up, they urgently needed Landor's written approval. The youngest brother, Robert Eyres Landor, wanting to travel to Italy himself, undertook to carry the documents to Landor and so it was that Robert arrived in Tours in October 1815.

Always chivalrous, Landor was on good terms with the women in the local market and his brother Robert noted that he seemed happy. Landor had become particularly friendly with the scholar Francis Hare who had come to the area to be close to his dying father and there were other Englishmen in the area with whom he was on friendly terms.

Perhaps for the first time, Robert Landor and the rest of the family in England learned the truth about the whole Llanthony affair. When Landor had raised the huge loan of £3,000 from the Swansea bankers, the family had thought the worst of him and had imagined that the money was for his own use on the continent. It seems that only now did the enormous mismanagement of the Llanthony estate become apparent.

Robert was amazed when he learned the true extent of the dissembling which had gone on at Llanthony and how legal adviser after legal adviser had failed to do all that they should have done. On 4th October 1815 Robert Landor wrote to Henry,

"Walter appears to be very much altered in disposition & I never felt so sorry for him before. The threat of the Swansea bankers hangs upon his mind ... he has made a solemn resolution never to spend more than £450 a year,

even after my mother's death, till every guinea is paid off & his wife joins him in this resolution."

Within a few days of Robert's arrival, the brothers had decided to leave Tours which was becoming very unsafe. Almost all the English families had gone and if France was occupied by the allies who had fought against Napoleon, the Swansea bankers might have been able to arrest Landor for debt after all.

Taking advantage of the cheaper living in Tours, Landor had his own carriage and it was decided to use this for the flight. They set out through German-occupied territory and travelled post – *" Walter and myself on the dicky, his wife and her maid within,"* as Robert described the events.

There then followed a most amazing journey across France with the occupying armies close by and the Landors staying in poor inns or whatever accommodation they could find. Robert reported to the family in Warwick how they had passed from Tours to Lyons, a distance of four hundred miles through two hundred thousand troops including Austrians, Prussians, Bavarians, Wirtembergers and Hessians.

When they arrived in Savoy, Landor and his wife thought of settling there, but they decided to go on. A bargain was struck with a voiturier that he would convey them across the Alps, first to Milan then Como, free of charge, with all their food and lodgings thrown in, in return for the ownership of Landor's carriage.

The long and uncomfortable journey over several weeks seemed to bring out the worst in the two brothers and the young wife. Walter Landor was worried, Julia tired and resentful and Robert Landor jealous of his eldest brother's pretty wife! Robert wrote to brother Henry,

"He (Walter) *is seldom out of a passion or sulky fit excepting at dinner when he is more boisterous and good humoured than ever. Then his wife is a darling, a beauty, an angel, and a bird. But for just as much reason the next morning she is a fool. She is certainly quiet, patient, and submissive … if he loses his keys, his purse, or his pocket handkerchief, which he does ten times an hour, she is to be blamed; and she takes it all very quietly."*

Cynical people might have guessed that young Julia, still only twenty one and probably ordered by her mother (who might other-wise have had to support her in Bath) to rejoin her husband only months earlier, was playing a part and biding her time. If her husband Walter Landor spent all day reading and writing, then she felt alone and neglected.

Having passed through the Alps by Napoleon's new road over Mount Cénis and thence via Turin, Robert Landor left the oddly matched married couple at Milan and they proceeded to Como in the same carriage, whilst he waited for its return to take him to Rome. If Landor and his wife thought that all their troubles would be behind them, how wrong they were!

It is a well known fact that the Prince Regent (later George IV) detested his wife Caroline and wanted her out of his life. When Walter and Julia Landor arrived in Como, attended only by Julia's English maid, they found that Caroline, attended by a whole retinue of servants, was also in the area.

Because he still feared that the Swansea bankers might get word of his whereabouts, Landor kept his life secretive and quiet. He and his wife settled quietly and mixed little in society, but because of this he soon attracted the attentions of the authorities, who suspected him of being a spy sent to reveal the secrets of Caroline's bedchamber so that the Prince Regent could obtain a divorce more easily. There were many who sympathised with the plight of Princess Caroline who had given birth to Princess Charlotte in 1796, the year after her marriage which had been arranged for political reasons. However the unscrupulous Prince Regent had determined that he would never again live with her or admit her to be his queen. Back in Warwickshire Samuel Parr in his Hatton Church regularly disobeyed instructions and had Caroline's name included in the list of the Royal family mentioned in church during each service. This later brought Parr official recognition from Caroline's supporters, but in 1815, only six years before the unfortunate Queen was to attempt to attend her husband's coronation and be barred, sympathies on the continent were mixed.

Within an English enclave in an Italian city, there was bound to be gossip and Landor believed, probably wrongly, that Princess Caroline was much at fault. He was appalled at being taken for a spy and he then took refuge in telling everyone where he lived and being openhearted about everything. However gossip being what it was amongst the English in Como, the poor Princess could hardly obtain any efficient servants and before long, Julia Landor's maid had been enticed away to join the royal entourage.

Robert called again on his return from Rome in June 1816 and by then Walter and Julia Landor were installed in a comfortable house in Como. They found that the small sum that Walter's mother had allowed them (four hundred and fifty pounds a year) was more than ample for gracious living, yet Julia was thin and talked of dying or returning to Bath.

Living in a beautiful place, in a comfortable house seemed to be scant comfort for Julia Landor who must have realised by then that she did not love her husband, if indeed she ever did. Perhaps the seeds of resentment which were to surface so unpleasantly in later years were sowed then.

In June 1817 Landor's friend Southey, the Poet Laureate who felt the need to travel after the death of his eldest son the previous year, visited Landor in Como. Although their views differed on many subjects, in their hearts Southey and Landor were truly kindred spirits as they both testify. How Southey must have treasured the diverting moments he spent that hot summer with Landor who was a very amusing companion indeed, famous for his loud, infectious laugh. Afterwards Landor described these times in the Imaginary Conversation between himself and Southey, published in the later 1820s.

"**Southey**. *Well do I remember our long conversations in the silent and solitary church of Sant' Abondio (surely the coolest spot in all Italy) and how often I turned my head toward the open door, fearing lest some pious passerby, or some more distant one in the wood above, pursuing the pathway that leads to the tower of Luitprand, should hear the roof echo with your laughter, at the stories you had collected about the brotherhood and sisterhood of the place.*"

In March 1818 Landor was overjoyed for Julia gave birth to their first son and at last he had an heir. Landor named the boy Arnold Savage after a speaker of the House of Commons centuries previously, thinking that perhaps he had been an ancestor of his mother. It must be supposed that Julia had had a difficult pregnancy for Landor wrote to his mother that she had been bled seventeen times in the last six months of her pregnancy. Having suffered from miscarriages in the past, Julia Landor could hardly be blamed if future childbirth seemed something to be feared. Yet Landor reported happily to his mother that both mother and baby seemed well and that Julia had an abundance of milk and planned to breastfeed for eleven or twelve months.

Despite the fact that he now had a six month old son to be

considered, by the middle of the year 1818 Landor was thinking of leaving Como but as things turned out his hand was forced. A famous Italian poet had written a sonnet attacking England and Landor, feeling the honour of his country was at stake, had written a Latin reply, which he attempted to publish anonymously with several other similar verses. The local officials summoned Landor to a meeting, accused him of writing an insolent letter and a massive row developed.

Landor said that the word insolent should never be applied to any gentleman, whereupon the local official grew angry and hinted that the matter might need to be settled with swords in the square! Always prone to meet anger with anger, Landor laughed in the man's face when he attempted reconciliation and he can hardly have been surprised when he was ordered to leave the Como area. Always wishing to prove his point, Landor stayed a week longer than he was officially permitted to do, but then he left quietly and settled for a short time near Genoa.

Soon the family moved on to Pisa, for they had heard it was a cheap place to live. Such was not the case, but it was a warm and congenial place for the young mother and her infant to pass the winter. Hoping to move to Florence in the near future, Landor found his plans thwarted and it was not until 1821 that the family were able to make the desired move.

In the meantime young Arnold grew sturdy and Landor made plans for his education. He wrote to Southey,

"He begins to walk. I am anxious for the time when he will talk as much nonsense to me as I have to him ... My plan (regarding education) is to have no plan at all. I shall teach my son Latin and Greek, as I teach him Italian and English, by practice ..."

On March 6th 1820 two years almost to the day after Arnold had been born, Landor's daughter Julia Elizabeth was born in Pisa. Mother Julia seemed fit and well and Landor reported enthusiastically to his mother.

At one stage whilst the Landors were in Pisa, the poet Shelley was also in the area. Shelley let it be known that he would like to meet Landor, but Landor refused as he believed rumours of misconduct which surrounded his fellow poet. Landor was to regret this decision greatly in the years that followed.

Whilst still in Pisa, Landor again became caught up with the scandal connected with Caroline, Princess of Wales. Gossip was rife in Pisa but although he thought Caroline guilty of much, Landor refused to condemn her, writing to Southey,

"*… not knowing her guilty, I am not authorized to prejudice her: proofs alone constitute guilt.*"

Landor knew that Dr Parr still actively continued to take Caroline's part, but although he disapproved of this, he condemned those who hounded the woman so much.

It was well that Landor was out of England at this time, for there might have been a huge family row had he been in Warwick. His brother Robert Eyres Landor was actively condemning Caroline and there must have been constant arguments between the brothers. As things were, Landor wrote a letter to 'The Times' saying that he would never repeat any gossip and this Robert Eyres Landor read with disgust.

Robert Eyres Landor was then a Chaplain at the important Hughendon Estate (where he had family influence) but he used his brilliant classical brain and literary style to write various letters to the Courier newspaper under a clever pseudonym. The letters were so vitriolic against Caroline that the newspaper was accused of libel. Apparently Henry Eyres Landor had offered to go to prison in place of Robert should the identity of the letter writer be discovered, and once again, a family letter indicates just how little the family understood of the educated and correct stance adopted by Landor.

Robert wrote to Henry Landor in December 1820,

"*Elizabeth will tell you of Walter's letter in the Times, if you have not already heard of it. He is the most whimsical creature on earth since the times of Puck. His indignation against the government is so great that it has half consumed his former hatred for the Queen, as a fire is supposed to burn out a scald. But, however, his letter is just what one could have wished in one respect, it is too magnificent to be intemperate.*"

Eventually, the following year, poor Queen Caroline was shut out of her husband's coronation and she died two weeks later in July 1821. Those, like Robert Eyres Landor, who had condemned the queen so harshly, possibly lived to be ashamed of their actions for as the years passed it became evident that the king had behaved in a most unkind and ungentlemanly manner.

Eventually Landor and his family moved to Florence and in 1821 the first apartment rented by the Landors was the Palazzo Lozzi. However a row with the owner led to the Landors moving to an apartment in the Palazzo Medici a few months later in November

1821. At that time, there were a number of impoverished nobles in Italy who were only too willing to rent out their property and sell their paintings.

This grand apartment, one of several owned by Marchese de'Medici-Tornaquinci, was in Borgo degli Albizi, not far from the Bargello and the rent was around fifty pounds a year. Landor described in a letter to a friend how he had furnished the apartment in late 1821.

"Furniture is very cheap in Italy, and sells for above two -thirds, after much using. I furnished the Palazzo Medici, fourteen rooms, for about six hundred pounds – there were however the carpets and girandoles – and my dinner service cost seventy. There were three or four rooms remaining which were left bare. Everything here is cheaper here than in England, except the wages of the servants. I pay my coachman nearly the same as at Lantony and the maids are paid more."

Julia Landor could hardly complain that she was living in impoverished circumstances! By all accounts the apartment was an extremely beautiful one and the furnishings, busts and pictures were all of the highest quality.

Landor himself came to love the city of Florence and his wife appeared to enjoy the social life. English visitors seemed to flock to Landor and as far as writing went, it was a very productive period. On 13th November 1822, about a year after the Landors had moved, a second son, Walter Savage Junior, was born. Friendships with Francis Hare, Keats' friend Charles Armitage Brown and the painter Seymour Kirkup helped to make this period a happy time for Landor.

Through Francis, Landor became friendly with all the Hare brothers, meeting Augustus in 1821 and having much correspondence with Julius from 1822. Julius was exceptionally helpful over the publication of the "Imaginary Conversations" but Landor did not actually meet him until 1832.

The artist Seymour Kirkup became a very faithful friend in later years and he grew to understand Landor extremely well. Kirkup gave a delightful description of Landor and Francis Hare as they were when they conversed together in the 1820s.

"It was a constant struggle of competition and display between them, both often wrong, although men of strong memory. They used to have great disputes often on questions of history ... Hare was often astounded at being corrected. He was thought infallible."

Besides sharing Landor's independent spirit, Francis Hare spoke most European languages and had a wonderful memory, being able to quote perfectly pages of books he had read. It must have been marvellous entertainment for their friends to hear Hare and Landor discourse together.

Charles Brown too was a very good friend to Landor at this time and when Leigh Hunt and his wife arrived in 1823 to live in Maiano near Florence, Brown introduced him to Landor.

In 1824 the first of his "Imaginary Conversations" were published and fame began to come to Landor at last. Having written the conversations over a period of years, Landor entrusted the manuscripts to Julius Hare, whom he knew only through Francis. Julius Hare found a publisher Taylor who was willing to publish at joint expense (author and publisher sharing expenses and profits) and Southey helped enormously in getting the work published. Taylor had originally objected to lines such as,

"I must piss upon these firebrands before I can make them tractable."
which came in the conversation between Walter Noble and Oliver Cromwell. In vain did the publisher point out that such words would affect sales and that one word might make the difference between one thousand copies being printed and seven hundred and fifty. Southey was negotiating on behalf of his friend and in the end Landor had his way and "piss" was in the first two editions. However later editions substituted "spit" for as the nineteenth century wore on, language became more refined and some robust words which had been in use in the 18th century were deemed impolite and unusable.

This somewhat amusing incident concerning the word "piss" serves to illustrate how passionately Landor cared about the English language. In some later "Imaginary Conversations" Landor allowed his characters to give voice to his ideas concerning reformed spelling and style.

The Landors stayed in the splendid apartment in central Florence for several years and life for them both seemed good. In the Renaissance City, surrounded by the beautiful countryside of Tuscany, Landor seemed to mature, his confidence grew and with his own young children he appeared to find a happiness hitherto only dreamed about.

In February 1824 when her brother had paid a visit Julia had almost decided to go on a visit to England. The plan was that Julia and the two eldest children would travel back with her brother, so that she could see two of her sisters again, perhaps for the last time before they went to live abroad. Landor himself purposely put no pressure on his wife either way, although he said that, being the one to stay in Italy with toddler Walter Savage, he would miss the other two children enormously. However Julia's visit did not take place for she found herself pregnant again and Landor's mother never saw her grandchildren, although she repeatedly begged Landor to send Arnold back to England for his education. Old Mrs Landor even offered to pay for Arnold's school fees for Rugby, but always Julia seemed reluctant to let the children go. Both she and Landor seemed happier when they were together with all the children.

Landor's third son Charles was born on August 5th and the pregnancy proved to be a difficult one. Mrs Landor's face, fingers and legs often swelled and her condition, then described as dropsy, may have indicated the problem known as pre-eclampsia today. The baby was born two months premature, but despite that Landor was able to write home to his mother in Warwick that he "*was doing well and even strong*". Called Charles Savage after Landor's maternal grandfather, it was not long before Landor began using the pet name Carlino for the baby.

Life again seemed good for the Landor family. In March 1824 the first two volumes of the "Imaginary Conversations" had been published and as the months went by, Landor achieved a degree of fame, as he was sought out by a variety of visitors to Florence. Julia Landor had four healthy children, a fine apartment and a high social standing in Florence and yet ... The truth was perhaps that no amount of fine trimmings could disguise Walter and Julia Landor's growing unsuitability for each other.

They were both devoted to the children and neither parent wanted to be parted from them for even a single day. Julia Landor had several servants to make her domestic load a light one, however that did not prevent her developing a kind of hysteria and as the years went by, a nurse was often in attendance at their apartment. It seemed that the trigger for much of the trouble was her husband and perhaps modern psychologists would say that Julia Landor did not like being the wife of a writer. It may well have been that she resented the fact that she and the children were often asked to give Landor the peace and solitude in which to write and that instead of a nurse or doctor, what she really needed was undivided love. Also it would have been quite understandable if Mrs Landor had been scared of future pregnancies, bearing in mind her bad experience with the last, and that may well have made her decide that sexual intercourse in the future was too risky.

In the summer months when it was hot in Florence, Landor usually rented a house in the hills, away from the heat and disease of the city. Realising how much better it was to live in the Tuscan countryside, he said he would have made the move to the country a permanent one, except that his wife wanted to be part of the social life of the city for at least part of the year.

The steady procession of visitors continued. One morning in March 1825 William Hazlitt had arrived without an introduction and his fashionable attire had caused quite a stir. Mrs Landor had described it as "*A dress-coat and nankeen trousers halfway up his legs, leaving his stockings well visible over his shoes.*" Years later Seymour Kirkup recalled the incident.

"*I perfectly remember Hazlitt's being here. He wished to pay Landor a visit, but was advised not, unless he was well introduced. Armitage Brown, who was Landor's greatest friend here, offered him a letter; but Hazlitt said he would beard the lion in his den, and he walked up to his house one winter's morning in nankeen shorts and white stockings; was made much of by the royal animal; and often returned – at night; for Landor was much out in the day, in all weathers.*"

Hazlitt and Landor got on famously despite their differing views on dress. Already Landor, perhaps like the absent-minded scholar he sometimes was, often dressed shabbily, sometimes to the extent of being taken for a beggar by servants.

Seymour Kirkup recalled,

"*… He often was shabbily dresssed, and I have known servants offend him by taking for a beggar or poor devil. He had the reputation of being a violent man, and no doubt was so. But I never saw anything but the greatest gentleness and courtesy in him, especially to women. He was chivalresque of the old school. At Lord Dillon's in Florence we used to meet often, and there we made the acquaintance of Lamartine. Landor was much attached to Lord Dillon, in spite of his being a poet; for he was always reciting, and people laughed at him. Not so Landor. He showed the most courteous attention; and often gave him a word of advice, so gently as never to offend him. He used to say that Lord Dillon's smiling handsome fair face was like a ray of sunshine in Florence.*"

By piecing together snatches of the reminiscences of various literary people, a quite delightful picture of Landor's life at this time can be obtained. Landor took Hazlitt to dinner at Lord Dillon's and afterwards Hazlitt said,

"It was the first time I had dined with a lord; and by gad, sir, he had all the talk to himself. He never waited for an answer. He talks as much as Coleridge; only he doesn't pump it out."

That Landor was well known for being sympathetic towards Lord Dillon speaks volumes for his character, as did his great friendship with Gould Francis Leckie, an old acquaintance of Lord Byron. Leckie it seems was always playful, waggish and satirical and Landor loved his company, as much as Mrs Landor hated it.

In November 1825 the writer Thomas Jefferson Hogg paid a visit and gave the Landor family a great deal of amusement. Landor later wrote to his mother,

"A Mr Hare, a very learned man, was sitting with me one morning when Mr Hogg sent in his card with Dr Lambe's name also on it. I showed it to Hare and told him I now thought myself La Fontaine, with all the better company of the beasts about me. He was delighted."

Landor's mother wrote back to say that she could imagine him laughing as he made the remark! So she was laughing too and enjoying the mention of Dr Lambe of the Warwick of previous days.

A trip to Rome with Francis Hare in January 1826 was a total delight – so much so that planned for two weeks, it soon lengthened into four. A letter from Charles Armitage Brown to Joseph Severn, one of Keats' friends, brought Landor into contact with Severn and during the trip they enjoyed each other's company. From that time on, Brown's letters to Severn often contained messages from Landor.

Whilst Landor was away, Arnold sent his *"Dearest papa"* a letter and in return Landor wrote

"I shall never be quite happy till I put my cheek on your head. Tell my sweet Julia that if I see twenty little girls, I will not romp with any of them before I romp with her; and kiss your two dear brothers for me ... God preserve and bless you, my own Arnold. My heart beats as if it would fly to you, my own fierce ceature. We shall very soon meet. Love your Babbo."

Some might feel that Landor was in danger of spoiling Arnold and his brothers and sister. Visitors to the Landor apartment in the late 1820s certainly felt that Arnold's behaviour left much to be desired.

Lord Normanby too was an old friend of Landor and in late 1826 Landor had written home to his mother

"We are very gay here at Florence. Last night we were at a private play

given by Lord Normanby. He and Lady Normanby act admirably. Arnold was very much flattered by being invited, and the more, as he was the only one of his age who received an invitation."

In 1827 Lord Blessington called on Landor whom he had known many years previously in Bath and a delightful friendship grew up between the Blessingtons and Landor. Francis Hare had been staying with the Blessingtons in Pisa when he learned that Landor was confined to bed with quinsy – a nasty complaint from which Landor suffered at intervals when an abcess formed on or behind the tonsils. Landor was lying on a sofa in an inner drawing room of the beautiful apartment in the Palazzo Medici, when a servant announced Lord Blessington. Before Landor could reply that he knew no one of that name, the Earl was at the door saying,

"Come, come Landor! If you don't know Blessington, you may remember Mountjoy."

A few days later the Earl brought Lady Blessington to see Landor and make him well again – indeed it would be difficult to imagine anyone more likely to inspire the invalid than that beautiful lady! Herself a formidable literary presence, Marguerite Blessington had also known Dr Parr (whom she had met in London) and Byron whom she had met a number of times.

A couple of months after the Blessingtons and Count D'Orsay arrived in Florence, Landor was persuaded to accompany Lord Blessington on a trip to Naples in his yacht. Although Arnold had just recovered from a fever, Mrs Landor and the children seemed well enough to be left, but within twenty four hours of his sailing Landor's wife had become seriously ill. Describing the matter later to his sister Elizabeth, Landor wrote,

"The complaint was a malignant fever of the very worst kind. She took three emetics in one day, and in the first two days of her illness she was bled twice in the arm, and in the succeeding days wih leeches. Besides all these tortures she had mustard, and God knows what, applied to her feet and legs."

Baby Charles caught the fever from his mother and for around three days it was thought that he would die. However the doctor visited the patients every day (once sleeping at the villa overnight) and gradually both began to improve. Quick thinking by Lady Blessington had saved the day as far as the rest of the family was concerned for she had driven out to the villa from Florence taking young Julia and Walter back with her, thus preventing them catching the illness. By the time Landor arrived back, his trip having been cut short because he had had no letter from home and guessed something was wrong, his wife was a little better, but still unable to speak coherently.

Towards the end of September 1827 Mrs Landor was well enough to be moved back to Florence but she was still very weak. Anxious to move back the three miles or so to the city, she was brought part of the way *"by means of oxen on the sledge, and upon two mattresses,"* as Landor later described.

Once Mrs Landor was recovered, Landor could resume his normal life and until November, when they left for Rome, he was in the habit of visiting the Blessingtons in their apartment in Florence every evening. Lady Blessington wrote in her journal,

"The shades of night send us home to enjoy iced tea and sorbetti in our charming pavilion over looking the Arno, where a few friends assemble every evening. Walter Savage Landor seldom misses this accustomed visit, and his real conversations are quite as delightful as his imaginary ones. In listening to the elevated sentiments and fine observations of this eloquent man, the mind is carried back to other times; and one could fancy oneself attending to the converse of a philosopher of antiquity, instead of that of an individual of the nineteenth century; though to be sure, one of the most remarkable persons of this, or any age."

In the spring of 1828 the Blessingtons again took up residence in Florence for a time and Landor resumed his evening visits. For the Blessingtons and Landor it was an idyllic time, before some of the sad times in the not too distant future.

Changes of residence several times in 1827 and 1828 then led indirectly to Landor's threatened expulsion from Florence in April 1829. In that month Landor was robbed of seventeen pieces of silver plate and when he reported the matter to the police, a disagreement soon developed over Landor's remarks about a previous alleged theft. The police felt they could not ignore the remarks and as a face-saving exercise ordered Landor to leave Florence within three days. The Florentine authorities were angry with him for several comments written in the "Imaginary Conversations" but eventually after Landor had spent time out of Florence in Lucca and his wife had petitioned the Grand Duke and friends had tried to smooth things on his behalf, Landor was allowed back.

Sir Robert Lawley, later Lord Wenlock, an old friend of the Landor family, was in Florence and he had used his influence, as had Lord Normanby. Landor was persuaded that he must try to avoid confrontation in future. Whilst out of Florence, Landor had received the news that Lord Blessington had died suddenly of apoplexy in Paris and life suddenly seemed serious.

During the summer of 1829 Landor went house-hunting with a friend Joseph Ablett whom he had met in the spring of the previous year, when Mrs Dashwood, Hare's cousin, had introduced them. Ablett was a great admirer of Landor's work and in Llanbedr in North Wales he had a great estate. Ablett and Landor walked to view a cottage to rent with twelve acres of ground near Fiesole, but then Ablett persuaded Landor to inspect a much grander villa nearby. As the owner wanted to sell, not rent, Ablett begged Landor to arrange the purchase on his behalf, but then said that he would like Landor to have the villa and repay the purchase money (around two thousand pounds) when he was able. It was a generous gift and Ablett refused to take any interest whatsoever on his money.

Named the Villa Gherardesca, the villa and small estate was one of the finest in the Fiesole area. Situated about a quarter of a mile east of San Domenico, it was said to have links with the Italian writer Boccaccio.

Before he could be well settled in the villa however Landor received a sad letter from Warwickshire. The death of his mother in October 1829 gave him a nasty reminder of how far from England he was and how long it had been since he saw any of his family in Warwickshire. For some time his mother's death set him thinking about his past and all the old family friends.

A couple of years later however, when he was well settled, Landor wrote to his sisters Elizabeth and Ellen in Warwick sending them a marvellous description of the new estate.

"*The front of the house is towards the north, looking at the ancient town of Fiesole three quarters of a mile off ... The hall is 31ft by 22 and 20 feet high. On the right is the drawing room 22 by 20 and through it you come to another 26 by 20. All are 20 feet high. Opposite the door is another leading down to the offices on right and left; and between them to a terrace walk about a hundred yards long, overlooking Valdarno and Vallombrosa, celebrated by Milton.*"

Landor goes on to describe how the place had four good bedrooms, plus a smaller one on an upper floor and two for servants. He had two gardens "*one with a fountain and one with a jet d'eau.*"

Visitors arrived with even greater frequency. Crabb Robinson came in 1830 and also John Kenyon (Elizabeth Barrett's cousin) who came with his wife. Landor invited his two sisters who still lived in the family home in Warwick to come to stay, promising them the best bedrooms if they made the journey. However the two sisters did not come – only Edward Wilson Landor, a second cousin, a few years later.

Crabb Robinson, a retired barrister, roughly the same age as Landor, had come with an introduction from Southey and Wordsworth. For the latter part of his long life, he was friendly with many literary figures and later his published diaries made interesting reading. After their first meeting, Robinson said of Landor,

"He was respected universally. He had credit for generosity, as well as honesty; and he deserved it, provided an ample allowance was made for caprice. He was conscious of his own infirmity of temper, and told me he saw few persons, because he could not bear contradiction. Certainly I frequently did contradict him; yet his attentions to me, both this and the following year, were unwearied."

A very amusing episode in the life of the Landor family came about because of Landor's preoccupation with improving the estate and planting many trees. He tried to recreate an English garden, similar to that in Warwick, but of course all these plans needed water, which in Italy is in far shorter supply than England. The daily watering of the plants, not to mention the daily use of a family of six, plus guests, placed the water supply of the villa under severe strain and the little brook which had previously flowed from the estate of the villa to the neighbouring property, owned by a Frenchman, Monsieur Antoir, dried up.

Anyone with a grain of common sense would have perceived the problem at the outset, but once his ideas for creating a garden were in full flow, Landor was unstoppable!

The authorities received complaints from both sides and the stalemate eventually resulted in Monsieur Antoir challenging Landor to a duel. Landor was an excellent fencer and a crack-shot with a pistol and so it seemed was Monsieur Antoir. It was in the spring of 1831 that the duel was averted as was Landor's possible banishment from Tuscany, for duelling was against the law and carried the strictest penalties. Seymour Kirkup the artist, who was designated to act as Landor's second, made a discreet agreement with Count de Garay, the French Minister who feared a diplomatic incident. Kirkup pledged to pacify Landor and the Count did the same for Antoir.

However this was not the end of the matter and Monsieur Antoir began a lawsuit which went on for many years and was eventually settled in 1841 when Landor had to pay between two and three hundred pounds.

On his side, Landor could not leave the matter alone, but instead took the writer's way and included the arguments and lawsuit in the work "High and Low Life in Italy," which he was currently writing. This work contained many topical references and recognisable figures and was eventually published in England in 1837, fortunately after Landor had left Tuscany. Leigh Hunt, who had undertaken the publication, was asked to keep the work anonymous, but it was quite clear from the instalment "The Cardinal-Legate Albani and Picture Dealers" that the work was Landor's.

In this witty dialogue Landor gives a very amusing picture of himself at the time the watercourse row broke out. The Marchese Scampa says

"*The proud Englishman had bought a villa and a couple of farms under Fiesole; rooting up olives, cutting down vines, the madman! A Frenchman was his neighbour. He had the right to the waste water from the proud Englishman's fountain. The proud Englishman, in his spite and malignancy, not only shaved every morning, and ordered all his menservants to the number of five, to shave also just as frequently, but he washed his hands and face several times in the day, and especially at that season when the water is most wanted. In like manner did all his children, four of them; and all four bathed: all four Eminence! all four! every day! the malignant father setting them the example.*"

A little further on comes a description of Landor's garden. "... *this one committed the injury through wanton extravagance, shaving washing bathing, beside watering two hundred orange, lemon citron trees and then laurels and myrtles, and rhododendrons and magnolias and all the fantastical flowers imaginable. No wonder there was little waste water. The Frenchman cited him before the tribunals.*"

By now, any readers then as now, would say "Typical Landor" and laugh. Indeed Landor could laugh at himself and frequently did, as was illustrated in that passage. However that did not mean that he gave up fighting, which was why the lawsuit dragged on for so long.

Not long after the Landors had moved to the Villa Gherardesca, one of Landor's oldest friends came to visit Florence with her family. Landor could not do enough for the wealthy young widow and her children and so it was that he personally supervised the renting of a fine apartment for her in the best part of Florence and during her visit, often walked down to have breakfast with her and her family. She and her children from her second marriage, who were of a similar age to Landor's children, romped around at the villa and what pleasure it must have given Landor to be once more in the presence of his Ianthe. The friendship begun in 1803 in Bath was renewed.

The love of his life had returned to it. Although they were destined never to marry, what a boost Landor received from contact once more with this person, who, above all others, was his kindred spirit, his calming influence, his contact with his youth.

Ianthe was given a very special task to perform at the villa one evening after she and her family had dined with the Landors. With the help of Francesco the gardener, Ianthe and her three daughters were asked to plant some mimosa trees, and her son William was asked to compose a poem to celebrate the occasion. When the time came, Landor planned that his body should be laid to rest there. Amidst the fragrant trees planted by her fair hand, Landor hoped to be united in death with her spirit.

It was a sentimental idea, readily understood the world over by those lovers destined never to be able to marry the partner of their dreams. However by all accounts the evening was far from being a sad one and when Landor improvised some verse as they stood on the hill-side, his own laughter mingled with that of his guests.

Some little time later Landor composed a serious verse about his intended grave.

> Lo! where the four mimosas blend their shade,
> In calm repose at last is Landor laid;
> For ere he slept he saw them planted here
> By her his soul had ever held most dear,
> And he had lived enough when he had dried her tear.

What Julia Landor thought of the mimosas is not recorded – suffice to say that no poems exist which Landor wrote for his wife. Despite the fact that Mrs Landor enjoyed her husband's excellent social standing amongst the English in Florence and sometimes was able to use a box at the opera which Sir Robert Lawley kindly offered, below the surface their marriage was crumbling away. It was said that more than once Julia had locked Landor out of her bedroom and that in fact soon after their move to the villa, they were living not as husband and wife, but rather as brother and sister.

In February 1832 Landor suddenly decided to pay a visit to England. Perhaps his journey was influenced by the fact that many English friends such as Sir Robert Lawley had gone back or perhaps it was the political situation, with the Reform Bill at last about to be passed, which attracted him. Had they known, close friends might have conjectured that Ianthe's presence in Brighton had something to do with the journey.

Landor planned to take fourteen year Arnold with him, but at the last minute his mother would not let him go. The boy was disappointed and how much this non-event affected his later judgement can only be imagined. Up until the age of thirteen Landor was boasting that Arnold was not ashamed to fling his arms round his father's neck and kiss him over and over again. How much then would a serious broken promise have affected his view of his father? Did emotional Arnold come to despise his father for not standing up to the wiles and pleas of his mother, or had Julia Landor even then attracted the boy to her side in the arguments?

Landor said,

"I promised my dear Arnold to bring him with me, but his mother would not let him go. He was grieved at the disappointment, but bore it heroically. Dear good divine creature!"

Landor travelled alone and buying a phaeton and horse, drove himself to Dieppe, where he sold the horse and carriage. At that time, early 1832, cholera was rife everywhere and some idea of the difficulties of travel can be obtained from the fact that as he had just missed the weekly steamship in Dieppe, he was obliged to wait nearly another week for the next.

After crossing the Channel and arriving in Newhaven, Landor made straight for nearby Brighton where Ianthe and her family were enjoying the social whirl.

When he came to write his memoirs "*Wilhelm's Wanderings*", some years later, Ianthe's son William Swift described the occasion. Landor he said had burst in on their company "*with pristine friendliness and almost boyish spirit.*" Fifty seven year old Landor felt young again and spent two days in Brighton with Ianthe "*in the midst of music, dancing and fashionable people turned radicals.*" In the euphoria of many, as the long-awaited Reform Bill became law, Lady Bolingbroke said that her husband would never enter the House of Lords again.

After reluctantly tearing himself away from Brighton, Landor met up with his great friend Joseph Ablett in London and then proceeded with a whole series of visits which took him to Denbighshire, Cumberland to meet Southey and Wordsworth, Warwick to meet his brothers and sisters and many other places. By the end of September however, it was time for him to return abroad.

It was probably on the 1st of October that Landor and Julius Hare and another friend Thomas Worsley took the steamboat for Rotterdam. Thus began an interesting journey which took in the art treasures of Belgium and Holland, the battle field of Waterloo, Bonn and Frankfurt. Afterwards Landor wrote jokingly to Robinson (who had been brought up in Germany and revered Goethe)

"Today I passed before the house of your friend Goethe – the house where he was born. I lifted off my hat and bowed before it".

The journey continued to Augsburg, Munich and the Tyrol where heavy snow almost stranded them in Innsbruck. Able to continue, although with some difficulty, they spent three days in Venice where Landor bought some paintings for himself and others for Hare to take back to Herstmonceux. These included St Catherine by da Udine and a lovely head of St Cecilia by Perugino or Raphael. Then it was Padua to admire the Giottos, Vicenza, Bologna – the trio enjoyed all until they arrived at Florence in December. Hare and Worsley stayed at the villa Gherardesca until almost Christmas and Landor was at home, happy to be with his children once more.

However on his return Landor noticed a change in Arnold who seemed to have grown more sullen and was far less co-operative than previously. Little has been written about Mrs Landor, but when Arnold was left behind, might she not have comforted the teenager after his father had left, telling him that she alone cared for him and that Landor was selfish?

In the 19th century, it seems that few parents ever thought of the effect that some decisions might have on their children, it being generally assumed that the children would fall in line with their parents' wishes. Indeed Landor himself had had a temporary quarrel with his friend Charles Armitage Brown because he had allowed his son to do as he liked when growing up. *"He is the wickedest boy I have ever known"* declared Landor at one stage. It would seem that then, in the mid 19th century, the management of difficult teenagers was just as hard as it is today. Perhaps in the case of Arnold Landor and his brothers and sister, the fault lay in the fact that Mrs Landor seemed quite incapable of making sensible decisions, with or without the help of Landor.

Whatever undercurrents lay below the surface in the Landor household, on the surface things seemed to be quite normal. In mid 1833 not only Julius Hare and Worsley on their return trip called on the Landors, but also Henry Francis Carey, an old schoolfriend. Landor had not seen the studious Carey for some time, but he later achieved fame as the translator of Dante. The American Ralph Waldo Emerson was also given an introduction. Afterwards Emerson wrote of Landor,

"He praised the beautiful cyclamen which grows all about Florence; he admired Washington; talked of Wordsworth, Byron, Massinger, Beaumont and Fletcher. To be sure he is decided in his opinions , likes to surprise and is well content to impress, if possible, his English whim upon the immutable past."

In the summer of 1833 a young man fresh from Cambridge University arrived with a letter of introduction from his former tutor Julius Hare. Soon after his arrival in Florence Richard Monckton Milnes fell ill with a fever and Landor invited him to stay at the villa. Milnes stayed some weeks and he wrote to his mother,

"Mrs Landor was as attentive to me and kind as if I had been at home"

Milnes was very impressed with Landor and he noted how his host loved dogs. At this time Landor had a magnificent mastiff named Parigi and he would often take Parigi's head between his knees and say

"Ah, if Lord Grey ... had a thousandth part of your sense how different would be things in England"

In November 1833 the writer Lytton Bulwer (later known as Bulwer Lytton, 1st Baron Lytton) called on Landor with an introduction from Lady Blessington. In October 1834 Lady Blessington wrote from Seamore Place, Mayfair, London to Landor,

"Mr E.L. Bulwer's new novel, 'The Last Days of Pompeii,' has been out a fortnight; it is an admirable work, and does him honour. He refers to you in one of the notes to it as 'his learned friend Mr Landor,' so you see you are in a fair way of being praised (if not understood) by the dandies ..."

The footnote referred to was in Chapter 3 and concerned a suggestion by Landor that a certain table had been made of mahogany wood.

One of the staunchest of Landor's friends at this time was the

novelist G.P.R. James who rented a nearby property, the Villa
Palmieri, at Fiesole. Many years younger, the usually reserved James
seemed to be enlivened by Landor's conversation and he invited the
older man to be godfather to his son born in 1832. In 1837 James
dedicated the novel "Attila" to Landor.

A most important visitor to Florence in 1834 was Mrs Paynter, the
half sister of Lord Aylmer, and now a widow. Landor had first seen
Sophia walking on the sandburrows at Swansea in 1796 together with
the legendary Rose Aylmer, her half-sister, and later Sophia had
married David Paynter of Dale Castle in Pembrokeshire. In 1834
Mrs Paynter took rooms for herself and her two daughters in the
Piazza Santa Croce.

By now the fifty-nine year old Landor had his thoughts set firmly
on visiting England again and in November 1834 Landor wrote to
his sister Elizabeth that he hoped to see her again in the April or May
of 1835. The plan was for the whole family to travel to England.
Landor would take Arnold and Julia with him and Mrs Landor
would take the two youngest children and stay with her mother in
Richmond. Arnold was then seventeen and grown moody and
sullen, although Landor still maintained that "*never was there a more
perfect being in temper and principle.*" Joseph Ablett was pressing
Landor to come to England and it seemed that plans were being
made.

Although most of their friends maintained a discreet silence,
marital affairs at the villa were worsening in 1834. For some years,
Julia Landor had verbally lashed out at her husband when she felt
like it and this was generally in company when she had an audience.
In front of servants, or even guests, she would contradict her
husband and parade his faults, perhaps jealous that at no time did
her husband have much real affection for her.

The actual break-up came during a dinner at the villa in March
1835 when Charles Armitage Brown was invited to dinner. Also
present at the dinner were the older children, Arnold and Julia
Landor. For about an hour Mrs Landor grumbled about her
husband, hardly pausing for breath and when she did eventually stop
Landor with great composure said in a quiet voice

"*I beg, madam, you will, if you think proper, proceed; as I made up my
mind, from the first, to endure at least twice as much as you have yet been
pleased to speak.*"

Charles Brown later admitted to Landor that he had never seen him behave towards his wife in anything but "*the most gentlemanly demeanour.*"

For a time, after that dinner, Landor left Fiesole and stayed alone in Florence, but eventually he went back to the family. Finally, some weeks later, he left his villa. He asked his wife,

"*Mrs Landor will you allow me the use of your carriage tomorrow morning to take me the first stage out of Florence?*"

She did and Landor left. He was aged sixty.

In the months which followed his departure from the villa, reports from friends told him that the children were quite wild and that young Julia, an exceptionally pretty girl, desperately needed her father's protection. A young second cousin, Edward Wilson Landor of Rugeley, visited the villa in 1836 and fell in love with Julia. Her mother was quite in favour of the match and it was resolved that when he returned to Rugeley, Edward should ask Landor.

Cholera regulations delayed Edward's journey home and in the meantime Arnold, maliciously informed his father of the cousin's attentions. Landor immediately took steps to prevent the marriage. Perhaps the saddest of all the documents in the Landor collection in Warwickshire County Record Office are those connected with this love affair of Julia and Edward. A poem from Edward to Julia and a letter from Julia to her father (never forwarded, so un-read) remind us of the unhappiness of this young couple. Forbidden by Landor to make overtures to his daughter and forbidden by his own family to marry such a young and unsuitable bride, Edward Wilson Landor went abroad. By the time he came back years later, it was no longer thinkable that he should marry Julia for by that time she had borne an illegitimate child.

In the meantime, over a period of many years, Mrs Landor continued to let it be known that she would like Landor to return to Fiesole, but his mind was made up, he had left forever.

7. BATH, BRISTOL AND THE WEST
Visits to Bath and Clifton.
A Bath Celebrity 1837–58

If all the happy days which Landor ever spent could be added up, there is no doubt that by far the greatest number of these would have been spent in Bath, Bristol and other places in the western counties of England, such as Worcestershire and Gloucestershire, besides various places in South Wales. To these western havens he returned again and again in his life, at different periods.

Perhaps the first place in which Landor spent any length of time apart from Warwickshire was Ripple in Worcestershire where he stayed with Fleetwood Parkhurst, a schoolfriend from Rugby. Fleetwood Parkhurst senior owned a house, Ripple Court, close to the banks of the Severn, five or six miles to the north of Tewkesbury and Landor often used to stay at this house in the school holidays. Even after Landor had left Rugby, he was still invited to visit and he continued to do so until 1801 when Fleetwood Parkhurst senior died.

On one of these visits Landor had the chance to visit his old headmaster Dr James who had retired from Rugby a couple of years after he had left. Landor wrote in a note to "Simonidea," published in 1806.

"I called on James while he was living at Upton, and of my own accord offered him my right hand, which he freely accepted."

This was a very brave and forgiving thing to do, especially after Dr James had forced him to leave Rugby School, but at least it showed that there was no bad feeling on either side.

By the early years of the nineteenth century, Landor was already fond of living in Bath and Clifton. Both were then fashionable places, with plenty of good country walks nearby. The opportunities for lively meetings in the evening made for an interesting life. Never fond of dancing, gambling or blood sports, Landor preferred to spend his time visiting friends or discussing topical questions over dinner.

In the nineteenth century the United Kingdom was a very class

97

conscious place, but Landor had no problems on this score for his parents were counted amongst the old landed-gentry of Warwickshire. His father had long been a magistrate in Warwick, serving alongside people such as the Earl of Warwick and the family name was often enough to secure numerous invitations. His expectations of great inheritance in the none too distant future, also made Landor a welcome guest at many gatherings.

In South Wales, in the 1790s, Landor had been friendly with various members of the Irish aristocracy and in Bath he continued this association. Landor often frequented the house of Lady Belmore, the widow of the first Earl who lived with her sister Miss E. Frances (Bess) Caldwell. Bess Caldwell was an old friend of Landor's mother which may have been how he came to be invited into her social circle in the first place.

Landor said of Lady Belmore,

"I liked her frankness so much, that I overcame my abhorrence of routs and went at her desire to hers, although to no others."

Like many self-conscious and rather insecure characters, Landor often went to the other extreme when at small dinner parties. Not only was his laughter often excessively loud, but he seemed to take a delight in shocking people with immoderate outbursts, just as he had when a boy. Proof that his character was unusual lay in the words of an acquaintance who sometimes dined in the same company. This gentleman, a Major Tickle, said that it amazed him how Landor managed to get away with making provocative statements.

"We were occasional guests at the same public table in Bath two winters, where there were other military men; and if I had talked as he talked, there would have been half a dozen bullets through my body, if the first five had been insufficient."

Landor was fast becoming known for outrageous statements, a knowledge of the classics, a fiery temper and love poems! Life with him was never boring.

In 1803, probably at Lady Belmore's house, Landor met the love of his life. Already he had had several serious love affairs and flirtations, but this was different.

By this time, Nancy Jones, the Tenby girl with whom he had fallen in love in 1793, was almost certainly dead. Also another girl, heiress to a large fortune, had ended the courtship, preferring to marry a titled suitor instead of Landor. In the way of many sensitive people, he could not bear rejection, brooded on the matter and became depressed, complaining to a barrister friend, William Rough, of sleepless nights. William Rough, who was also friendly with the other Landor brothers and the family in Warwick wrote back to Landor,

"Come, come, rouse yourself and write...If you must die, it is at least your duty to leave something behind you; and though "Gebir" will do much, yet I am persuaded it is in your power to do still more."

Eventually Landor, then a young man of twenty eight, took his friend's advice and began to write again. He had been inspired by a wonderful woman!

The young lady with whom Landor fell in love was Jane Sophia Swift, the daughter of Richard Swift of Lynn in Ireland, a descendent of the family of Jonathan Swift, the writer. Miss Swift, whom he called his 'Ianthe', was dark-haired like Landor himself, had beautiful blue eyes and possessed a wonderful sense of humour. However she was not free to love or marry him and although Landor went on frequent walks and other outings in her company, within a few months she returned to Ireland to marry a distant cousin, as was the custom in her family.

To begin with Ianthe amused and flattered him and they enjoyed each other's company. Typical of their many happy walks was one taken along the towpath of the Kennet and Avon Canal in Bath, around 1803. Landor often stayed at Sydney House and the canal traversed the gardens adjoining the house. Ianthe was very tender-hearted and she soon became troubled because a schoolboy on the opposite bank was throwing stones at some ducks on the canal. She begged Landor to intervene and he shouted across to the boy to stop. However the boy took no notice and Landor, suddenly losing his temper as he was apt to do, shouted across,

"You scoundrel! If I was on the other side I would fling you headlong into the canal."

Now although of a fairly stocky build, twenty eight year old Landor was no more than medium height and he was beside himself with rage when the boy retorted,

"It would take a man to do that!"

It was at this point, with Landor's rage boiling over, that Ianthe began to laugh. Soon Landor was laughing too and many years later Ianthe's son related this anecdote in his memoirs.

Sometimes during these first few years of the new century Landor stayed in fashionable Clifton, near Bristol and one of his favourite views was that from Clifton Hill, near Old Clifton Church. Perhaps Clifton around 1803 held special memories for Landor for pinned inside the lid of his writing desk shortly before his death many years later, John Forster found an engraving of the view from the church. It was obviously a view Landor had enjoyed since he was a young man in Ianthe's company.

Despite the fact that many of their friends suspected otherwise, in all probability Landor and Ianthe were not lovers in a sexual way. Rather their friendship was deep, platonic and everlasting. Landor thought of himself and Ianthe in a similar situation to Petrarch and Laura in fourteenth century France. Petrarch had fallen in love with beautiful Laura in a church but she was not in any position to return his love. So he wrote sonnets in her praise and through the medium of the poems, the lives of the lovers were remembered. Landor presented Ianthe with a copy of Pertrarch's sonnets and naturally a manuscript poem accompanied the book.

It was probably in late 1803 that Ianthe returned to Ireland to marry but she returned to Bath several years later. Landor was always very chivalrous and called on her and her young family whenever possible.

When his father died in November 1805 Landor was recovering from a wound to his leg in Hot Springs, Clifton, where there was a good surgeon. For the next few years he was to frequent Bath whenever possible. In a letter to Robert Southey some years later Landor wrote of his love for the city.

"*The South Parade was always my residence in winter. Towards Spring I removed into Pulteney Street – or rather towards summer for there were formerly as many nightingales in the garden and along the river opposite the South Parade, as ever there were in the bowers of Schiraz. The situation is unparalleled in beauty and surely the warmest in England. I could get a walk in the country without crossing a street which I hate. These advantages often kept me in Bath till the middle of June and I always returned in the beginning of November.*"

After purchasing the estate of Llanthony in Monmouthshire, in 1808, Landor found a wife in Bath in 1811. For years his family in Warwick had been hoping he would marry and settle down, and quite out of the blue, he courted and married a very pretty seventeen year old girl, whom he met at a ball, held at the Assembly Rooms.

Julia Thuillier was one of the older daughters of a Swiss banker who had lost most of his money because of the wars with France.

Julia's father, Jean Pierre Thuillier, the son of a general in the Austrian service, was descended from an old and respected French family, the Barons de Nieuville and later in life Landor used to refer to his wife as "My little baroness". Before he died, over 25 years after the marriage of Landor and his daughter, Monsieur Thuillier had once again restored the family fortunes so that his surviving nine children each received a handsome legacy of one thousand, five hundred pounds.

However when Landor married Julia she was penniless. He wrote to Southey in 1811,

"I have found a girl without sixpence, and with very few accomplishments. She is pretty, graceful and good tempered – three things indispensable to my happiness."

Julia was exceptionally pretty and had of course the beautiful long, golden hair that Landor had always admired. She was five feet two inches tall and had more curls on her head than any other girl in Bath, according to Landor!

The wedding, which was arranged by Julia's mother as her father was out of the country, took place quietly on Friday 24th May 1811 at St James' Church, in Bath. The Landor family knew little about the wedding until afterwards, and by then the couple had left for a three week honeymoon in Rodboro' and Petty France, not far from Bath. On their return, the young couple left for Llanthony straight away to await the arrival of their first guests.

In early 1812 the Landors returned to Bath, after travelling to Warwickshire and Gloucestershire, because Mr Thuillier was returning home for a brief period. Landor and his father-in-law got on very well and when the Thuillier's last and eleventh child was born in 1813, the boy bore the name of Henry Edward Landor Thuillier.

Sadly the next visit of the Landors to Bath was not so happy. It was in May 1814 that Landor passed through Bath prior to fleeing abroad to escape his creditors after financial difficulties in Llanthony. His wife was left in Bath with her mother until such time as he could find a home for her. It was a tremendously difficult time for them both and it may have been at this time that the seeds of discontent were sown, which were to turn the marriage sour.

Eventually Julia followed Landor abroad and she was never again to set foot in England, although from time to time she would reminisce about the happy life she had led in Bath.

In 1832, eighteen years after he had fled from his creditors, Landor was once again back in England and naturally he visited Bath. Although he arrived in England in May 1832, he had so many visits to crowd in elsewhere that it was late August or early September by the time he arrived, amazingly having met his brother Robert en-route, purely by chance in an inn-yard in Evesham, where the stage coach from Warwick had made a stop. Time did not permit a long stay in Bath and after some days Landor was off on his travels again and he returned to Italy in October.

At the end of 1835 Landor again came to England, this time having left his wife and family for good. After visiting various friends elsewhere, being sad and unsettled, he took lodgings in Smith's Lodging House on Clifton Hill, planning to spend the winter there. He wrote to the Countess of Blessington,

"*Clifton is the best climate on this side of Nice and climate is everything to so Italianised a piece of machinery as I am.*"

Although not many of his friends knew this, widowed Ianthe, his love of earlier days, was also living in the area with her children and grandchildren. The friendship was temporarily renewed.

Later in that year of 1836, Landor settled at Penrose Cottage, Clifton and within a month or so, in November 1836, he was visited by Robert Southey and his son Cuthbert. The Southeys stayed at Bedminster with publisher, Joseph Cottle, an old friend, but Landor saw a great deal of them during their week-long visit. At that time, Southey was under tremendous pressure as his wife had gone insane and was in a mental institution and the purpose of the visit to Bristol was to show young Cuthbert the haunts of his father's boyhood and to introduce him to such old friends as remained.

Southey wrote "*On Tuesday 8th we walked with Landor about the finer parts of the neighbourhood but the house which I inhabited for one year at Westbury and in which I wrote more verses than in any other year of my life, has been pulled down.*"

Cuthbert Southey wrote,

"*We spent several delightful days* (in Landor's company) ... *He was one of the few with whom my father used to enter freely in conversation and on such occasions it was no mean privilege to be a listener ...*"

The friends visited Southey's old school and also an old aunt and when they crossed College Green and saw some workmen Landor remarked to Southey,

"Some day workmen may be busy on this very spot putting up your statue but it will be twenty years hence."

"If I ever have one I would wish it to be here" answered Southey.

That happy visit in 1836 was the last time Landor ever saw Southey. When the Poet Laureate died less than seven years later, in 1843, in vain did Landor re-iterate that Southey wished his monument to be in the open on College Green. A committee of those who thought they knew better, took little notice of the ageing Landor.

Living in lodgings, with his mind very much on his children in Italy, Landor was very lonely at this time. He had become friendly with a scholarly man Charles Elton, who had a large family of three boys and eight girls and he visited them often.

One of the girls wrote to an older brother, *"nothing occurred – only old Landor called oftener than ever ..."*

Landor at that time was sixty two years of age and he really missed the company of his own four children, the youngest of whom was eleven. Landor would arrive at the Eltons around dinner time at six o'clock and ask leave to sit in the room without dining, as he preferred to go home to a later dinner. He would sit in an armchair and chat to the family, no doubt easing his own immense loneliness in the process. He was fondest of the two youngest girls who were around the age of fifteen which was that of his own daughter Julia.

During the following year 1837, Ianthe had moved elsewhere and the Eltons decided to move to Southampton, where around a year after their move Landor visited them. One of the girls, Mary Elton had written a short story and she was flattered when Landor took the trouble to read it and send it to Lady Blessington who included it in the "Book of Beauty" which she edited. Mary Elton was paid five pounds for her contribution and how delighted she was!

By November 1837 Landor had settled at 35 St James's Square in Bath and the next six and half years were perhaps some of the happiest in his entire life. With his wife and family still living in the large villa in Florence and enjoying the bulk of his income, Landor managed to live simply and cheaply on his own in the quiet square, which had several beautiful trees in its pleasant garden in the centre. For perhaps the first time in his life, he was free to write with no worry about future expectations or finance. First of all he looked up old friends, but he found a somewhat dismal situation to begin with. He wrote to Lady Blessington,

"Most of my old acquaintance are dead, most of my younger married and gone elsewhere. Poor Lady Belmore, whom I have known the longest of any is totally blind. Her sister, Miss Caldwell, still sings and plays on the guitar, but like Anacreon, she has changed all the strings. Two or three people have recollected me, whom I had utterly forgotten, not that I am less changed than they are but because my memory of faces is a most unloyal one. I may converse a whole evening with a person and forget both his features and his name before the next."

His lodgings in St James' Square were not far from the Assembly Rooms where Lady Belmore and Miss Caldwell still presided over the dances. Although he did not dance, Landor loved to go to some of the balls to watch the dancing prowess of a new acquaintance Rose Paynter, who with her sister Sophy, provided him with some excellent company. Landor had known Mrs Paynter, the mother of the girls, many years before in South Wales for she was the half sister of the long-lamented Rose Aylmer. Now in 1836, the widow and her daughters lived in Great Bedford Street, very close to Landor's lodgings.

A letter to Rose Paynter in June 1840 clearly explained the Irish charm of Bess Caldwell and one can imagine that Landor, with his great sense of humour, adored the ageing hostess all the more because she made him laugh. Landor described how Bess Caldwell had said to him,

"Sure, Landor, it is a beautiful book, your 'Periwinkle and Asparagus'; but faith! I've no time to read it."

It is said that Landor loved to retell this anecdote about his book "Pericles and Aspasia" and in the letter he goes on to explain,

"Bess Caldwell was a well – known and loved Mrs Malaprop. She lived with her sister, the Dowager Countess of Belmore, at Bath. Sir William Gell, when they were at Naples, compiled – and I believe published – a book called "Caldwelliana" of her remarkable sayings."

After Landor had visited the Countess of Blessington at Gore House in London a few times, he had an entirely new set of literary acquaintances and many of these, notably John Forster, called on him from time to time. Whenever possible, Charles Dickens came with Forster and they sometimes stayed overnight for there were several spare beds in the lodgings so that visitors could be accommodated. In turn, Landor introduced the Paynters to Dickens and Forster, and the girls visited the Dickens family more than once in London.

During the winter months, Landor dined very regularly with the Paynters and afterwards Rose used to sing, which pleased Landor immensely for he adored opera and beautiful singing. In the summer when the Paynters were abroad or at some sea-side resort, Landor wrote to Rose and her mother or sister quite frequently and these letters were particularly interesting, as they gave many details of famous people and events.

Landor was extremely fond of music in general and Bath often had some excellent concerts. He actually delayed a visit to London so that he could hear Thalberg, Balfe and Miss Birch perform in Bath and he was very friendly with Henry Field, a local music master. Often Landor would visit houses and halls where Field was playing and singing.

Landor's long love affair with Clifton took a severe knock in 1839 and from then onwards he spent little time in the place. In late July 1839 he wrote to Mrs Paynter in Paris,

"I took lodgings for a week in Clifton, but stayed only two days. The place is utterly ruined by that detestable bridge, and they have cut a deep hollow-way to it and thrown the soil over the grassy slope with its pinnacles of porphyry-looking rock surmounting it – now no longer."

Landor's irritation at losing some of his favourite views were perhaps shared by many others. Designed by Brunel and begun in 1832 the bridge was not finished till 1864, the year of Landor's death, decades later.

Another great friend at this time was Colonel William Napier to whom Landor was introduced by the Paynters. Napier was married to a niece of Charles James Fox and he and Landor discussed politics past and present. At the time when they met in the late 1830s, William Napier was writing his "History of the Peninsular War" and Landor considered him a very great historian indeed. The Napiers lived in Freshford about seven miles from Bath and Landor often walked there to visit them. William Napier and his family left Bath in 1842 when he became Lieutenant-Governor of Guernsey and Landor greatly missed their company.

In a footnote in "Historic Houses in Bath and their Associations" (page 85 Vol 2 1884) R.E. Peach gives a glimpse of how Landor and Napier spent some of their time in Bath.

"At the time Napier was in Bath, he, Landor, Leader, Sir W. Molesworth, Roebuck, Dr Thomas Falconer and others, used to meet at the library of the late Miss Williams in Milsom Street. In the midst of them was this famous

woman, and the more radical the sentiments uttered, the more she applauded."

In 1844 Landor left his lodgings and he moved from 35 to 1 St James' Square. In September 1846 he moved from 1 to 2 or 42 and in December he moved to number 36 St James' Square. Having found a locality he liked, Landor was loth to leave the square, but leave it he had to in March 1849 when he moved to 3 Rivers Street. This last address was not far from his favourite square and the move was brought about because of alleged pilfering by the servants in his previous lodgings. However his new rooms looked out into St Catherine's Place which had a small garden and his back window looked out into the house garden. It was a smaller house but Landor proved to be very happy there.

By this time he had lost the pleasure of the company of the Paynter sisters. Sophia had married Mr (later Sir) Henry Caldwell in 1839 and Rose married Mr (later Sir) Charles Graves-Sawle of Penrice in Cornwall in Feb 1846. Landor visited her and her family several times and later wrote poems for Rose's daughter Rosina.

By 1848 Landor was becoming lonely for many of his friends had moved or died. It seemed that just when he needed a friend most, his daughter Julia sent him a Pomeranian puppy from Italy.

All his life, Landor had loved animals, especially dogs, and soon the new arrival and his master were well known on the streets of Bath. Pomero, as the beautiful white dog was named, followed his master everywhere and on morning calls the two of them would sit quietly together, the dog under his master's chair. However on a given signal, usually words spoken in Italian, Pomero would leap up onto his master's lap and would then jump up and sit on his partially bald head! Whenever Landor went on country walks, for he was accustomed to walk perhaps eight miles a day, even when he was in his eighties, Pomero would accompany him. Landor used to compose his poetry whilst walking and he would march off quite preoccupied, leaving Pomero to follow behind. The two became quite famous locally with the popular remark in Bath being that the dog had the better coat! It was well known that Landor did not spend money on clothes unless he was forced to do so. His income was small and clothes came well down on the agenda.

For much of his life Landor had been friendly with the Hare family, Augustus, Julius and Francis. In his later days in Bath the young Augustus Hare (son of Francis) visited him quite often and around Easter-time 1849, young Augustus dined with Landor.

"First we went out to order the dinner, accompanied by Pomero in high spirits ... We stopped first at the fishmongers, where, after much bargaining, some turbot was procured; then, at the vegetable shop, we bought broccoli, potatoes, and oranges; then some veal to roast; and finally a currant-tart and biscuits. Mr Landor generally orders his own little dinners, but almost all this was for me, as he will dine himself on a little fish. He has actually got a new hat because he says all the ladies declared they would never walk with him again unless he had one, and he had a hideous pair of new brown trousers. Pomero was put out of the room for jumping on them, but when he was heard crying outside the door, Mr Landor declared he could not let his dear child be unhappy, and he was obliged to let it in; upon which the little creature was so delighted that it instantly jumped on the top of his master's head, where it sat demurely, looking out of the window."

Whenever Landor travelled to London or elsewhere, he always left Pomero behind in the care of his landlady because he was convinced that the pretty cream-coloured dog would be stolen in London. Amongst some sections of the London poor at that time, ransom demands for pet dogs previously stolen, provided a steady income and Landor had no doubt heard many tales of dog-napping.

Eliza Lynn first met Landor in July 1847. The daughter of the Vicar of Keswick (who also owned Gad's Hill Place near Rochester) Eliza was starting a career as a writer when she went to Bath to stay with Dr Brabant and his sister Miss Hughes. They had gone to visit the Museum or "Old Curiosity Shop" of Charles Empson in The Walks. Eliza wrote afterwards,

"In came a noble-looking old man, badly dressed in shabby snuff-coloured clothes, a dirty old blue necktie, unstarched cotton shirt...and knubbly boots (full of bumps and bosses like an apple pie.) But underneath the rusty old hat-brim gleamed a pair of quiet and penetrating grey-blue eyes; the voice was sweet and masterly; the manner that of a man of rare distinction."

When Miss Hughes whispered *"That is Mr Landor"* Eliza Lynn rushed up to him and he smiled and took both her hands in his and said *"And who is this little girl I wonder?"*

In fact the two got on so well together that ever afterwards Landor called Eliza his *"Dear Daughter"* and she called him *"Father"*. As other biographers have pointed out rather cynically, it was a platonic friendship to benefit Eliza Lynn in particular as she was then struggling to become known as a writer. However it was she who later recorded for posterity some of the most vivid descriptions of Landor at this time and undoubtedly their friendship was a true meeting of like souls. To her credit, for the rest of her life, Eliza Lynn was a staunch friend and later she was a zealous guardian of Landor's memory. She was a competent journalist and when she was placed on the staff of the 'Morning Chronicle' in 1849 she was said to be the first woman newspaper writer to draw a fixed salary. Later she wrote many pieces for periodicals such as 'Temple Bar', 'Saturday Review', 'Literary Gazette' and 'Cornhill Magazine'. On 30th January 1849 Eliza Lynn, who was staying with Landor, was able to meet Dickens and Forster who came for the day. Later she was to write many pieces for Dickens' periodicals 'Household Words' and 'All the Year Round' and it says much for her literary work that Dickens considered her a very reliable journalist and reviewer. She also wrote various romantic novels and it was for these that she became remembered.

Perhaps it was the female attention to detail or perhaps it was her journalistic skill, but the picture Eliza Lynn painted of Landor and Pomero seems particularly full of vitality.

"At one moment he (Landor) *would have him between his strong but soft and tenderly gripping hands, burying his face in the little fellow's coat, kissing him, calling him "darling" asking him where "he got his pretty yaller tail from?" and was "his mother a fox?" The next he had thrown him on the floor for a "little noisy, troublesome devil," for whom one would have expected the hangman's cord as the logical ultimate. He was always losing Pomero, and always giving some unprincipled scamp half a crown for his return."*

1849 saw Landor temporarily reunited with his beloved Ianthe, which presumably was why the new hat and other clothes, described by Augustus Hare were bought. Ianthe and her seventeen year old granddaughter Luisina de Sodré often travelled together for Luisina's mother (Ianthe's third daughter) had died many years previously. Luisina's father was a Brazilian diplomat and Ianthe, together with other members of her family, spent much time in Paris. Whilst Ianthe was in Bath, Landor visited her every day and when Eliza Lynn was staying with him for a day or so, she would accompany him. She recalled some very touching scenes saying that Ianthe was,

"evidently very proud of her old lover's affection, very fond of him, and somewhat afraid. And his behaviour to her was perfect." (She was) ... *"a gentle sweet natured, but by no means wise old woman in these days; but*

though she used to say the most inconceivably silly things, Landor never lost his temper with her and always listened to her with grave attention and courteous respect. Her grandchildren were his great delight and he used to play with the younger of them by the hour together."

Landor's great love of good music was enhanced when the performer was Luisina herself and a delightful picture is given of one performance in a letter he sent to John Forster. Landor explained how he had taken Pomero to hear Luisina sing.

"Pomero was deeply affected and lay close to the pedal on her gown, singing in a great variety of tones, not always in time. It is unfortunate that he always will take a part where there is music, for he sings even worse than I do."

Sometimes Landor and Ianthe and the family went out in the carriage and on one occasion at least they went to nearby Widcombe, a favourite place from decades previously. When Ianthe admired the view from the churchyard of Widcombe Church, just as she had done soon after they had first met, Landor determined to be buried there, to be near her in spirit, if nothing else, for all eternity.

After that happy summer of 1849 Landor never saw his Ianthe again. She and her family returned to Paris and she died in Versailles in July 1851. Greatly affected by news of her death, Landor consoled himself that at least he could arrange to be buried at Widcombe, but sadly, a few years later, he had to abandon this idea.

At the end of July 1850 the writer Thomas Carlyle visited Landor at Rivers Street. The two had met several times before at Lady Blessington's and elsewhere, but as Carlyle was passing through Bath, Landor invited him to stay. Carlyle described how he found Landor *"in a poor lodging, though in a fine, quiet street, waiting for me attended only by a nice Bologna dog. Dinner not far from ready, his apartments all hung round with queer old Italian pictures; the very doors had pictures on them, Dinner was elaborately simple. The brave Landor forced me to talk too much, and we did very near a bottle of claret, besides two glasses of sherry; far too much liquor and excitement for a poor fellow like me."*

In the evening after dinner, Landor conducted Carlyle through the park and the Crescent, showing him the sights of Bath. However around ten o'clock, Landor drew out his watch, announced that it was his bedtime and after fixing the time for breakfast, left Carlyle to go through the streets, smoking on his own!

When it was time for Carlyle to leave the next day, things did not go smoothly. It was arranged that after breakfast, an omnibus would stop and take him to the railway station where he would catch the 9.15 train for Bristol. Carlyle recalled,

"For some reason the omnibus did not appear and the time drew on, – at last Landor, though he was proud as a duke or an emperor, seized my bag, and was for carrying it himself to the station. I shall never forget him; the old man felt I was his guest, and he would carry my bag, therefore; tho' if a king had asked him to carry his …!. Happily just then the vehicle appeared."

In 1846 Carlyle had tried to introduce Margaret Fuller, a much respected American writer to Landor, but the meeting could not be arranged and he promised to try again next time she was in England. When Landor read of her death by drowning a few years later, he wrote a poem in her memory which was published in 'The Examiner' of 8th May 1852. Afterwards Emerson wrote to Carlyle,

"She had such reverence and love for Landor that I do not know but at any moment in her natural life she would have sunk in the sea, for an ode from him; and now this most propitious cake is offered to her Manes."

Born at Cambridgepont, Massachusetts in 1810, Margaret Fuller, her husband the Marquis of Ossili and their young child had all been drowned on the sand-bars of Long Island in 1850 as they sailed back to America. In the poem *"On the Death of M. D'ossili and His Wife Margaret Fuller"* Landor had written,

… Rest, glorious soul,
Renowned for strength of genius, Margaret!
Rest with the twain too dear!

No wonder that Emerson felt that she would have been delighted.

In early 1852 a second edition of Carlyle's "Life of John Stirling" was published and the author straight away sent a copy to Landor bearing the inscription,

To Walter Savage Landor Esq
    with many respects and regards
        T. Carlyle
Chelsea, 12 Jan, 1852

(This same copy of Carlyle's book is now owned by the Landor Society of Warwick.) Many authors sent inscribed books to Landor who once he had read them, often sent them back to his sons in Italy.

Interesting details concerning Landor's life at Rivers Street can be obtained from the 1851 census returns. Mrs Bishop the widowed landlady (who had been born in Invernesshire) was aged forty nine, whilst Landor himself, aged seventy five, was described as a "Landed Proprietor". A young married couple, Walter and Frances Brownjohn, both in their early thirties, were also renting rooms (presumably on the second floor) along with Charles Gale, a twenty five year old solicitor and brother in law to Walter Brownjohn. Naomi Wickham, a general servant aged twenty, was also living in the house.

As far as is known, Landor was renting the first floor of the house at a rent of thirty pounds a quarter, which included payment for the lodgings and servants. As his income was seventy five pounds a quarter, provided he lived economically, Landor had plenty for his needs and very often he gave small sums of money to people who needed it. Eliza Lynn noted when she stayed with him that on some occasions Landor would deliberately leave his dinner, so that it could be sent to a poor, old woman who lived close by. Quietly, and without any fuss, Landor was often very generous to those he knew who were in genuine need.

Sadly as the 1850s wore on Landor became more and more lonely. Many of his old friends were dead or ailing and in 1853 he saw the last of his family in Warwickshire for on 24th February 1854 his sister Elizabeth died and later that year the old family house in Smith Street was given up.

Also earlier in February 1854, Bess Caldwell had died. Her sister Lady Belmore had died a short time before, and poor Landor was left to reflect that friendships which had lasted since the early years of the nineteenth century were ended.

Some indication of Landor's sombre frame of mind at this time may be gleaned from a letter and poem he sent to John Forster on 8th April 1854.

"Last evening I walked in the park, and saw the sun gradually illuminate the whole of Marlborough-buildings, window after window, six or seven at the time. Many of my old friends lived there, and went away in like manner, one after another. This evening I took my usual walk a little earlier, and, sitting afterwards without candles for about an hour as I always do, I have had the same feeling as I watched the twilight darken on my walls, and my pictures vanish before me. I make no change in these lines, but write them as they have risen to my mind."

My pictures blacken in their frames
   As night comes on,
And youthful maids and wrinkled dames
   Are now all one.
Death of the day! a sterner Death
   Did worse before;
The fairest form and balmiest breath,
   Away he bore.

In March 1856 Landor suffered a terrible blow when his beloved Pomero died. The dog was buried in the garden of the house in Rivers Street and Landor wrote sadly to Forster,

"Everyone in this house grieves for Pomero, the cat lies night and day on his grave; and I will not disturb the kind creature, even though I want to plant some violets round it and have his epitaph placed around his little urn."

In fact Landor did give the much-loved dog an epitaph, CANEM AMICUM SUUM EGREGIE CORDATUM QUI APPELLATUS FUIT POMERO, SAVAGIUS LANDOR INFRA SEPELIVIT. Landor also wrote a short verse in Latin.

A short time later he wrote to a friend, Miss Boyle,

"Pray for me and Pomero. Some people are wicked enough to believe that we shall never meet again."

Without his canine companion Landor had no appetite for walking and when Mrs Crosse, an old friend, visited him she found the sight of Landor sitting still and quiet in his armchair *"infinitely pathetic"*.

Sadly, in late 1856 a somewhat different friend began to see much of the eighty-one year old Landor. Eliza Lynn was rarely in a position to visit any more and it seemed that an Irishwoman, Mrs Yescombe, who had known Landor very slightly for a few years, set her sights on using the old man to help her and a young friend obtain money.

Mrs Yescombe lived at Green Park buildings in Bath with her husband the Rev. Morris Yescombe and their five children. Next door lived a family called Hooper, and Geraldine, the sixteen year old daughter of the Hoopers became very friendly with Mrs Yescombe who listened to the tales of grievance the girl had against her mother.

In November and December 1856 Landor was ill with bronchitis but despite this he was asked to give evidence in a trial at Bath County Court which the Yescombes had brought against another family in Bath, who it was alleged had enticed away their governess.

LANDOR'S VILLA AT FIESOLE, NEAR FLORENCE, IN TUSCANY. He bought the Villa Gherardesca in 1829 with the help of Joseph Ablett.

GORE HOUSE IN KENSINGTON GORE, LONDON A FEW YEARS BEFORE IT WAS BOUGHT BY THE COUNTESS OF BLESSINGTON IN 1836. Despite its somewhat ordinary appearance, for nearly thirteen years the house was the venue for many gatherings of distinguished people, especially those from the literary world. When staying at Gore House, Landor had his own special room and his favourite seat in the magnificent garden was on the terrace between two fragrant lilac trees.

XVIII

MARGARET (GENERALLY CALLED MARGUERITE), COUNTESS OF
BLESSINGTON WAS THE MOST FAMOUS LONDON HOSTESS OF HER DAY.
Her great beauty, generosity, intelligence and ready Irish wit made her an unforgettable
character. She and Landor held a deep respect for each other.

XIX

AN ENGRAVING OF THE DILAPIDATED SHAKESPEARE'S BIRTHPLACE
FROM AN 1847 APPEAL LEAFLET PRESERVED BY THE LANDOR FAMILY.

GUY'S CLIFFE HOUSE, WARWICK AS IT WAS WHEN LANDOR DINED
THERE ON NUMEROUS OCCASIONS IN THE 1840s. Sadly today the house is in
ruins.

XX

THE CHAPEL OF GUY'S CLIFFE, WARWICK IN THE MID-NINETEENTH CENTURY. Guy, Earl of Warwick, a legendary Saxon hero, is reputed to have lived as a hermit here in the tenth century and to have been buried beneath the chapel. The standing figure in armour, nearly nine feet high, is said to represent Guy and is carved out of the natural rock face. Landor was interested in old legends and referred to the chapel in a short poem dedicated to Miss Isabella Percy, whose family owned the house and chapel in the nineteenth century.

XXI

IT IS PROBABLE THAT LANDOR WALKED WITH IANTHE ALONG THE CANAL-SIDE IN SYDNEY GARDENS IN BATH. This delightful view shows the curving tow-path and part of the gardens around 1820.

A RECENT VIEW OF THE PULTENEY BRIDGE IN BATH. Landor's two favourite cities were Bath and Florence. Begun in 1769 the Pulteney Bridge has been compared with the Ponto Vecchio in Florence.

ST JAMES' SQUARE IN BATH IN 1860. Landor's lodgings at Number 35, where Dickens conceived the character of Little Nell, are just off-picture to the right hand side.

A RECENT PHOTOGRAPH OF 3 RIVERS STREET IN BATH WHERE LANDOR LIVED FOR OVER NINE YEARS FROM 1849 TO 1858. Thomas Carlyle and other friends stayed overnight with him and Landor's famous dog Pomero was buried in the back garden.

XXIII

IT WAS ONE OF LANDOR'S DEAREST WISHES THAT HE SHOULD BE
BURIED IN THE PICTURESQUE CHURCHYARD OF OLD WIDCOMBE
CHURCH, NEAR BATH. *The view from the churchyard was quite stunning and the place
had many associations with Ianthe. However, although his grave was prepared at Widcombe
in 1861, two days after his death in September 1864, Landor's body was buried in a
cemetery close to where he had died in Florence. In this print of 1837, the Manor House can
be seen to the left and the Garden House of Crowe Hall to the right.*

XXIV

*A RECENT PHOTOGRAPH OF "THE WHITNASH OAK" WHICH MARKS THE
BOUNDARY BETWEEN WHITNASH AND BISHOP'S TACHBROOK IN
WARWICKSHIRE. Landor loved trees, especially oaks and as this outstanding ancient tree
is only around a mile from Savage's House in Tachbrook and close to the main road from
Leamington Spa, he must have passed it many times and doubtless knew it well. When
Landor was born in 1775, this tree was already around seventy-five years old.*

CHARLES DICKENS IN 1855. For nearly 25 years, the much younger Dickens and Landor were loyal friends.

THE JOURNALIST AND NOVELIST ELIZA LYNN LINTON AS SHE WAS WHEN LANDOR'S GRANDSON VISITED HER AROUND 1890. Eliza Lynn first met Dickens in Landor's apartment in Bath in 1849 and later when she inherited Gad's Hill Place in Kent, she sold it to Dickens in 1856. Despite an age difference of around 47 years, she and Landor were extremely good friends in his later years.

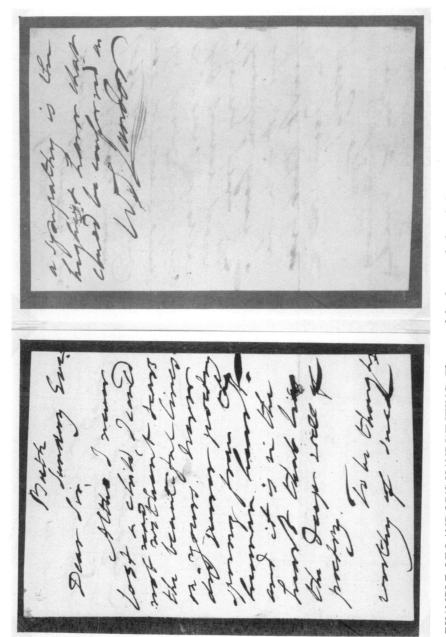

AN EXAMPLE OF LANDOR'S HANDWRITING. The text of this letter, which includes some interesting remarks on poetry, appears in the chapter containing a selection of Landor's prose.

XXVII

ROBERT BROWNING IN 1858.

ELIZABETH BARRETT
BROWNING IN 1858.

XXVIII

JOHN FORSTER, SHOWN HERE IN AN ENGRAVING OF 1869 WAS LANDOR'S FRIEND, LITERARY AGENT AND BIOGRAPHER.

NO-ONE REVERED LANDOR MORE THAN ALGERNON SWINBURNE WHO REGARDED HIM AS A GREAT SPIRITUAL FORCE. This photograph shows the enthusiastic, twenty-six year old Swinburne who travelled to Florence to meet his hero, only six months before Landor's death.

XXIX

A NINETEENTH CENTURY VIEW OF ST CHAD'S CHURCH, AT BISHOP'S TACHBROOK, IN WARWICKSHIRE, WHERE MANY OF LANDOR'S FAMILY WERE BURIED. The church contains a memorial to Landor himself besides various of his ancestors. The thatched roof to the left is that of the New Inn.

IN THE YEARS WHICH FOLLOWED LANDOR'S DEATH MANY PROFESSIONAL PHOTOGRAPHERS TOOK PHOTOGRAPHS OF THE HOUSE IN WARWICK IN WHICH HE HAD BEEN BORN. This excellent photograph by Francis Bedford was probably taken around 1889 and is simply entitled "Landor's Birthplace". Eastgate is to the left and the Castle Arms on the right.

XXX

ONE OF THE MOST ATTRACTIVE FEATURES OF LANDOR'S BIRTHPLACE IS
THE FRONT DOORWAY WITH ITS PAINTED STONE SURROUND. *The sign
"Landor Born 1775" was erected on 30th January 1888, nine years after the house had
been offered as premises to the King's High Shool for Girls. This photograph was taken
around 3 p.m. on 30th January 2000 to mark the 225th anniversary of Landor's birth.*

THIS FINE MEMORIAL TO WALTER SAVAGE LANDOR IS IN THE NAVE OF ST MARY'S CHURCH, WARWICK. The Landor crest of a dexter arm, holding a fleur-de-lis and the arms of both the Landor and the Savage family are shown above the bust of pink alabaster which was designed by Edmund Ferry R.A. and executed by James Forsyth. The memorial was erected by the direction of Landor's second son Walter Savage Landor 2nd, who inherited his father's estates in 1871.

XXXII

Rev. Yescombe sought fifty pounds in damages – the maximum allowed in a County Court, but in reality the case appeared to be no more than a ruse by which to obtain money.

Landor and Geraldine Hooper were summoned to appear as witnesses for the Yescombes. Landor was ill but, despite doctor's orders, insisted on going and had to be helped into court on 3rd January 1857. Although he gave his answers clearly and briefly, the counsel for the defence was typically unkind, and said that "*it was a miserable exhibition to bring the poor old man into the box to talk the twaddle he had.*" The Bath Express and other newspapers loved it all and even printed special editions, because Landor's name as a literary celebrity had made the petty affair gossip-worthy.

The result of the case was that Roche was found guilty of harbouring the governess, but the damages were set at a farthing. The Yescombes had to pay their own costs, as did Mr Roche.

Her first plan to obtain money having failed, Mrs Yescombe tried again and this time she targetted Landor, who was known to be generous to his friends. For a while Landor dined regularly with the Yescombes and he appeared to trust them as friends, although they were outside his usual social circle. In March 1857 (as recounted by R.H. Super, a previous biographer) Landor made out his will naming Rev. Morris Yescombe as sole executor. However the Yescombes were in need of cash immediately and so was Geraldine Hooper who had run up debts all over Bath, perhaps for clothes. So a further plan was devised.

When Landor asked to be excused from dining at the Yescombes, as he hated dining in public, Mrs Yescombe brought Geraldine Hooper round to Rivers Street to dine once a week. Landor soon became fond of the girl and gave her some of his pictures, as he often did to friends. On her birthday he gave her a locket. Mrs Yescombe had words with Landor's landlady and said that if anything happened to the old man, he had given orders that all his pictures were to be taken round to her house straight away. She also added that she thought he was a "*bit cracked*", but kindly Mrs Bishop knew better for she had grown quite fond of her elderly lodger.

Geraldine appealed to Landor's sense of chivalry and he believed her and tried to help when he heard how cruelly she claimed to have been treated by her mother. In the spring of 1857, Mrs Yescombe told Landor that Geraldine's affairs had become critical and that she might run away from her family. Landor had just received one hundred pounds as a legacy from the will of his old friend John Kenyon who had died in December 1856 and he gave this to Geraldine. Mrs Yescombe then told Landor that she had set two of his poems to music in order to sell them for Geraldine's benefit and that the publisher needed twenty three pounds to go ahead. Landor gave her fifteen pounds which was all he had, but shortly after this his suspicions were aroused.

In those strict Victorian times when chaperones were necessary, Geraldine never came to see him alone but a few days later she did come alone and asked for eight pounds, which she claimed was to pay the music publisher. Landor became suspicious, made enquiries and discovered that the music publisher had already been paid, the entire bill having been only eight pounds.

Landor made more enquiries and found that Mrs Yescombe had been suspected of pilfering more than once and a shoemaker signed a statement saying that she had stolen seven shillings from his counter. Further enquiries revealed that a letter to Eliza Lynn which Landor had written the previous summer enclosing a five pound note and which Mrs Yescombe had insisted on posting, had been the only letter, out of three thousand and more letters which he had sent from Bath, to go astray.

Immediately Landor wrote to Geraldine's parents outlining his suspicions of Mrs Yescombe and Mr Hooper replied on 17th May 1857, but only after his daughter had been sent to Cheltenham to stay with relatives. He said he had written two letters to Mrs Yescombe's husband, Rev. Yescombe but received no reply. He had received one brief note from Mrs Yescombe denying all knowledge of the one hundred pounds. Mr Hooper went on,

" *Yet I have so far succeeded in obtaining the confidence of the dear child as to receive her confession, by this morning's post, that she gave £50 of it to Mrs Yescombe to pay Mr Slack's (her solicitor) bill for the trial of Yescombe versus Roche.*"

Mr Hooper stated that sixteen year old Geraldine was very ill at that time and he felt that she had been imposed upon by Mrs Yescombe. Of course Landor could not consider prosecuting Mrs Yescombe because Geraldine would need to be involved. Even if it had gone to court it would have looked bad for Landor for people might well have misconstrued the gift of one hundred pounds to a teenage girl.

Morris Yescombe insisted on being addressed as "Reverend" but this could have been a bogus title as his name did not appear in any directory of Clergy. Already Landor had given away over one hundred and fifteen pounds but if she could only keep her nerve Mrs Yescombe felt she could obtain more.

Landor then began receiving anonymous letters repeating slanderous statements against him and he became angry, perhaps angrier than he had ever been since his Llanthony days, It is quite conceivable that these letters were concocted by the Yescombes to push Landor into publishing something rash, so that they could sue him for libel. In a way he fell into their trap. He gathered the statements together and published them in a pamphlet "*Walter Savage Landor and the Honourable Mrs Yescombe*". The pamphlet was printed by the printers of the 'Bath Express' in early June 1857 and for that newspaper the rows and gossip were excellent news! The Yescombe's solicitor Mr Slack wrote to threaten legal proceedings and in late June, Landor published another pamplet "*Mr Landor Threatened.*" The Yescombes were then able to begin proceedings for libel.

During May, Landor had been ill, which was hardly surprising considering all the stress of the last few months, and when John Forster learned of all the trouble, he tried to persuade Landor to settle with the Yescombes out of court. On 27th July 1857 Forster came to Bath, used illness as a mitigating plea and eventually Landor agreed to sign a retraction.

Whilst John Forster felt sorry for Landor in one respect he was not pleased to learn that Landor intended to publish another book of poems comprised of odd verses which had been returned from various sources and some poems which had been composed for the young Geraldine. Landor claimed that Mrs Yescombe was showing poems round Bath which she said were written by him and he felt that the only way to give a lie to her actions was to publish a new book of his poems himself. Forster advised against it, but Landor found a publisher in Scotland and went ahead anyway.

For a few months, the whole affair went quiet. The new book "Dry Sticks Fagoted by Walter Savage Landor" was published in January 1858 and friends said they enjoyed it, but on 14th January, Orsini attempted to assassinate Louis Napoleon in Paris and Landor unwittingly became drawn into the recriminations. Landor wrote to Forster,

"*Miserable Orsini! He sat with me two years ago at this table at which I am now writing. Dreadful work! Horrible crime! To inflict death on a hundred for the sin of one!"*

The trouble was that Orsini had had fellow conspirators in England and it was suggested that Landor was one of them because he had theoretically advocated tyrannicide in letters to newspapers and it was true that Orsini had once called on him in 1856. Following a report in the 'Times' hinting that he had approved of Orsini's attempt, Landor wrote a letter to the paper saying,

"Assassination I consider is the basest of crimes".

However as with all false reports, a little of the mud still clung to him and when he began to receive a number of letters about Orsini, friends advised Landor to sue one newspaper editor and reporter for libel.

Landor steadfastly refused to read the articles, yet they must have worried him. On March 24th 1858 he was worried further when Eliza Lynn married the penniless engraver and political writer William J. Linton, whom she had met when she nursed his first wife. Landor offered her money as a wedding present, as he knew that the marriage was causing a worsening in her financial situation and eventually she accepted a token amount.

It can have come as no surprise with all this worry that on 27th March 1858 Landor was found unconscious in his lodgings following a serious stroke. His landlady immediately sent for his niece Kitty who had moved to live at 3 Belmont, very close to Rivers Street. Two doctors were summoned who continued to attend throughout that day. After twenty four hours Landor was slightly better but it took two more days for him to improve sufficiently for the doctors to be hopeful of his recovery.

During these few anxious days there was a stream of friends who called at the house to enquire after Landor's health – Sandford, Caldecot, Lady Caldwell (Sophy Paynter), Mr Pitman, Mr and Mrs Hughes, Captain and Mrs Brickman, Empson, Mrs Gollop and various others, His doctors and nieces must have realised that Landor was recovering when, on being told of the numerous visitors, he was struck by the name of Mrs Gollop. Asking for a pencil and paper, Landor feebly scribbled a brief rhyme.

When she asks, good Mrs Gollop,
Say with me that all is all up.

Niece Kitty sat with him most of the time as he slept, for he liked the reassurance of seeing her when he woke. His rooms were cluttered with books on the chairs and Kitty often sat on the window sill keeping a watchful eye on her patient. Her sister Sophy had come from Tachbrook, but when it became clear that Landor would pull through she returned to Warwickshire to look after her Uncle Henry.

Gradually Landor grew stronger until he was able to take short drives out. Realising that it might be worth their while after all, Mrs Yescombe saw another opportunity and took out a further action for libel – this time over the contents of some poems in his latest book.

Three poems in particular were cited as evidence; one being *"The Pilfered to the Pilferer"* which began,

MOTHER PESTCOME! none denies
You were ever true … to Lies.

Landor wanted the case defended in court, but the solicitor whom Kitty engaged thought only of his fee in case Landor should die or the case go against him. A barrister in London was consulted and he thought it would go against Landor. The doctors feared if Landor appeared in court the trauma would kill him, so Kitty was persuaded to take her uncle out of the country in a hurry because (wrongly) it was pointed out that he could be sent to jail.

Kitty felt she had no time to lose. She had to decide what to do and she opted for flight. She sent Forster a telegram saying that she and Landor would be arriving later that day and they left Bath very hurriedly at 8 a.m. on 12th July 1858, the day after she had been given the prognosis of the trial.

First they went to Forster's house at Montague Square in London and then after a week or so, Kitty conducted her eighty three year old uncle to France. There Landor was met by his son Walter and eventually taken to the family villa at Fiesole, where they arrived on August 27th.

Whilst this journey was being undertaken, the libel case was heard in court. On Monday 23rd August 1858 the case was tried at Bristol Assizes, before Baron Channell and a special jury. Phinn, the barrister engaged by Landor's solicitor, offered little evidence and none of Landor's friends were called as witnesses. After a short trial the Jury found in favour of Mrs Yescombe and Landor was ordered to pay a total of one thousand pounds in damages.

On 24th August 1858 the 'Times' carried a leading article on the trial and in the days and weeks that followed, other newspapers and periodicals followed suit. All Landor's critics climbed on the bandwagon and the result was a public outcry against him which took his friends by surprise.

The article in the 'Times' said,

"How ineffable the disgrace to a man of Mr Landor's ability and reputation at the close of a long life to be mixed up with so disgraceful a transaction."

The 'Saturday Review' was more outspoken.

"Filth and obscenity are never so unnaturally nauseous as from the chattering lips of age, and a tottering and toothless satyr generally keeps his foul life and conversation to himself and his associates."

Since Landor was neither toothless nor senile, all this was hard to bear! Eliza Lynn Linton wrote to Forster asking him to undertake a public defence of Landor. Forster however felt that there was little he could do without becoming involved himself, but behind the scenes he tried to use his influence.

The 'Daily News', the 'Critic' and 'John Bull' all carried articles which were hostile and the 'Examiner' and the 'Spectator' carried articles without comment. Only one brave paper printed anything in Landor's favour. Eliza Lynn Linton's friend, Shirley Brooks, wrote a bold article in the 'Literary Gazette' and in it he suggested that a public subscription should be made to pay off Landor's libel award. More outcry followed this article however and in the end the whole thing subsided.

Afterwards appeals were made by the trustees of Landor's estate and no money was actually paid till three years afterwards, but by then the amount had increased and in the end the Yescombes were awarded one thousand eight hundred pounds. All the money Landor had was the three hundred pounds annuity he was allowed from the estates and this was paid to the Yescombes for the rest of his life, by which time in total they had collected around one thousand four hundred pounds.

How did such a dreadful happening occur to a man of Landor's strong principles and chivalry? Privately his friends were loyal to him, but it seemed that there was little they could do except ride out the storm. The circumstantial evidence was against him and his principles of being chivalrous had led him to defend a manipulative girl with large debts and few scruples. Landor blamed Mrs Yescombe for almost everything, but privately Mrs Paynter thought that *"the abominable girl was at the bottom of it all and I dare say it was to save her that Mr Landor was induced from first to last to act as he did."*

The fact that Geraldine Hooper's father had had to place an advertisement in the 'Bath Express' in July 1857 saying he would no longer be responsible for his daughter's debts would seem to bear out the truth of Mrs Paynter's statement. Maybe from late 1856, Landor had been marked out as a potential source of income by two unscrupulous women.

Some previous biographers of Landor have criticised John Forster for not doing more to help Landor. There was no need for Landor to be sent abroad and a proper defence should have been mounted at his trial. Landor had plenty of friends in Bath, most of whom were taken entirely by surprise by the turn of events, but young Augustus Hare confided to his mother that he had known Mrs Yescombe for years and that he

"Always prophesied that she would be the ruin of Mr Landor some day."

In many ways Landor showed his true fighting spirit in this libel action and posterity has been very glad that he fought back via his pen. His spirit remained unbroken by all the trouble and several years after fleeing the country, when it was pointed out that if he apologised to the Yescombes he could return to Bath, Landor wrote to Eliza Lynn Linton,

"I would rather go and live in Siberia!"

In short Landor behaved courageously, in accordance with his principles, and the newspapers, acting rather as the tabloids might do today, were happy to condemn him and destroy his reputation. At least Robert Browning was staunch in his defence of Landor and he wrote to a friend,

"I – for one – am profoundly grateful to the author of the "Conversations", and would not abuse him as all those wretched catch-penny 'Presses' 'John Bulls' and the like, do just now – if he had libelled me."

Whilst Kitty was helping Landor to flee abroad, Sophy was left with the sad business of clearing up her uncle's affairs in Bath. Some of his one hundred and fifty or so pictures were packed up and sent after him, but others were to be sold. Empson volunteered to oversee this task and at the auction in Manchester, the pictures brought in £109.

Landor had left few clothes or personal possessions, but there were some things, including Pomero's tail *"beautifully preserved"* as Sophy told Kitty. Some preserves Sophy divided with Mrs Bishop and, at Landor's request, his landlady was also given a dozen bottles of his brandy. The rest of the brandy (twenty nine bottles) and the five bottles of port and six of sherry which remained were taken to Kitty's house, along with several writing desks and two busts.

The bills were few although Mrs Bishop asked for an extra ten pounds to repair the damage to the walls done by Landor's heavy pictures. Mrs Bishop had her rent until Christmas; Hill a picture framer and gilder was paid what he was owed and Landor's subscriptions to "Household Words", "Punch" "The National Magazine" and "Art Union" were cancelled.

There must have been many in Bath who were sad to see Landor leave and one of these people was James Hall, a blind man. He said that Landor had helped him to go to St George's Hospital and also to learn the basket trade. Landor had also promised to give him a pound to set him up in business and Sophy paid the pound willingly, on behalf of her uncle, knowing the man's story to be genuine.

8. FRIENDSHIP AND ARGUMENTS WITH OTHER WRITERS
Southey, Wordsworth, Byron, Lady Blessington, Browning etc.

Coming as he did from a land-owning family in Warwickshire with few direct connections with the literary or artistic world, Landor had to learn to forge his own friendships with other creative people whom he admired. At Rugby School, although he was praised as a classical scholar, he was derided by the other boys for writing poetry. It was not until he was in his early twenties and had had books of his poems published, that he began to make friends with other serious-minded poets.

After "Gebir" had been published in 1798, very gradually other poets read the work and took notice. Southey (who was sent the book to review for the 'Critical Review') wrote enthusiastically about it in 1799. He also told his friends about it and on the eve of a voyage to Lisbon said to Coleridge,

"I like Gebir more and more; if ever you meet its author, tell him I took it with me on a voyage."

However it was not until years afterwards that Landor ever met Southey or had opportunity to meet many other writers. Although Landor and Southey were more or less the same age and had been at Oxford University at the same time in 1793/4 they did not actually meet till 1808 when they were introduced in Bristol. After having met Landor, Southey wrote to Grosvenor Bedford, an old friend, *"I have often said before we met, that I would walk forty miles to see him, and having seen him, I would gladly walk fourscore to see him again."*

Southey was in a mood to pay Landor the handsomest of compliments and in 1810 his poem "Kehama" carried the simple but direct dedication,

"To the author of Gebir, Walter Savage Landor, This poem is Inscribed, by Robert Southey."

This dedication was a source of pride to Landor and for the next thirty years the two writers did all they could to help each other, both

121

by assisting publication of each other's work and by being sincere friends.

At the time of their first meeting Landor was completing the purchase of the estate at Llanthony Abbey and three years later, only a month or so after he had married the seventeen year old Julia Thuillier, Landor and his bride entertained Robert and Edith Southey, the first friends to visit their picturesque estate. The Landors were in the process of having a new house built, but when the Southeys visited in 1811, temporary accommodation was provided in one of the towers of the abbey which had been refurbished.

For the remainder of their lives, until Southey could write no more, he and Landor wrote regularly, and although they rarely met, each regarded the other as a truly special friend. In June 1817 Southey visited Landor, then living in Como, and soon afterwards there broke out in print a furious row between Byron and Southey who had by then been created Poet Laureate. Byron accused Southey of saying highly derogatory things about him and in one of the early cantos of "Don Juan", (published anonymously in 1820) Byron hit back at the Lakeland poets.

> Thou shalt believe in Milton, Dryden, Pope;
>   Thou shalt not set up Wordsworth, Coleridge, Southey;
> Because the first is crazed beyond all hope,
>   The second drunk, the third so quaint and mouthy.

The row rumbled on for several years and in 1822 Byron wrote a satirical stanza in the eleventh canto of "Don Juan" when discussing claimants to the greatest living poet.

> Some persons think that Coleridge hath the sway;
>   And Wordsworth has supporters, two or three;
> And that deep-mouthed Boeotian "Savage Landor"
> Has taken for a swan rogue Southey's gander.

Happily these arguments did have a positive side, for Landor's name was brought to public notice in 1824 just at the time when the first editions of his "Imaginary Conversations" were being published. In the conversation between Bishop Burnett and Humphrey Hardcastle Byron was satirized, being referred to as Mr George Nelly. However Byron's sudden death in Greece in April 1824 made Landor sorry that he had made any criticism of him in his newly published work. When the second edition appeared in 1826 Landor added a note concerning Byron.

"Little did I imagine that the extraordinary man, the worst parts of whose character are represented here, should indeed have been carried off to the tomb so immaturely ... I had avoided him; I had slighted him; he knew it; he did not love me; he could not."

Later on when writing another imaginary conversation Landor called Byron *"the keenest and most imaginative of satirists."*

In fact Byron and Landor had met once, quite by chance when neither knew the other. In 1813 Landor had written to his lawyer about the meeting in London.

"I have seen Byron – once only. It was at Smith's the perfumers in Bond Street. Odd enough – he had just bought the very article I came to buy – attar of roses. He was more economical than I – he gave his one pound , I gave my five. Smith or whoever it was that served us, asked me whether I knew that young gentleman. On my replying in the negative, he said 'It is the young Lord Byron'. Not knowing he was somewhat lame, I thought he rolled about fantastically. He appeared to me remarkably handsome altho I could not see his noble forehead."

The friendship of Southey and Landor continued to flourish and they exchanged many letters. In 1824, Southey wrote to Caroline Bowles (who was to become his second wife in 1839) concerning his friendship with Landor.

"Differing as I do from him in constitutional temper, and in some serious opinions, he is yet of all men living the one with whom I feel the most sympathy in heart and mind."

In 1820 whilst living in Italy Landor refused to meet Shelley when both poets were in Pisa. Years afterwards Landor recalled the event.

"I was in Pisa the winter he resided there, and was told that Shelley desired to make my acquaintance. But I refused to make his, as, at that time, I believed the disgraceful story related of him in connection with his first wife. Years after when I called upon the second Mrs Shelley, who, then a widow, was living out of London, I related to her what I had heard. She assured me that it was a most infamous falsehood, one of the many that had been maliciously circulated about her husband. I expressed my sorrow at not having being undeceived earlier, and assured her I could never forgive myself for crediting a slander that had prevented me from knowing Shelley."

It was a great pity that Landor and Shelley never met, for when an undergraduate at Oxford Shelley had come by a copy of "Gebir" in Slatter's bookshop. Years later when visiting him in Italy, Thomas

Jefferson Hogg had told Landor the story of how Shelley had liked the book so much he had refused to be parted from it for several days. In her preface to "Queen Mab", Mary Shelley confirmed that Landor's "Gebir" was one of her husband's favourite books.

In 1832 Landor came to England for the first time for nearly nineteen years, and Joseph Ablett and other friends saw to it that he met as many writers and poets as possible during his stay. In June he visited Southey in the Lake District and was also taken to meet Wordsworth whom he had long admired.

Wordsworth and Landor had first corresponded when Landor had paid Wordsworth a great compliment in his Latin essay "Idyllia Heroica", published in 1815. Previously, various messages had passed via Southey, but in 1821 Wordsworth sent a letter via John Kenyon to Landor in Florence saying,

"It is high time I should thank you for the honourable mention you have made of me. It could not but be grateful to me to be praised by a Poet who has written verses of which I would rather have been the author than of any produced in our time – what I write to you now, I have frequently said to many."

In 1832 Landor spent the best part of two days in the company of Wordsworth, and his daughter Dora asked Landor to compose some verses for her album. Wordsworth seemed to like Landor and he wrote to Henry Crabb Robinson, a retired barrister and journalist friend, that Landor *"appears to be a most warm-hearted man, his conversation is very animated, and he has the heartiest and happiest laugh I ever heard from a man of his years."*

Landor reciprocated by sending a message back via Crabb Robinson saying how much he had enjoyed his time with Wordsworth.

Following their surprise visit to Wordsworth, Landor and Ablett went on to Keswick to make Southey and his wife very happy with an unexpected visit. In those days when swift communications were very difficult, Southey exclaimed that seeing Landor again after fifteen years was *"like a dream"*.

On 28th September 1832 Landor visited Charles Lamb at Enfield and the following day he visited Coleridge at Highgate. The brief visit to Lamb was a great success and Landor was much amused because Lamb played a wonderful trick on him. Landor was able to recall the event many years later.

"During my visit Lamb rose, went to a table in the centre of the room and

took up a book out of which he read aloud. Soon shutting it, he turned to me, saying 'Is not what I have been reading exceedingly good?' 'Very good' I replied. Thereupon Lamb burst out laughing, and exclaimed: 'Did one ever know a man so conceited as Mr Landor? He has actually praised his own ideas!' It was now my turn to laugh, as I had not the slightest remembrance of having written what Lamb had read."

Lamb asked Landor to write some album verses for his protégée Emma Isola, and Landor duly obliged a few weeks later. When the verses arrived Lamb was overjoyed and full of *'boyish delight'* according to John Forster who had called on him that day. In return Lamb sent Landor a copy of "Last Essays of Elia" and a letter in which he said he forgotten to thank him for various things including writing the poem Rose Aylmer *'which has a charm I cannot explain. I lived on it for weeks.'* It is said that, drunk or sober, Lamb was often to be heard reciting the poem!

Landor had visited Lamb in the company of Henry Crabb Robinson and it was this same companion who went with him to Coleridge. Landor recalled his visit when he wrote to his sister a couple of years later after the death of Coleridge.

"Coleridge had recovered his health when I saw him and told me he had not been better for years. Poor man! He put on a bran-new suit of black to come down and see me, and made me as many fine speeches as he ever could have done to a pretty girl. My heart aches at the thought that almost the greatest genius in the world, and one so friendly to me, is gone from it."

It was three years later in September 1835 when Landor again returned to England alone, and to start with he lived quietly with Joseph Ablett in Denbighshire for some weeks. He was unsettled and unsure that he wanted to travel to London or meet many people.

By February 1836 Landor had taken lodgings in Clifton but during May however he was plunged into a wonderful social whirl in London. Landor had known Lady Blessington and Count D'Orsay ever since the summer of 1827 when they had visited Florence. By all accounts Marguerite Blessington was a most intelligent and striking woman and soon after they had first met, Landor had written home to his mother,

"Lady Blessington is, without any exception, the most elegant and best-informed woman I have ever conversed with."

For her part Lady Blessington had written much of Landor in her journal "The Idler in Italy".

"The first glance at Landor satisfies one that he can be no ordinary person;

and his remarks convince one of the originality of his mind and the deep stores of erudition treasured in it."

After Lord Blessington had died suddenly of a stroke in 1828 Lady Blessington had settled in Seamore Place (Curzon Place) in London near Count D'Orsay, who had married her step daughter (one of four children from Lord Blessington's previous marriage). Lady Blessington's house became a meeting place for many literary and intellectual people in London. Whilst the handsome and striking looking Count was an accomplished artist, although thought a dandy, Lady Blessington herself was a talented writer and editor of the annual "Book of Beauty".

However, Lady Blessington had been the widow of an army officer and it was said that she had lived with another man afterwards, as his mistress, before her marriage to Lord Blessington. This apparent blot on her reputation meant that she was shunned by many in polite society and the fact that the French Count D'Orsay lived close by, if not with her, after his marriage had broken up, made matters worse.

Landor had feared that he would not be welcome or liked in literary circles, but when Lady Blessington wrote inviting him to London to stay in her new house in Kensington, eventually he decided to go. He arrived at Gore House on 2nd May 1836 and had a marvellous time for a month and more. Lady Blessington did all she could to make him feel welcome and she arranged outings and meetings galore.

Henry Crabb Robinson had been friendly with Landor since 1830 when he had called upon him in Florence and so had John Kenyon, a friend of Wordsworth and Southey. Although Robinson and Kenyon both lived in London and were members of the same club, it was their mutual friendship with Landor which helped to unite them. As it was, in early May 1836 Landor saw much of both friends. He stayed at Gore House and enjoyed the evening company of Lady Blessington and her guests, but during the day he visited such places as the National Gallery.

William Wordsworth came to London about ten days after Landor and thereby caused some rearrangements to Landor's plans. As Wordsworth did not approve of Lady Blessington (his daughter Dora had gone so far as to write to her father asking him not to visit Gore House) Kenyon persuaded Landor to stay with him for a time, to avoid all unpleasantness.

Landor and Wordsworth were often in the same company during this time. One afternoon a visit was proposed to view the Elgin Marbles and the temperament of the two writers seemed to be aptly demonstrated by their reaction. Wordsworth, who was after all nearly five years older than Landor, said he felt too tired to go. Landor went however, and was so absorbed in his study that Crabb Robinson got tired of waiting and left him there!

The literary event of 1836, of the decade, perhaps of the half century, was the glittering first night of Thomas Noon Talfourd's new classical play "Ion" at Covent Garden Theatre on May 26th, the author's birthday. The distinguished actor Macready and Ellen Tree took the leading roles and the whole evening was planned for the benefit of Macready himself. It turned out to be a social occasion on an immense scale for Talfourd was a lawyer and Member of Parliament besides being a dramatist and he had many friends and acquaintances. John Forster as the young drama critic for the 'Examiner' was there and he was interested to note that side by side in Crabb Robinson's box in the Dress Circle sat Wordsworth and Landor.

After the performance the two poets walked side by side up the road to Talfourd's house in Lincoln's Inn Fields where a great supper for around sixty guests was given. Macready, the guest of honour, was sitting with Landor on one side of him, Wordsworth on the other, with the young Robert Browning opposite. Macready, like Landor, was an old Rugbeian and the two men seemed to like each other very much. John Forster was also at this supper and afterwards he wrote a description of Landor, for it was the first time he had been able to have a good look at him.

"Landor was then upwards of sixty and looked that age to the full. He was not above middle stature, but had a stout stalwart presence, walked without a stoop and in his general aspect, particularly the set and carriage of his head, was decidedly of what is called a distinguished bearing ... What at first was noticeable, however in the broad white massive head, were the full yet strangely-lifted eyebrows; and they were not immediately attractive...The lips that seemed compressed with unalterable will would in a moment relax into a softness more than feminine; and a sweeter smile it was impossible to conceive."

On another evening Mrs Kenyon gave a large dinner party and both Wordsworth and Landor went, although neither enjoyed the large number of guests. Amongst the guests was Kenyon's cousin

Elizabeth Barrett (later Browning) and also her friend the writer Mary Russell Mitford. Afterwards Elizabeth Barrett recalled "*I never walked in the skies before; and perhaps never again shall, when so many stars were out!*" It seems that Landor gave her two Greek epigrams he had written and spoke to her for ten minutes. Wordsworth she found "*With a reserve even in his countenance, which does not lighten as Landor's does*"

Landor stayed in London until the first of June and for the remainder of his stay he returned to Gore House, the place where he felt most at home. The house, which stood close to the road at Kensington Gore was not an especially beautiful one, but it had a magnificent garden at the rear which included several old walnut and mulberry trees. The house had once belonged to William Wilberforce, the campaigner against slavery in the early 19th century, and many of the prominent politicians of the day had been frequent visitors. However, it was Lady Blessington who made the house internationally famous and in the late 1830s and 1840s, her salon became a mecca for literary people from all over the world.

On the whole Landor disliked London because he liked country walks, but as Gore House was adjacent to Hyde Park and had substantial gardens he felt more at home. Not only did he have his own room in the house, but he also had his own favourite seat on the terrace, between two lilac trees, one white and one purple.

The long-lasting friendship with Lady Marguerite Blessington seemed to be a source of great comfort to Landor, although he did not really see very much of her. Lady Blessington recognised in Landor a truly sympathetic friend of her beloved late husband and their letters in the 1830s often spoke of shared and happy memories.

In 1835 before Landor had left Tuscany to settle in England and before Lady Blessington had moved to Gore House, she wrote to Landor from Seamore Place,

"*You are associated in my memory with some of my happiest days; you were the friend and the highly-valued friend of my dear and lamented husband, and as such, even without any of the numberless claims you have to my regard, you could not be otherwise than highly esteemed. It appears to me that I have not quite lost him who made life dear to me, when I am near those he loved, and that knew how to value him. ... We, or properly speaking I, live in a world where friendship is little known, and were it not for one or two individuals like yourself, I might be tempted to exclaim with Socrates, 'My friends! there are no friends'.*"

With tender words like those, it was small wonder that Landor felt a deep attachment in a non-sexual kind of way for the serenely-beautiful, witty Irishwoman. Lady Blessington did all she could to aid publication of Landor's work (including on several occasions correcting proofs) and each time she produced books of her own, Landor was sent his special, early copy.

One only has to study the famous portrait of Lady Blessington by Thomas Lawrence, painted in 1822, which once hung in Gore House, to realise why first Dr Parr and later Landor were so attracted to her. Her lustrous dark hair and beautiful clear complexion help to form a memorable picture, together with the intelligent, kind, yet hauntingly-sad expression in her eyes. It is said that the portrait was the talk of London in 1822 when it was exhibited at the Royal Academy and the fact that it hung in Gore House where it would have been seen frequently by Landor makes it doubly interesting to a biographer of his.

The charms of Lady Blessington however did not inspire William Wordsworth and if Landor was on good terms with Wordsworth in mid 1836, by the end of the year all had changed. Landor had written a "Satire on Satirists and Admonition to Detractors" which was published in December 1836 and contained in this work was an attack on Wordsworth, largely because Landor believed that Wordsworth had uttered a criticism of Southey's poetry. Being an emotional man, Landor then widened the attack and included many other instances of where he felt Wordsworth had been cool towards him and his friends. At the first night of "Ion" Landor recalled that Wordsworth had been rather reserved and not wildly enthusiastic and the well-known fact that Wordsworth was largely preoccupied with his own poetry did not endear him to Landor or some other writers.

In 1837, despite their differences with Landor, Crabb Robinson and Wordsworth travelled to Italy and called on Mrs Landor and the children at Fiesole. However, despite both men entreating Landor to return to his family, he told them he could never do so.

When in London staying at Gore House, Landor often breakfasted with Crabb Robinson and other literary gentlemen. On 20th May 1838 Crabb Robinson made an interesting reference to Landor in his diary.

"*A good deal of rattling on the part of Landor. He maintained Blake to be the greatest of the poets; that Milnes (also present) is the greatest poet now living in England."*

Richard Monckton Milnes, who had visited the Landors in Florence in 1833, had just then published a book of poems which included one to Walter, Landor's second son, so it was small wonder that Landor was enthusiastic about his work. Landor's opinions concerning Blake however were far less superficial and they were reinforced by remarks by John Forster.

In his biography of Landor John Forster wrote,

"At an old bookseller's he picked up some of the writings of Blake and was strangely fascinated by them. He was anxious to have collected as many more as he could, and enlisted me in the service; but he as much wanted patience for it as I wanted time, and between us it came to nothing. He protested that Blake had been Wordsworth's prototype, and wished they could have divided his madness between them; for that some accession of it in the one case, and some diminution in the other, would very greatly have improved both."

Landor appears to have been genuinely interested in Blake, who at that time was not much known or revered. Well-schooled in the classics and interested in the writings of Milton, Landor perhaps found Blake's unusual ideas very stimulating. The remarks about Wordsworth however were consistent with the gradual cooling of Landor's former friendship for the well-known poet.

In December 1842 Landor sent an "Imaginary Conversation" to 'Blackwoods Magazine' and this contained another attack on Wordsworth. Crabb Robinson and Quillinan, Wordsworth's son-in-law, then determined to punish Landor and collaborated on a satirical "Imaginary Conversation Between Mr Walter Savage Landor and the Editor of Blackwood's Magazine" which was published in the issue for April 1843. The piece was clever, the London papers enjoyed it and it was even reprinted in America. Landor refused to retort, beyond severing all connections with Blackwoods. Wordsworth himself said he knew nothing about either article and he wrote to a friend,

"I knew nothing about it or the preceding article of Landor, that had called it forth, till after Mr Q's had appeared. He knew very well that I should have disapproved of his condescending to notice anything that a man so deplorably tormented by ungovernable passion as that unhappy creature might eject. His character may be given in two or three words: a madman, a badman, yet a man of genius, as many a madman is."

All these literary arguments however did not concern Southey for in March 1843 he died, after the most unhappy decade in his life. His first wife Edith Fricker (sister to Coleridge's wife) had gone insane and after a period in a madhouse in 1834 had died not long afterwards. Soon after his second marriage in 1839 to the writer Caroline Bowles, Southey's own mental state had deteriorated. Within days of Southey's death Landor sent a poem to the 'Examiner' which was included in its coverage of the death of the Poet Laureate and in November 1843 he sent an epitaph to the 'Examiner' and proposed a subscription for a memorial to Southey, saying that he would contribute twenty pounds. In vain did Landor write that Southey had told him in 1836 he would prefer a statue on the College Green in Bristol. Eventually a bust of Southey was placed in Bristol Cathedral minus Landor's epitaph.

Unfortunately Southey's family had been divided over his second marriage and his widow was left relatively poor. Wordsworth was appointed Poet Laureate in Southey's place and Landor was incensed that he did not use his position to try to obtain a pension for Caroline Southey. Landor wrote to her around this time hinting that Wordsworth was very mean concerning money.

"Wordsworth is a strange mixture of sheep and wolf, with one eye on a daffodil & the other on a canal-share."

Tired of all the wrangling over the publication of her late husband's letters and the erection of memorials, Southey's widow returned to Hampshire. Despite Landor's efforts, no state pension was given to her until 1852, when she was granted an annual pension of two hundred pounds just two years before she died.

If anything, in his sixties and seventies Landor seemed to have had more in common with the younger literary set and Landor's friendship with Robert Browning is a delightful story in itself. He first met Browning at Talfourd's supper in 1836 and soon afterwards Landor had opportunity to praise his work.

In the summer of 1836 Landor travelled to Heidelberg in a vain attempt to meet up with his sons and whilst waiting there he did a great deal of reading and writing. Landor was delighted to be introduced to Dr Paulus, one of the Professors at the University, and as Dr Paulus was uncomfortable speaking English, their conversation was carried on in Latin! In the 'New Monthly Magazine' at this time, Forster had written a very enthusiastic article about Robert Browning and after reading this, Landor sent a letter back to Forster containing some highly complimentary remarks about Browning's poetry. Forster cut this section from the letter and sent it to Browning who treasured the fragment till his dying day. Nine years later when he was courting Elizabeth Barrett, he showed the words to her and eventually the precious scrap of writing was preserved in the Baylor University Browning Collection, Waco, Texas. Kindly Landor had written to Forster of Browning,

"When you told us that the author of Paracelsus would be a great poet, you came rather too late in the exercise of prophecy – he was one already, and will be among the greatest. I hope he does not relax in that scirocco of faint praise which brother poets are fond of giving. Such as yours will brace him against it."

Whether Landor realised it or not, words such as those were likely to make all the difference to a young writer trying to build up confidence in his own abilities. Forster must have been pleased and Browning ecstatic!

In late 1836 "A Satire on Satirists ..." which caused so much indignation to Crabb Robinson and admirers of Wordsworth, Landor again praised Browning's "Paracelsus". Also in 1838 Landor wrote to Forster asking that he pass on a greeting to Browning and in 1840 Landor received a flattering letter from Browning, together with his new book "Sordello" which contained various complimentary lines of verse praising Landor as his *"patron friend"* and the giver of *"... that smile which went/To my heart."*

When Elizabeth Barrett and Robert Browning began to correspond in early 1845 Landor's name cropped up frequently in their letters. Indeed, unbeknown to Landor, Elizabeth had collaborated with Richard Hengist Horne over an essay about which appeared in "A New Spirit of the Age" in 1844. Horne had taken the trouble to obtain correct biographical details from Landor and Elizabeth Barrett had written a critical appreciation of Landor's works.

In November 1845 Browning sent Landor a copy of his "Dramatic Romances and Lyrics" and Landor's letter of reply was once again highly enthusiastic.

"What a profusion of imagery, covering what a depth of thought! You may stand quite alone if you will – and I think you will."

Landor also sent a poem *"To Robert Browning"* which appeared in the 'Morning Chronicle' a few days later. (see page 184) Such public praise must have delighted both Browning and Elizabeth Barrett. In March 1846, it was Browning's turn to flatter Landor and this he did in a dedication in the final number of his "Bells and Pomegranates". Landor's reply to this was a short but splendid note.

> *My dear Browning,*
>   *Let us agree to drop Sirs for ever,*
>   *... Go on and pass us poor devils! If you do not go far ahead of me I will crack my whip at you and make you spring forward. So, to use a phrase of Queen ELizabeth, 'Yours as you demean yourself'*

Forster (more or less the same age as Browning) reviewed the book very favourably in the 'Examiner'. Landor wrote to Forster *"Browning is a great poet, a very great poet indeed as the world will have to agree with us in thinking ..."*

Thus from 1846 onwards, Browning was under no illusions that his status and reputation as a poet owed much to the timely praise from Landor during the previous decade when he was relatively unknown and in dire need of public encouragement. Shortly after this in 1846, Browning escaped abroad with Elizabeth Barrett, whom he had secretly married, and the couple had cause again to thank Landor. He it was who had unwittingly enticed John Kenyon (Elizabeth's cousin who had introduced them and who might have guessed the secret of their flight) to visit him in Bath and then go on together to some friends in Somerset. Although Landor had no idea of the importance of the fact in 1846, it was very fortunate for him around thirteen years later, that the Brownings eventually made their home in Florence, only a few kilometres from Landor's villa in Fiesole.

Sadly, the good times at Gore House were soon to come to an end and Landor's last visit was in May 1847. Lady Blessington's sister, Lady Canterbury, had died in 1845 and then in early 1849 disaster struck. With the great depression in Ireland in the 1840s many rents were outstanding from Lady Blessington's Irish estates and she and Count D'Orsay ran heavily into debt. They fought off the creditors as long as possible but in the end Gore House and its contents were sold off in May 1849. Count D'Orsay had gone to Paris and Lady Blessington soon followed, only to die within a few months. The Count lived on until 1852 and Lady Blessington's nieces, the Misses Power remained abroad.

The world was changing rapidly in the 1840s. In 1846 Prince Louis Napoleon had dined at Gore House, entertaining his hostess, Count D'Orsay, Forster and Landor with tales of his escape but less than three years later all was gone. Dickens, Forster, Thomas Moore (the famous songwriter and poet dubbed 'Bard of Erin') a twelve year old pianist Anton Rubinstein, Sir Henry Bulwer Lytton, Monckton Milnes and many many more celebrities had graced its doors but no more.

To a friend Mrs Paynter, Landor wrote in 1852 of how the death of Lady Blessington had affected his life.

"The world will never more see united such grateful minds, so much genius and pleasantry, as I have met year after year under her roof. Since she was intercepted from me by the shadow of death, I have never enjoyed society, and have rarely and reluctantly entered it. Age has pehaps something to do in this change of temperament and disposition, but not very much."

Perhaps because of hypocrisy or moral criticism, history has not been kind to the memory of Lady Blessington. However there can be little doubt that she was a highly efficient and competent woman, who did her best to run her late husband's estates and pay the dozen or so annuities which he decreed should be paid to various relations. When the sad state of agriculture in Ireland in the late 1840s caused cash-flow problems, she ordered the sale of all her effects before retiring to France. Every one of the creditors was paid in full from the net amount of eleven thousand, nine hundred and eighty five pounds raised by the sale and there was money left over to provide cash sums for her nieces who had lived with her. Since he too knew what it was to have enormous debts, Landor was full of admiration for the successful way in which Lady Blessington had handled the difficult situation. Almost everything in Gore House was sold by Lady Blessington including the portrait of Landor by D'Orsay which hung in the drawing room and also a miniature of Madame de Maintenon which Landor had given her.

At the auction sale in Gore House in 1849, the famous portrait of Lady Blessington by Lawrence, so long admired by Landor and the other guests, was sold for three hundred and thirty six pounds. The buyer was the Marquis of Hertford who added the picture to his extensive collection. (Now part of "The Wallace Collection" housed in Hertford House, Manchester Square, London.)

In 1851 Gore House was used as a restaurant whilst the Great Exhibition was on and in 1852 the entire site was bought by the Commissioners of the Exhibition with some of the profits as a site for a new National Gallery. However, instead of an art gallery, the site was used for the building of the Royal Albert Hall in 1867.

Despite his reluctance to visit London once he could no longer stay at Gore House, Landor did visit the capital once or twice more, just to stay with old friends. In July 1851 Landor sat next to Macaulay at a dinner in Forster's chambers and in July 1852, whilst visiting John Kenyon, at dinner Landor was in the company of the Brownings, the Carlyles, Mrs Jameson (whose works he admired) and several others including the American publisher James T. Fields whose Boston firm, Ticknor, Reed and Fields, had already published some of Landor's work in America. Fields and Landor liked and respected each other very much and they corresponded during Landor's later years. (They were to meet again in Florence in 1860 when Fields called on Landor who returned the call, and invited Fields and his wife to dine with him the following day.)

Landor's last visit to London for pleasure was in July 1855 when he stayed at a hotel in Sydenham for a week and visited his old friend Sir William Napier and his family in Clapham. On one of the days, Landor and the Napier family visited the Crystal Palace, then permanently resited nearby. Forster was friendly with Sir Joseph Paxton, the architect of the building, who arranged for the great fountains to be playing in Landor's honour. It was a wonderful day for them all, despite Napier's lameness.

Outspoken, courteous, yet very emotional, Landor was a much sought-after acquaintance who seemed to stimulate many of his fellow writers into mentioning him in their letters and memoirs. However even old friends like Leigh Hunt occasionally felt the sharpness of Landor's pen. His poem (published in 1846) entitled "TO LEIGH HUNT, ON AN OMISSION IN HIS 'FEAST OF POETS' " began,

Leigh Hunt! thou stingy man, Leigh Hunt!
May Charon swamp thee in his punt ...

Landor was always ready to fight battles by means of his pen and other writers respected him for it.

However, it was probably Landor's sense of fun and vitality which endeared him most to literary friends such as Charles Armitage Brown and John Kenyon. In his biography of Landor, John Forster described why Kenyon in particular found him so amusing.

"*The laugh was encouraged till the room shook again; and, while Landor would defend to the death some indefensible position, assail with prodigious vigour an imaginary enemy, or blow himself and his adversary together into the air with the explosion of a joke, the radiant glee of Kenyon was a thing not to be forgotten."*

9. FOR LANDOR WITH MY LOVE
Landor's Friendship with Charles Dickens and John Forster

Although they were not able to meet frequently, there can be little doubt of the mutual love and respect between Walter Landor and Charles Dickens. Yet, on the face of it, a young ambitious writer in his late twenties would not be expected to develop a deep and lasting friendship with a writer from a totally different background, over thirty five years older.

The friendship between Landor and Dickens blossomed because of the friendship between Dickens and John Forster. As a busy and aspiring journalist, John Forster cultivated a large number of friends and acquaintances and he met Landor in May 1836, following the Gala Performance of Talfourd's "Ion". At the dinner following the performance, Landor sat next to Macready, the highly distinguished leading actor for whose benefit the play had been performed and they liked each other immensely. Forster and Browning were also present on this occasion and a few days afterwards Landor called on Forster, who he had learned was responsible for writing some favourable reviews of his work. Later that same year of 1836, Forster met Dickens at the house of Harrison Ainsworth.

Landor was a very old and trusted friend of Marguerite, Countess of Blessington and Count Alfred D'Orsay and sometimes stayed at Gore House, Kensington with them, where he had his own room. Soon Landor, Forster, Dickens, Macready and many others of dramatic or literary note moved in the same social circle, based on the gatherings at Gore House.

It was soon obvious that Landor and Forster could help each other with literary matters. Forster was the working journalist and reviewer of some of Landor's works in the 'Examiner' and other papers and Landor was an established, serious writer with impeccable social connections amongst the upper middle-class and landed-gentry.

In early 1839 the publication of Landor's "Andrea of Hungary" and "Giovanna of Naples" was held up because of trouble over the sudden resignation of Dickens from the editorship of 'Bentley's Miscellany'. After printing most of Landor's book, Bentley had stopped abruptly in February, not long after Dickens had relinquished his post. Forster had also severed his connections with Bentley and it was not until late summer that copies of Landor's book were widely available, barring advance copies that were being read aloud at Gore House by Lady Blessington, Count D'Orsay and Forster in mid April.

At this stage in their friendship, messages between Landor and Dickens were often routed via Forster. Concerning the printing of his book, Dickens advised Landor to write Bentley a contemptuous letter and around this time Landor asked Forster to convey to Dickens a complimentary remark about his novels.

"Tell him he has drawn from me more tears and smiles than are remaining to me for all the rest of the world, real or ideal."

It was obvious that when they did have time for lengthy meetings, Landor and Dickens were going to get along famously!

Having met Landor briefly in London, Dickens arranged to call on him in Bath, together with Forster, early in 1840. At the time of this first meeting, Landor was sixty five (ten years older than Dickens' father) whilst Dickens and Forster were twenty eight. Forster had probably visited Landor on his own several times earlier and no doubt both Dickens and Landor were keen to have the chance of a discussion with each other.

After a slight postponement of their visit, Dickens and Forster arrived on 29th February 1840 and they stayed at York House, then the largest hotel in Bath. On their first night in the city, they dined with Landor at his lodgings at 35 St James Square.

This first dinner proved to be quite a success as Landor was an excellent host. Like his guests, he was full of fun and he had a stock of very fine wine, much of it inherited from his father. Although he drank very little himself, whenever he had guests Landor opened a bottle of something special. Sometimes Landor would prepare a simple meal himself and he may have done so on this occasion.

On this first evening Dickens appeared pleased with his visit to Landor and the following day he wrote to his wife *"Although desperately learned and frequently first-person – singular-ish, we were much better than I expected. ... Indeed I was not bored ..."*

When three writers with different aspirations and skills feel they are helped by contact with each other, a deep friendship is likely to develop. For all creative people, interaction with others of like sensitivity, but different experiences, is perhaps the single most important stimulus and so it proved with Dickens.

At the side of the house in which Landor had rooms was an entry to a courtyard behind St James' Square and it is said that in this court Dickens observed an interesting girl who lived in a rather strange shop. This gave him an excellent idea. Thus the character of Little Nell was conceived in Landor's apartment and Landor himself used to joke about this in after years saying that he would like to have had enough money to buy the house and then burn it down in order that *"no meaner association should ever desecrate the birthplace of Little Nell."*

At the time of their first visit, both Dickens and Forster were on their best behaviour and, not wishing to offend their host; over one matter they kept their laughter silent till afterwards. Landor often bought pictures which some of his friends did not appreciate and he had bought a picture of a lion by Rubens a few months before the time of their visit. Naturally he showed off the picture to his guests, but they did not share his great enthusiasm. After the pair had left Landor's rooms around midnight, they walked noisily back to their hotel, laughing helplessly and crying out *"Roars for the lion"* at frequent intervals! However Landor himself, with his marvellous sense of humour, was not above putting on an act for the benefit of his friends and it may have been that the visitors were reacting to something which he had done earlier.

In the course of that first visit in 1840, Landor introduced Dickens and Forster to Mrs Paynter and her two daughters, Rose and Sophy, then living in Great Bedford Street, near St James Square. Thus began another friendship between the Paynters and Dickens and in after years they sometimes dined with him and his family when in London. Mrs Paynter was the half sister of Lord Aylmer and through her and her family, Dickens was introduced into other social circles.

Perhaps John Forster, being less emotional, was different, but, deep down Dickens and Landor appeared to share many characteristics and each would have recognised and appreciated the signs in the other. A fear of ridicule when young plus a feeling of being misunderstood is common to many ultra-sensitive and imaginative children and these emotions never entirely leave a person, no matter how successful they are in later life. So it was with Dickens and Landor, despite their different backgrounds. All his life, Landor was famous for the same loud laugh he had had in his youth, but Dickens also had had the same trait when young. Both writers ended up being married to wives who were not very capable and who did not understand them. Landor left his wife after twenty four years of marriage, when he was sixty; Dickens left his wife after twenty two years of marriage, when he was forty six. There can be no doubt that the two men sympathised very much with each other's matrimonial difficulties and Landor had given Dickens an example of how a fair financial settlement could make marital separation work, without causing public criticism.

It was an enormous help to Landor to have John Forster in a position of some literary importance, first as Literary and Dramatic Critic of the 'Examiner' and then as Editor of various liberal newspapers including the 'Examiner' from 1847 to 1856. Having been educated in history and law, Forster gave Landor a different insight into topical matters and he possessed the practical, organising skills which the older man lacked. Soon they began to understood each other very well and Landor began sending all he wrote to Forster who became his literary executor. Forster helped prepare Landor's collected works for publication in 1846 and certainly Landor would have found it impossible to produce these two volumes on his own. Landor realised the great debt he owed to Forster on this score and Volume One contained a dedication jointly to Julius Hare (who had been instrumental in bringing the 'Imaginary Conversations' to publication) and to John Forster "*By whose exertion and solicitude a complete edition of my writings is now laid before the reader.*" Both men were directed by Landor to "*Accept my thanks, retain, continue, and, if possible, increase your friendship for me, and receive for your own works all the favour that you would attract to mine.*"

Ever since his visit to Bath in February 1840, Dickens had corresponded with Landor and in August 1840 Landor sent Dickens an inscribed, presentation copy of "Andrea of Hungary" and "Giovanna of Naples" when it eventually appeared. On 8th Feb 1841 Dickens' second son was born and Landor was invited to be godfather. He was overjoyed and wrote back to Dickens around a week after the boy had been born,

"*All the men in Europe, uniting their forces, could not confer on me so great and acceptable an honour as you have done. First, let me wish the boy health – then, everything else which such parents can contribute. It creates in me a somewhat new sentiment, it makes me religious, to think of him.*"

Both men were busy, Dickens was ill and it was early December before the christening of young Walter Landor Dickens could be arranged. Landor stayed with the family at Devonshire Terrace and later Dickens recalled with great humour,

(I remember) *"that steady snore of yours, which I once heard piercing the door of your bedroom in Devonshire Terrace, reverberating along the bell-wire in the hall, so getting outside into the street, playing Eolian harps among the area railings, and going down the New Road like the blast of a trumpet."*

From time to time during the next few years, Dickens and Forster dined with Landor at his lodgings in St James' Square, these dinners often being arranged for Landor's birthday on 30th January. On 21st October 1842 Dickens brought the American poet Longfellow to dine with Landor, this being the last evening of the poet's visit before he sailed back to America from Bristol. On 30th January 1844 Dickens and Forster again came to dine, but soon after this Landor changed his lodgings to a house on the other side of St James's Square.

In 1845 Dickens and his family visited Italy and he asked if there was anything which could be brought back for Landor.

"An ivy leaf from Fiesole" was the answer and Dickens did his best to oblige. On April 2nd 1845 he wrote to Forster from Florence with a message and an enclosure for Landor.

After describing how he took a carriage to Fiesole Dickens described how he asked the coachman which was Landor's villa.

"He was a dull dog and pointed to Boccaccio's. I didn't believe him. He was so deuced ready that I knew he had lied. I went up to the convent, which is on a height, and was leaning over a dwarf wall basking in the noble view over a vast range of hill and valley, when a little peasant girl came up and began to point out the localities. 'Ecco la villa Landor!' was one of the first half-dozen sentences she spoke. My heart swelled almost as Landor's would have done when I looked down upon it, nestling among its olive-trees and vines, and with its upper windows (there are five above the door) open to the setting sun. Over the centre of these there is another story, set upon the housetop like a tower; and all Italy except its sea, is melted down into the glowing landscape it commands. I plucked a leaf of ivy from the convent-garden as I looked; and here it is. For Landor. With my love."

Naturally John Forster sent on the message and leaf, together with a covering letter from himself as soon as possible. Many years later, when, as biographer and literary executor, he opened Landor's writing desk, he found this same leaf, carefully preserved, together with the message and note, exactly as he had sent it.

When he saw him next Dickens reported to Landor that he had also met his wife, quite by chance, whilst she was walking along the road near the villa. The coachman had recognised her and had introduced him to 'La Signora Landora'. She was *"walking with a rapid and firm step, had bright eyes, a fine fresh colour and looked animated and agreeable."* When told of Julia's manner and appearance, Landor exclaimed *"And the Lord Forbid that I should do otherwise than declare that she always was agreeable – to everyone else but me!"*

On 30th January 1849 once again Dickens and Forster came to Bath to dine with Landor on his birthday and this time they were able to make the journey by train, returning to London very late in the evening. On this occasion Forster was not best pleased to find that Landor had another guest staying with him. This was Eliza Lynn, a young writer with whom Landor had become very friendly as she was a quiet and sympathetic companion.

Eliza thus described the evening in her memoirs.

"I found Dickens charming, and Forster pompous, heavy and ungenial. Dickens was bright and gay and winsome, and while treating Mr Landor with the respect of a younger man for an elder, allowed his wit to play about him, bright and harmless as summer lightning. He included me, then quite a beginner in literature, young in years and shy by temperament, and made me feel at home with him; but Forster was saturnine and cynical ... Dickens and Landor were his property, ... and he resented the introduction of a third person and a stranger."

It may well have been that Eliza Lynn and Dickens had much to say to each other for at that time, Gad's Hill Place, the house Dickens had dreamed of owning for a long time, was owned by her father Rev James Lynn who had leased it out. Whilst her father was Rector of Higham, as a child Eliza had lived in the house and in 1855 when her father died, Eliza inherited the house and sold it to Dickens, early the following year.

Besides being Landor's seventy fourth birthday, 30th January 1849 also marked the 200th anniversary of the beheading of Charles I. Various literary critics have remarked that pehaps it was no coincidence that Mr Dick, a character in "David Copperfield" which Dickens began to write not long after this dinner, had a fixation with Charles I.

The previous summer in the August of 1848 John Forster had played his part in making Landor very happy indeed by assisting with an addition to his household. By that time Landor had taken lodgings at 36 St James Square but as his movements in the summer were uncertain, a beautiful white Pomeranian puppy had been sent by Landor's daughter Julia to Forster to pass on to her father. Forster had duly sent the wicker basket on its way to Bath in a carriage and Landor had been overjoyed.

Landor's love of his dog and the fact that he gave it free rein in his rooms and actually encouraged it to sit on his head, was carefully noted by Dickens who based the character of Laurence Boythorne in "Bleak House" on Landor. In the book however, Boythorne had a canary, not a dog, which sat on his head and Dickens may have been recalling his own pet raven Grip which had died a few years before. "Bleak House" was published in instalments from March 1852 and during that year most of Landor's acquaintances would have recognised the clever pen-portrait.

Only a person sympathetic to Landor would have observed,
"He was such a true gentleman in his manner, so chivalrously polite, his face was lighted by a smile of so much sweetness and tenderness, and it seemed so plain that he had nothing to hide, but showed himself exactly as he was."

Since Landor detested hypocrisy above all else he could not have been anything but pleased with these words, yet those close to him said that he refused to read "Bleak House" and was deeply wounded by the shallowness of the character. As with so many of Dickens' characters, Boythorne was a caricature and showed Landor without any of his extensive learning or wise words. However it may have been that Landor felt embarrassed to have his idiosyncrasies paraded before the world by such a hugely popular writer. Boythorne's loud laughter, his massive grey head and frequent repetitions of "By My Soul!" were typically Landor as many knew him.

A few months after the appearance of "Bleak House" Landor dedicated his book "Imaginary Conversations between the Greeks and Romans" to Dickens. This must have pleased the younger man greatly.

As Dickens grew busier and more tired, he had less time for visits and letters, but he liked to keep Landor in touch with his godson's progress. In 1853 he again visited Italy and once again he promised he would visit Fiesole. In early July 1856, whilst on another trip abroad, he wrote to Landor from Boulogne.

"My dear Landor,
... you see many I daresay and hear from many I have no doubt, who

love you heartily; but we silent people in the distance never forget you. Do not forget us and let us exchange affection at least ... I write to you so often in my books."

In 1857 tragedy in the form of a libel suit overtook Landor. He felt that a certain woman had tricked him and he had produced pamphlets putting forward his views. It appeared to some that the whole proceedings were no more than a means of obtaining money from Landor, then aged eighty two and living alone in lodgings. On July 25th 1857 John Forster and his wife arrived in Bath and found the situation very serious. Using his expertise as a trained lawyer, Forster persuaded Landor to sign a recantation drawn up by himself, but at the last minute, after Forster had gone back to London, an addition to the wording was made by a lawyer in Bath. These additional words were to cause a great deal of trouble the following year.

Soon afterwards Landor, who could not let the matter rest, sent details of a proposed pamphlet to Forster who wrote back advising strongly against publication. Landor wrote back in the autumn of 1857,

"Of all the kind letters that ever were written yours is the kindest and I feel confident it is equally wise. I do again promise to obey you throughouot. Let me hope you will, at some future and not distant day, permit it to be published, to my honor and the discomfiture of my enemies."

However Forster was busy and left to his own devices in Bath, Landor did not keep quiet for long. In the summer of 1858 the same trouble again resurfaced and this time, Landor's nieces and the firm of solicitors they engaged advised the old man to quit the country without delay. Another book of poems by Landor had been published, this time without any consultation with Forster, and once again Landor was being sued for libel by the same woman in Bath.

The 12th July 1858 was the last time Dickens met Landor when he arrived at Forster's London house accompanied by his niece Kitty who had telegraphed notice of their arrival. He stayed for a few days until arrangements could be made to smuggle him out of England. On that first night when Landor and his niece had arrived so unexpectedly, Dickens and a number of other people were dining with Forster and his wife. Landor felt too worn out by the journey from Bath to join the others at dinner, so Dickens went upstairs to the old man's room to talk to him and sympathise with his plight. Afterwards a friend recalled what Dickens' reaction had been on his return to the assembled company. He had laughed and said that he had found Landor very jovial. Instead of the crisis in which he found himself, Landor's talk had been all of "*Catullus, Tibullus and other Latin Poets.*"

A few weeks later, when Landor was safely out of the country, news of the libel trial in Bristol was carried by many newspapers. As far as many were concerned, Landor's reputation was in shreds. Happily Dickens took the opposite view and he wrote to his daughter,

"*You must not let any new idea of poor dear Landor efface the former image of the fine and brave old man. I would not blot him out, in his tender gallantry, as he sat upon his bed at Forster's that night I lately told you of, for a million of wild mistakes at eighty-four years of age.*"

For the first year of his return to Florence, Landor was thoroughly miserable and in some part he blamed Forster for what had happened. Perhaps it would have been better to fight the libel action for it seemed to the old man that the tricksters had won hands down. Publication of a another book was delayed and he felt Forster did not have his best interests at heart. Thus in December 1859 all correspondence between the two was broken off and it was not until December 1863 that Landor wrote a reconciliatory letter asking Forster if he would consent to be his biographer.

"*Well do I know the friendship you had for me, and have grieved over its interruption. I would not now write but for the promise you once held out to me that you might consent to be my biographer. Last week I received a most insolent letter from a Mr –, containing a note from a person connected with him informing me that he was writing my life. He gave me a specimen full of abuse and falsehood ... If you still retain a thought of becoming my biographer, I hope you will protect me from this injustice. ...*"

Happily Forster did agree to be Landor's biographer and during the next few months a number of short letters passed between the two.

On 9th May 1864 a weary and ailing Landor wrote to Forster.

My dear Forster, This is the last letter I shall ever write to anybody. My kind friend Mr Twisleton will carry it, with my others last received to England. My love to noble Dickens, with, to yourself, your ever affectionate
W. Landor's

Apart from this, only a couple of very brief notes were sent by Landor to Forster, the last being dated 9th September. This was in answer to a letter from Forster dated September 5th in which

Dickens had asked him to say that the very first person to whom his completed book would be sent was his *"honoured and dear friend Landor."*

Sadly Landor did not live long enough to receive a copy of "Our Mutual Friend" for he died on 17th September 1864 just nine days after sending his last note to Forster. It was a pity for Landor would have loved the book in which Dickens satirised Forster in the character of Podsnap a smug, well-to-do businessman who *"stood very high in Mr Podsnap's opinion"*.

Forster eventually wrote the biographies of both Landor, (two volumes published in 1869) and Dickens (three volumes published in 1874). However although Dickens favourably reviewed Forster's biography in 'All the Year Round' there were many who disliked the way in which Forster levelled criticism at the character of his former friend. Robert Eyres, Landor's youngest brother, was consulted a great deal and his rather unsympathetic attitude perhaps influenced Forster. When Eliza Lynn Linton read Forster's biography, she was angry that he had omitted the poems Landor had written for her and had made hardly any mention of her friendship. She wrote later, *"I thought this Life a disgraceful thing for a friend to have written ..."* and it *"was a cold and carping and unsympathetic biography."*

10. THE FINAL YEARS
Libel. Exile in Florence.
Befriended by the Brownings.

With the libel action from Mrs Yescombe pending, Kitty felt that she had no option but to try to take her uncle abroad. Acting on the advice of Landor's solicitor, uncle and niece hurriedly left Bath by train early on 12th July 1858, leaving most of Landor's friends, as well as those who sought to sue him, in blissful ignorance of their flight.

They reached London and went immediately to 46 Montague Square, the house of John Forster and his wife, who had earlier been sent a telegram telling them of the situation. Forster seemed to be very kind, but perhaps his disinclination to be involved in the libel action clouded his judgement and made him go along with the plan, when the most sensible course of action might have been to allow Landor to live quietly in England.

It was decided that Landor should stay with the Forsters, whilst Kitty and Sophy (who arrived a day later) were found lodgings nearby. It took a few days for arrangements to be made but Kitty and Landor eventually left for Folkestone and crossed to Boulogne on 23rd July 1858. There they settled into a hotel to wait for the arrival of young Walter to escort his father on the rest of his journey. For weeks he did not come and Kitty was worried because the Hoopers, including Geraldine, were also in Boulogne. However, fortunately, their paths did not cross and eventually young Walter arrived and accompanied his father back to the family villa near Florence.

To begin with Landor had planned to settle by himself in Genoa or some other place which he liked, but young Walter convinced him that his wife Julia and the rest of the family wanted him to return to the villa. So he went but he was cruelly disappointed when he arrived there.

After a week, eighty-three year old Landor wrote to his niece Kitty,

"Here I am told that there is no place for more pictures and that it would

147

hurt the walls of my bedroom to drive nails into them. Walter, so attentive to me in France and on the journey, made me remember that the house is Arnold's. There was no question or mention on my part about it ... The closet where I formerly kept my few books is not vacant ... My head tells me that paralysis or worse will soon befall me ... At the next incivility, I walk into Florence and remain there."

Thankfully, Landor was given his own drawing room, but when Arnold found out that no extra money was forthcoming from his father's estate, he tried to charge him for board and lodging. There was no sympathy, except from young Walter and Charles who were often out anyway. His wife, his eldest son and his daughter were distant, if not downright bitter and unhelpful.

Landor learned that the trial verdict had gone against him in a letter from his friend Captain Brickmann, which arrived at the villa about a week after his arrival. Forster wrote too and also Taylor, Landor's solicitor.

In the months which followed, unhappy, and becoming increasingly frustrated by the uncaring attitude of the family in the villa, Landor tried to leave and do what he had always intended to do, which was live independently. The problem was that he had no money at all of his own and his eldest son refused to make him an allowance of any kind. Landor found himself in the plight suffered by many other old people, in that his wishes were totally disregarded in almost everything.

Still his one thought was to publish something in his own defence, but Forster advised against it and this helped to cause a gradual cooling in their friendship. The stress made Landor very ill in November 1858 and for weeks he could not leave his room. His whole mind was taken up with the unfairness of the situation and the fact that no real defence had been offered on his part. Although Landor had asked W.J. Linton (Eliza Lynn Linton's husband) to print a pamphlet, he had declined and Landor had to approach others.

Happily in March 1859 this side of the affair at least had a happy ending. The radical publisher George Jacob Holyoake agreed, on payment of five pounds, which was all Landor could muster, to undertake publication of the pamphlet Landor had written and to send out copies as directed to friends and the newspapers. Holyoake ran a great risk of being caught in the libel action himself, but he admired Landor and was flattered to be asked to help. Holyoake had the manuscript copied at his own home, in order that Landor's handwriting could not be identified and his brother did the typesetting. *"Mr Landor's Remarks on a Suit Preferred against Him, at the Summer Assizes in Taunton, 1858"* eventually appeared at the end of May 1859 with the title page removed and without any means of identification.

Sadly the newspapers took little notice, in their usual way. Having already damaged Landor's reputation, they felt his troubles were old news and Landor's friends were a little puzzled and perhaps even embarrassed to receive such a publication. However Landor felt happier to be fighting back and at least the pamphlet had made his enemies angry. A two hundred pound reward was offered in the newspapers for the name of the printer, but this was never discovered. (Many years later Holyoake chose to reveal the information in his memoirs – no doubt with some satisfaction.)

Thus Landor passed the better part of a year living in his villa in Fiesole. He felt unwanted by his family and old friends who called often, tried in vain to cheer him. However, Landor did find four beings in the household in Fiesole who were sympathetic to him. Three of these were large dogs and the fourth was a girl of around ten years whom he was told his daughter Julia had adopted. If Landor recognised the girl, Ada Bishop Landor, as his illegitimate granddaughter, he said nothing and got on well with the child, spending many happy hours talking and playing with her.

In the meantime many more things were done to annoy Landor and he found that the mimosas so carefully planted by Ianthe all those years ago were dead and gone. When he was ill and asked for a bell to be placed by his bedside, an excuse was found to prevent this and the old man realised that he would have no peace of mind until he left.

The Brownings had returned to Florence in the Spring of 1859 and on 1st July Landor called at the Casa Guidi to voice his grievances against his family. However, when he called on that occasion, the Brownings were out. Both Robert and Elizabeth had good reason to be kind to Landor and at the time of the trial Browning had written sympathetically.

Later in July 1859, when workmen disregarded his wishes and white-washed some stone lions and prepared to alter a paved walk, things came to a head. Arnold was being forced by the English courts to relinquish his father's annuity (transferred to his name in an effort to keep it safe) to pay off the libel award. The atmosphere in the villa had sunk to an all-time low and Landor was determined to leave. Later he wrote to Eliza Linton and another friend, Arthur Walker, about the events.

"*On this I left the house the day after, without a single word of remonstrance ... but was assailed by Mrs L. in language such as a prostitute could scarcely assail a thief with ... When the chancellor distrained my rents, after what was settled on them, my worthless wife and eldest son, finding that I could add nothing to the luxuries of the house-keeping, treated me with every unkindness and indignity.*"

All Landor's anger and frustrations against his eldest son he put into a tremendously sad poem entitled 'Ingratitude" and there is no doubt that he thought of himself as a latter day King Lear.

Thus it was that Landor, at the age of eighty-four, one day in July 1859, forced himself to walk the two and half miles down the hot, dusty road into Florence. He stopped for a while in a hotel on the banks of the Arno, but had hardly any money in his pocket. Then he staggered on in the hope of a meeting with Robert Browning.

This time luck was with the exhausted Landor! He met Browning in the street near to Casa Guidi and found his troubles were over. Browning addressed the situation clearly and decisively. Straight away he took Landor into his house and did what he could for his comfort and he wrote immediately to Forster asking if Landor's brothers would provide enough money for the old man to live independently, with some dignity. Forster wrote back by return saying that until he could arrange things with Landor's family, he would be responsible for all expenses which might be incurred on Landor's behalf. Forster said he saw no problem as Henry and Robert Landor were "*noble, honourable gentlemen, and wealthy to boot, and will never bear indignity to their family's head.*"

Until Browning's intervention, the family in England had not understood how bad the situation in the villa had become. In any case Henry Landor felt that it was Arnold's place to assist his father, but on the realisation that this was never going to happen, he accepted the situation. Henry and Robert Eyres Landor agreed to send a regular sum of money to enable their eldest brother to live independently for the rest of his life. In addition Henry cancelled the two thousand pounds legacy that he had intended to leave young Julia in his will and instead he used the money to build and endow a school in the Warwickshire village of Whitnash, where he was Lord of the Manor. (Just over eighty years later, I was lucky enough to attend this village school.)

Never again did Landor enter his villa and true to form, Mrs Landor and Arnold showed their intense bitterness when asked by Browning to send on Landor's things. He had no clothes with him when he left and when Browning tried to obtain some, the family refused all his requests. Finally Mrs Landor called on Browning "*all butter and honey (save an occasional wasp's sting ... when she occasionally designated our friend as 'the old Brute')*" and agreed to allow Seymour Kirkup, Landor's painter friend to collect the clothes the next day. The other items, Landor's books, plate and pictures, which he had brought with him from Bath, were to be sent as soon as possible. When the Brownings brought over the things as packed up by Mrs Landor, Landor was humiliated to receive a rough bag (such as peasants used for corn) with a tangled mass of clothing and a few books stuffed inside. From that time on, he had very little to do with his wife or eldest son and daughter ever again. Of course they all declared that Browning had set the old man against his family, but the relatives in England by now knew better.

Luckily, the American sculptor William Wetmore Story, whom Landor had known in Bath, was renting a villa in Marciano, about three miles from Siena and he invited Landor to stay for a while. Until other arrangements could be made, the members of the Story family were glad to make Landor welcome.

When he arrived, Mrs Story recalled that Landor had looked "*old and almost as shabby and dusty and miserable as a beggar,*" but soon he had begun to recover his health and strength in the congenial surroundings. Landor was in the habit of rising very early during his stay, before even the servants were up, and he could often be found sitting under the cypress trees in the garden, reading or writing. Over breakfast he might read his compositions aloud to the family and then present Edith, Story's fourteen year old daughter, with the manuscript. Later in the day they often took a walk in the countryside round the villa and Landor began teaching Latin to Edith.

This period of Landor's life was a real Indian summer. He entertained the Storys with anecdotes of years ago and he forgot the pain of the recent past by seeming to dismiss it from his mind. Story told a friend, "*Landor's face would glow with enthusiasm as he rolled out some favourite choice lines in his deep low voice,*" and the two men often strolled together in the garden, discussing various topics. William Story must have been delighted to find another man who shared his love of flowers but disliked picking them as much as he did.

Besides completing several drawings of Landor at this time, Story painted a vivid picture in words. He recalled that Landor was "*the most impatient man with himself I ever saw … he was furious if he did not remember at once any passage of a book, or any name, or date, and would immediately begin to abuse himself, crying out in his sharp, high voice, 'God bless my soul! I am losing my mind, I am getting old'.*"

Landor stayed for three weeks as the guest of the Story family, leaving eventually to move to other accommodation not far away. Mrs Story recalled afterwards that they were all sorry to see him go. She wrote, "*his courtesy and high breeding never failed him; he was touchingly pleased and happy with our life, and so delightful and amusing that we ourselves grieved when it was at an end.*"

The Brownings rented a villa near the Storys and when Elizabeth Barrett Browning was well enough in September to join in, there were some very happy gatherings. Two young American visitors, Isabella Blagden and Kate Field, stayed with the Brownings, whilst Landor took an apartment in a cottage nearby as an experiment to see if he could live alone. An artist, Hamilton Wade, visited the Storys and was so struck by the marvellous company and surroundings that he painted a picture. The Storys, Elizabeth and Robert Browning, their son Pen and Landor were all pictured sitting round the tea-table in the garden. (Sadly this painting was destroyed in a fire in Boston some years later. Had it survived, it would have provided a magnificent record of those happy summer days.)

Many years later Edith Story recalled the pleasure that Landor had given her when he had worn a flowered waistcoat given him by Count D'Orsay in honour of her birthday. She also recalled the intense discussions which Landor and Mrs Browning had over Louis Napoleon, the French Emperor. Elizabeth Browning had a great admiration for Louis Napoleon, whilst Landor was full of mistrust. Edith Story recalled,

"*Mrs Browning, with her face hidden under her large hat and curls, would be stirred past endurance by these assaults on her hero … and would raise her treble voice even to a shrill pitch in protest, until Mr Browning would come into the fray as mediator.*"

Other friends noted how amused Mrs Browning would be at some of Landor's monologues when he had lost something and how the numerous choruses of "*God bless my soul*" would make her laugh.

Despite some trouble over his food, by and large Landor seemed contented in his cottage and he wrote to Forster,

"*You will have heard that I am now in a cottage near Siena, which I owe to Browning, the kind friend who found it for me, whom I had seen only three or four times in my life, yet who made me the voluntary offer of what money I wanted, and who insists on managing my affairs here, and paying for my lodging and sustenance. Never was such generosity and such solicitude as this incomparable man has shown on my behalf.*"

At the end of this wonderful summer, the Brownings and the Storys returned to Rome leaving Landor behind in Florence. Once again Robert and Elizabeth Browning were marvellous and before they left they arranged for the long-term care of their elderly friend. Wilson, Elizabeth's maid, who had fled with her from Wimpole Street, had married Ferdinando Romagnoli, an Italian servant of the Brownings, and she was to be paid thirty pounds a year to look after Landor. A small house, not far from Casa Guidi in Florence had been found and refurbished and Landor had three rooms and a book closet on the first floor, whilst Wilson and a servant girl had the ground floor rooms. The expenses, including the rent of one pound a week, were to be paid from Landor's allowance and Wilson was entitled to have whatever was left from his rations. Every quarter Forster transferred to Browning fifty pounds from Landor's brothers; in addition there was a reserve fund of fifty pounds in case of necessity. Browning acted as guardian over the finances for the rest of Landor's life and each quarter he made out an account of the expenses, which was certified by Landor's old friend Seymour Kirkup.

Making sure that Landor was comfortable delayed the Brownings' departure to Rome till late November, but when they did leave they had every confidence that he was in good hands.

Sadly that first winter in the new apartment was difficult and Landor was often miserable. The rooms were not so warm as the villa had been and he and Wilson had some arguments. She was driven nearly to hysterics by his pictures and his eccentricities and, when faced by a woman with fire in her eyes, Landor could be very difficult. All his life he had suffered from outbursts of temper and when depressed or under stress, his temper often became worse and stories of plates and dinners flying out of the window abounded at that time. Mrs Story had remarked that even when difficult, Landor might be managed "with civility", but Wilson found the elderly writer almost impossible at times.

In the spring when the Brownings returned, they had to sort out the situation, after listening to complaints from both sides. Eventually Landor and Wilson came to understand each other very well, for neither of them was in any position to make alternative arrangements. Wilson learned how to humour Landor and in return she was well paid and able to save money, which was her main consideration at the time.

Whilst in Siena in 1859, the Storys had given Landor another dog and this one he called Giallo. Once installed in the lodgings in the 2671 Via Nunziatina (now 93 Via della Chiesa) near the back of the Carmine monastery, he set about teaching Giallo some of the same tricks that Pomero used to do. In 1860, although eighty five years of age, Landor could manage short walks very easily and he and his little light-brown Pomeranian were a familiar sight in central Florence as he crossed the Ponte Vecchio to see old friends or leave his visiting card. Amongst the visiting intellectuals, Landor was very much a celebrity and in April 1860 when William Burnet Kinney, the former American minister to the Court of Victor Emmanuel 11, called with his wife, she recalled her visit to him as being "*one of the highest privileges which the lover of genius can enjoy*" in Florence. Although he was inclined to ramble and talk too much, his lively mind and firmly-held views about a wide variety of subjects made him fascinating to many younger people. Senator Winthrop and the Boston publisher, James T. Fields, came and there was renewed interest in Landor's works in America.

Fields, who had known Landor for some years, hoped at one time to publish a complete edition of Landor's work in the United States and during 1860 various manuscripts were placed in his hands. However the outbreak of the American Civil War made such a project unworkable and at the beginning of 1862 Landor's manuscripts were sent to Arthur Walker in London. Walker was an old and trusted friend and during this period he performed many useful services by way of preparing material for publication.

Good as it was to be sought out by interested young American visitors, Landor still enjoyed the friendship of a number of old friends. Seymour Kirkup, the artist, not only helped look after Landor's finances, he also visited regularly and, having become interested in spiritualism, tried to interest Landor too. It amused many, notably Mrs Browning, that deaf as Kirkup was, he could actually hear Landor's loud laughter when spiritualism was mentioned! Other visitors included the sculptor Gibson, Sandford (a friend from Bath) and Charles Empson who had kept the Museum in the Walks in Bath.

The Americans Isa(bella) Blagden and Kate Field often called on him and both became special friends. Kate had travelled to Italy at the age of twenty with her aunt and uncle, arriving in 1859 and becoming friendly with the Brownings soon afterwards. Like Mrs Story, Kate wrote down many things about Landor and later in her life she wrote about them in articles in American periodicals. When she came to Florence, Kate had been chaperoned socially by Tom Trollope's wife Theodosia, whom Landor had known many years earlier as Theodosia Garrow. Landor would pick Kate some roses or camellias from the tiny garden at the rear of his apartment and he would teach her Latin or reminisce about days of old.

Although the happy summer gathering in Siena in 1859 had been repeated in 1860, that was the last of such holidays. In 1861 Landor lost several very good friends and he was much saddened. Despite the fact that Elizabeth Barrett Browning seemed stronger when the family returned to Florence in early June 1861, she died on June 29th quite suddenly. As soon as he heard the news Landor wrote a short note to Browning,

My dear Browning,
Of all your friends who lament your irreparable loss, not one grieves more deeply than I do.
I will not say more, I can say nothing more true. Let these few lines, if they can be but of small or no comfort to you, at least manifest the affection of your affectionate
W. Landor.

Landor did not go the funeral, but discreetly kept his distance and when he did meet Browning at Isa Blagden's, he sent a note of warning lest Browning should think the visit indelicate.

Browning left Florence for good on 1st August 1861 and Landor never saw him again, although with Kirkup's assistance he continued to oversee Landor's finances.

Between May and August 1861, Landor often went out in a hired carriage with Kate Field and her mother. Once they drove to Fiesole and Kate recalled the emotive occasion for the eighty six year old writer.

"*Once we drove to aerial Fiesole; and never can I forget Landor's manner while in the neighbourhood of his former home. It had been proposed that we should turn back when only half way up the hill. 'Ah go a little farther,' Landor said nervously; 'I should like to see my villa.' Of course his wish was our pleasure, and so the drive was continued. Landor sat immovable with head turned in the direction of the villa Gherardesca. At first sight of it he gave a sudden start, and genuine tears filled his eyes and coursed down his cheeks. 'There is where I lived,' he said, breaking a long silence and pointing to his old estate. Still we mounted the hill, and when, at a turn in the road, the villa stood out before us clearly and distinctly, Landor said, 'Let us give the horses a rest here!' We stopped, and for several minutes Landor's face was fixed upon the villa.' There now, we can return to Florence, if you like,' he murmured finally with a deep sigh. 'I have seen it probably for the last time.' Hardly a word was spoken during the drive home.*"

Later in August 1861, Kate Field and her mother had to return to America rather suddenly and Landor was greatly downcast at the news. When Kate and her mother called to say goodbye, Landor not only insisted on accompanying them downstairs to the carriage, he also gave Kate a wonderful parting gift. Often Landor had tried to press gifts on Kate, but she had always refused. However this time, she felt to refuse would hurt his feelings very much, especially after he had staggered down the steep stairs from his apartment with it and had laid it carefully on the carriage seat. Landor insisted on riding back to their lodgings with the ladies where he saw them to their door.

Kate knew well what Landor had given her for they had looked at the album of one hundred and forty drawings many times in the past and once, because she had admired a particular pair of paintings by Turner, Landor had gone in search of scissors to cut them out! Now he had given her the entire album which he said he had bought for fifty guineas from Thomas Barker of Bath some years previously when the artist had been in urgent need of money.

"*I shall never see you again, and I want you to think of the foolish old creature occasionally,*" Landor had said when he gave Kate the album and, when he parted from her and her mother at their door, he murmured, "*May God bless you,*" before departing sorrowfully homewards.

Reading about Kate Field in "Notable American Women, 1607–

1959" Vol 1, it is easy to see why she and Landor, despite an age diffence of sixty three years, were able to pass many happy hours together. Small, intelligent and attractive, she possessed courage and humour and her father, like so many of Landor's friends, had been born in Ireland. Her mother had been an actress and it was small wonder that Landor found their company quite invigorating.

The contrast between the honourable behaviour of Kate Field and her mother and that of Geraldine Hooper and Mrs Yescombe must have struck Landor at that time. His female visitors in Bath had been only too keen to take home paintings and accept gifts, even that of one hundred pounds, but Kate Field was worried about accepting the album which she thought might be very valuable. In the end she found she could not carry it with her to America and worried in case she was depriving Landor's family of it, she left it in the custody of Tom Trollope. He sent it on to her two years after Landor's death and Kate kept it carefully during her lifetime. It was not properly catalogued until her death, when its full beauty and significance was realised. (see page 165)

After Browning had departed to England, Landor thought he might save a deal of trouble if he allowed his son Charles to find him a room. However when Landor wrote to Browning with the suggestion he said he was content where he was if that was what Browning thought best.

"Whatever you decide on I will do ... At no time have I for a moment felt an inclination to remove from my present quarters, being perfectly content with wife and husband equally."

Thus Mrs Romagnoli and her husband continued to care for Landor throughout his last years. Landor's sons Walter and Charles later did much to help their father.

In the latter part of 1861 and early part of 1862 Landor had suffered yet another great blow when his dream of being buried in Widcombe Churchyard near Bath was dashed. The Vicar of Widcombe wrote to tell him that the burial ground around the church was being closed and if he still wished to be buried there, a brick grave must be made for him at once. Landor asked for the work to be done and his friend Sandford, now back in Bath, advanced the payment of ten pounds five shillings. Landor wrote to Browning to ask for the money to repay Sandford, but this time there was no money forthcoming as brother Henry felt that it was Arnold's duty to pay it. Landor felt humiliated when Arnold refused to pay and in the end young Walter paid the debt. However, after an attempt to sell pictures in England caused more difficulty and Browning was left with the problem as to who was going to pay the six pounds shipping charge, Landor was persuaded by Browning to agree to be buried in Florence. This would be far cheaper and there could be no arguments about the payment. Thus Landor had to end his dream of being buried in a place dear to Ianthe and this saddened him greatly.

Deafness, weakness and illness overtook Landor frequently in his last years, but he did not give up writing or preparing work for publication. In December 1859 a new edition of "Hellenics" had been published, just in time for Landor's great friend General Sir William Napier to have knowledge of the dedication to himself before his death and in October 1863 "Heroic Idyls" was published. Throughout his last years, Landor continued to read a great deal and the plays of Shakespeare, the novels of Anthony Trollope, Harriet Beecher Stowe and the works of his friend G. P. R. James (now dead) were swiftly digested and re-read. The works of Anthony Trollope were chosen because although Landor was visited fairly often by Thomas Trollope who lived in Florence, brother Anthony had also called on Landor once. Landor had thought him "*a clever-looking man*".

Arthur Walker and his sister, the Countess Baldelli, were good friends to Landor in his last few years. Walker had been a friend of Arnold Landor many years previously, but in later life had visited Landor over a long period of time, both in Bath and Italy. At one time Landor intended that Walker should be his biographer and with this in mind he sent him his writing desk containing some papers and two miniature paintings, one of his beloved Ianthe and the other of her granddaughter, then married to Mr O'Donnell of Baltimore. Landor had been worried in 1863 that he had not heard from Luisina for some time and he hoped she had not become tangled up in the American Civil War. Since the death of Ianthe over ten years previously, contact with her granddaughter was to him an important link.

However trouble with Walker over the publication of "Heroic Idyls" led to a reconciliation with John Forster in the last few months of Landor's life and it was he who received the final papers prior to a writing of the official biography.

The Countess Baldelli continued to visit Landor almost up to the time of his death. She often took her three little children with her and she promised to give Giallo a good home whenever it was needed.

In the final year or so of Landor's life, he saw more and more of his sons Walter and Charles, but Arnold suffered a stroke in 1863 and for some time it looked as if he might not survive his father. To begin with, Walter and Charles came merely to dine with their father, but later one or both of them would come each day as the old man grew weaker and needed more help. Browning effected an introduction for a new friend Edward Twisleton, a younger brother of Lord Saye and Sele and a pioneer of educational reform, and his visits gave Landor much pleasure when he was left alone during the day.

In January 1863 Landor was very upset to learn in his birthday letter from Kitty of the death of Mrs Paynter some time before. Landor had been her friend for over sixty five years and yet another link with the past was gone.

In March 1864 a young man called at Landor's apartment with a letter of introduction from Lord Houghton (previously Monckton Milnes) but the visit was not a success. Landor who used to spend most days alone sitting in his chair, once his sons had dressed him, seemed not to hear or comprehend who the young man was. The young Algernon Swinburne, who had come to Italy expressly with the idea of meeting his idol, sadly withdrew and back in his lodgings sent Landor a note of apology and explanation, describing his immense admiration for him.

Happily this generous praise from a twenty-six year old poet, as enthusiastic as Landor had been in his own youth, brought about a temporary transformation in the old writer. Landor sent Swinburne a note inviting him to call again and the younger man did not need to be asked twice!

The second visit was a huge success and Swinburne remembered for the rest of his life the half-hour he spent with his alert, brilliant host, who for a brief time seemed to recapture some of his former mental energy as they discussed immortality. When Swinburne rose to go, Landor gave him as many copies as he wished to take of the Italian Conversation published to help the cause of Garibaldi some time before and the young man left in a haze of wonder and exhilaration.

Afterwards Swinburne wrote to Lord Houghton,

"I have got the one thing I wanted with all my heart. If both or either of us

die tomorrow, at least to-day he has told me that my presence here has made him happy. … I should like to throw up all my other things on earth and devote myself to playing valet to him for the rest of his days. I would black his boots for him if he wore any … I can hardly tell you what pleasures I have had today in a half-hour's intercourse with him."

Very wisely, after this visit Landor decided that any repeat peformance would be unlikely to be as good and he wrote a note to Swinburne a few days later.

My dear friend,
So totally am I exhausted that I can hardly hold my pen, to express my vexation that I shall be unable to converse with you again. Eyes, intellect fail me – I can only say that I was much gratified by your visit, which must be the last, and that I remain ever, Your obliged
W. Landor

Swinburne was to revere Landor's memory for the rest of his life.

A few other friends called in these last days including young Augustus Hare, the son of Julius, and nephew of Francis and Augustus, who had been such great friends of Landor in days gone by. The young poets Aubrey De Vere and Coventry Patmore called, and like Swinburne were glad to have the chance to meet the old writer, but they could not inspire him as he had done.

In these last days, Landor was helped up by Charles and Walter about noon and then he sat in his chair until six when he went to bed. Until the light evenings arrived in the summer, one of his sons would stay the night because Landor was afraid that they would be attacked by brigands when returning to the villa in the dark. When on his own during the day he would have a plate of strawberries on a high stool and pens and ink on a table where he could reach them.

On 1st May 1864 Landor rang the bell at two in the morning, asked Mrs Romagnoli to open the windows, light the lamp and bring him some writing materials. He wrote a few lines of verse then said, "*I shall never write again,*" and apart from a few letters that was how it was.

The last letter Landor ever wrote was to Forster dated 9th September. On 17th September, only eight days later, he died.

For some days Landor had had a bad cold and had eaten very little. On Friday 16th September he felt so ill that he stayed in bed and on Saturday 17th Walter arrived at 8 a.m. and Charles came at 11 a.m. with the doctor. Some time later that day, with both his younger sons present, a bad fit of coughing weakened Landor's heart and he died.

Later that day his daughter Julia came down from the villa to see her father for the last time. It is said that he looked like a majestic marble statue.

In the evening of Monday 19th September he was buried in the English Cemetery in Piazza Donatello, at Florence, not far from Elizabeth Barrett Browning. Only Walter and Charles, his two younger sons followed the body to the grave.

An upright stone was placed above the grave which read,

> Sacred
> to the Memory of
> Walter Savage Landor
> born 30th day of January 1775
> died on the 17th September 1864.
> This last sad tribute
> of his wife and children.

In the weeks that followed Sandford wrote from Bath and offered to assist in burying Landor in the grave at Widcombe, but Mrs Landor replied, "*We think he may as well be left where he is*". Landor's friends in Bath then proposed to erect a stone at Widcombe "*His long cherished desire to lie in this churchyard was frustrated by his death in Florence 17 September 1864,*" but it is believed they were unable to do this, for no stone exists today.

The will which Landor made in October 1859 was eventually proved in England, although a later will (invalid in England because Walter and Charles were beneficiaries and they had also been witnesses) was also taken into account. Landor had little to leave except his paintings and a few books and in the will Sophy was left all Landor's books, papers, pictures and plate and Kitty was left the rest. Both nieces realised the need to be flexible and they distributed things as they thought their uncle would have wanted. Walter and Charles certainly had some of their father's pictures for some remained in their families for many years afterwards.

Browning guessed that Mrs Landor would try to cause trouble and one day some weeks later, she stopped Tom Trollope in the street in Florence. She was furious over the will since it made no mention of any of the children. She was especially angry over the fact that Browning was an executor.

Long before his death, Landor had already sent the books he had promised to Browning's son Robert (Pen) and Browning had given each a suitable inscription. Although he would not accept any of Landor's property for himself, he did his best to see that all items were disposed of sensitively and correctly. He wrote,

"I have been more than rewarded for my poor pains by being of use for five years to the grand old ruin of a genius, such as I don't expect to see again."

11. IN THE YEARS THAT FOLLOWED
After Landor's Death in 1864

Arnold, Landor's eldest son, remained paralysed for the rest of his life and died in 1871 aged fifty three.

Walter Savage Landor 2nd then inherited the Ipsley Court and Llanthony Estates. All his life he was interested in painting and drawing and in later life he painted many modernistic pictures. In the 1880s he asked the family in Warwickshire to arrange a suitable memorial to his father in Warwick and the Rev. Rashleigh Duke (Sophy and Kitty's brother in law) duly obliged. At Walter's cost, a bust of his father, in a niche of Italian marble, was unveiled in St Mary's Church, Warwick, before a group of local dignitaries and friends on 30th January 1888, the 113th anniversary of Landor's birth. On the same day a sign was also erected over the door of Landor's birthplace in Eastgate (now Landor) House in Warwick. A memorial plaque had already been placed in Bishop's Tachbrook Church, close to that of Landor's maternal grandparents. Walter Savage Landor 2nd eventually went to live in Geneva where he died unmarried in 1899 aged seventy seven.

Charles Savage Landor, the youngest son, inherited Ipsley Court and Llanthony Abbey on the death of his brother in 1899. In the house in Florence where Charles lived were a number of pictures left by his father including works said to be by Botticelli, Paul Veronese, Rubens, Van Dyck, Carlo Dolci, Michelangelo and Salvatore Rosa. Charles died in Florence in 1917, at the age of ninety one, and the property then passed to his son Arnold Henry Savage Landor who was by then a well known artist, explorer and writer. His travel books, copiously illustrated by his own paintings, were very popular in the first quarter of the twentieth century and many are collectors' items today. In his autobiography "Everywhere" A.H.S Landor described how he travelled to London and met the famous writer Mrs Eliza Lynn Linton on 24th September 1888 at her apartment in Queen Anne Mansions, London. Although she was old, he warmed to her kindly expression and melodious voice. In her beautiful apartment, full of interesting things and rare books she entertained many of the best-known literary people of the day. She brought about a meeting between A.H.S. Landor and Algernon Swinburne who was thrilled to meet Landor's grandson. Both Eliza Lynn Linton and Algernon Swinburne remained devoted to Landor's memory all their lives and both were incensed by numerous inaccurate statements which were published after his death. Eliza Lynn Linton died in 1898 at the age of seventy six.

Shortly after Landor's death, Swinburne dedicated a book to his memory and wrote a poem "In Memory of Walter Savage Landor" which was quoted in full by Forster in his biography. A later ode "Song for the Centenary of Walter Savage Landor" was dedicated to Eliza Lynn Linton. Swinburne was not able to write a biography of his hero, but in 1882 he was given the task of writing the article on Landor for the 9th Edition of the Encyclopedia Britannica. After giving Landor's dates, Swinburne began the article with the memorable sentence,

"In the course of this long life he had won for himself such a double crown of glory in verse and in prose as has been won by no other Englishman but Milton."

When Landor's grave-stone in Florence was refurbished in the mid-twentieth century, a flat marble slab carried the last eight lines of Swinburne's poem "In Memory of Walter Savage Landor".

And thou, his Florence, to thy trust
    Receive and keep,
Keep safe his dedicated dust,
    His sacred sleep.

So shall thy lovers, come from far,
    Mix with thy name
As morning-star with evening-star
    His faultless fame.

Mrs Julia Landor, Landor's wife, lived out the remainder of her life at the villa with her daughter Julia, who never married. In 1876 Eliza Lynn Linton had visited Florence and mother and daughter had called upon her and invited her back to the Villa Gherardesca. Mrs Linton reported to a friend, *"Old Mrs Landor is really not unlike the dear old man himself. Her hair is white now, not golden, and she speaks something in the same way as he did."* Concerning the villa Mrs Linton said *"It is full of pictures – a beautiful place, and there were the terraces and walks and myrtles, etc, that the dear old man used to speak of.*" Mrs Landor died less then three years later on 17th April 1879, at the age of eighty four, and daughter Julia died only five years afterwards. Mother and daughter were both buried in the Protestant cemetery in Galuzzo, near Florence.

Landor's villa was then inherited by Julia's daughter who had married a Count Negroni in 1867. The villa was sold towards the end of the nineteenth century.

In Warwickshire, Henry Eyres Landor died at Tachbrook in 1866 at the age of eighty six and his niece Sophy inherited Savage's House at Tachbrook. Eventually she and her sister Kitty lived at Tachbrook together and on several occasions Arnold Henry Savage Landor visited them when in England. Sophy Landor died in 1889 at the age of seventy four and Kitty at the same age in 1892. Both Sophy and Kitty were buried in the same grave as their uncle and the three of them share a tombstone in Bishop's Tachbrook churchyard.

Robert Eyres Landor, Landor's youngest brother, died in 1869 at the age of eighty seven and was buried at Birlingham, Worcestershire, where he had been Rector for many years. Before his death he was contacted by John Forster who used some of his reminiscences when writing the official biography of Landor. Robert Eyres Landor had many valuable pictures in his collection, including some said to be by Rubens, Holbein, Raphael, Titian and Caravaggio, and a few of these had originally been bought by Landor himself. Also a published writer of some renown, Robert had a library of over 1,600 books and the auction sale of his effects raised over four thousand pounds for the restoration of the church in Birlingham. John Forster attended Robert Eyres Landor's funeral and was bequeathed four historical portraits by unknown artists in his will.

John Forster died in 1876 at the age of sixty four, after completing biographies of both Landor and Dickens.

In America interest continued in the life and works of Landor and various Americans who had met Landor in his later years in Florence recalled his genius and wrote books and magazine articles. Kate Field became a well known and respected journalist and actress. After her death in 1896 in Honolulu, Hawaii, from pneumonia, at the age of fifty seven, the album given her on their last meeting by Landor was catalogued by Major General Charles Greely Loring, Director of the Boston Museum of Fine Arts. In his opinion it contained some "*very rare gems, – heads by Raphael, flowers from Leonardo da Vinci, a landscape in oils by Salvator Rosa, sixteen sketches by Turner, a number by Gainsborough, and others by Claude Lorraine, Poussin, Allston, and several artists of the early Italian school.*"

As to Landor's estates, Ipsley Court continued to be leased out until the early 1920s when it was sold off by Landor's family. It is believed that the Llanthony Abbey estate continued to be owned by Landor's descendants until the 1970s when the estate was sold off, largely to the sitting tenants.

The ruins of the abbey themselves are now cared for by the Department of the Environment and many of the trees planted by Landor around 1810 to 1812 are now fine specimens nearly two hundred years later. Sadly some trees were lost in the storms of 1977, but many still remain and are much admired. The local Tourist Bureau in Abergavenny frequently acknowledges the huge debt they owe to the planter of the trees.

In Bath a few of the buildings connected with Landor were damaged during the Second World War. Number 3 Rivers Street sustained slight damage during a bombing raid but St James' Church was severely damaged and later demolished. Very early in the Twentieth Century a commemorative plaque was unveiled outside 3 Rivers, Street, which already had the name 'Landor House' painted over the door by the owner. Today this plaque is no longer in situ but there are plaques to both Dickens and Landor outside 35 St James' Square.

Also during the Twentieth Century a memorial to Landor bearing his quatrain "I strove with none …" was erected in the Chapel at Rugby School in Warwickshire, alongside memorials to other Old Boys famous in the literary world.

And finally, not long after Landor's death, Giallo was claimed by Countess Baldelli who treasured him for another eight years. Eventually the dog, by then blind and his hair having fallen out, died on November 29th 1872. Much saddened by the dog's death, the Countess erected a tombstone at her villa to "The last dog of Walter Savage Landor."

12. A PERSONAL REFLECTION
The Landor Trail. Does Landor
Deserve More Popularity?

"Few men have impressed their peers so much, or the general public so little, as WALTER SAVAGE LANDOR".
So wrote Sidney Colvin in the opening sentence of his excellent biography of Landor in 1881.

In the few decades after his death, Landor's works were recognised by studious people like Professor Sidney Colvin to be truly great in many respects. Landor's prose style in particular was admired and students were required to study his works for examinations at school and university. At this time, Landor's family in England spent much time being proud of him and they compiled details of his ancestors and other documents for posterity.

As time went on, more and more books about Landor appeared, Day-books of short quotations from the "Imaginary Conversations", selected books of poetry and other books of biographical anthology were published. Between 1927 and 1936 "The Complete Works of Walter Savage Landor" were published in sixteen volumes and many delightful and hitherto unknown pieces were included. In 1957 what is generally considered to be the definitive biography of Landor was published. It was the work of R.H. Super, an American who worked for twenty years before he produced a book of over six hundred pages, with around a third of the book occupied by notes. Not to be outdone, a previous biographer, Malcolm Elwin, felt that in all the mass of detail, Super had lost sight of the wonderful character of the man himself and so he wrote in 1958 a second biography, A REPLEVIN. in an attempt to restore Landor's vitality and reputation.

I freely acknowledge my debt to R.H. Super and M. Elwin in particular for they both wrote splendidly detailed accounts of Landor's life and quoted from many of his works in an effort to give a rounded picture of the man. However both these works are now available only on the second-hand book market and apart from a few

Latin poems and short selections of his poetry and prose in anthologies, none of Landor's works are now in print.

Perhaps each generation needs to discover afresh the strengths of each great writer, for the needs of readers change and the priorities of each decade are different. If any of my readers think my account of Landor's life is rather one sided, I can only reply that I am a personal writer and must write from my own enthusiasm. If my words paint a too flattering picture, then perhaps they will balance some of those gone before. I think Landor has suffered very much at the hands of some biographers and I believe it is time for a re-assessment of his work.

His first biographer, John Forster, infuriated many of Landor's friends by making unsympathetic remarks in his original biography, Some of the facts related by Forster had been told to him by Robert Eyres Landor, Landor's youngest brother, then still alive, but Robert had always been rather jealous and was probably vindictive. Eliza Lynn Linton and Algernon Swinburne remained staunch in their unwavering defence and admiration of Landor, but many other biographers were more influenced by the original work done by Forster. Mrs Lynn Linton in particular was doubted because she was thought to be a rebellious female who wrote romantic novels. Even Sidney Colvin, pro-Landor as he was, was not able to give details about the libel case in 1858 and only in the relative freedom of modern times has it been possible to discuss such topics as the widespread abuse of the elderly, which always seems to have been prevalent.

I have pored over many books dealing with Landor, but now that I too have written a biography, I like to think that I am adding something to the study of this remarkable man. If nothing else, I am putting forward the female point of view and also that of a local historian, born and bred in Warwickshire, and able to consult the Landor family documents in Warwickshire County Record Office. My ancestors, living side by side with Landor and his family in Warwick, may easily have passed him or his family in the wooded Warwickshire lanes and town streets, and I believe this gives me added insight. I grew up imbibing the same influences as Landor, for I attended school in the very house where he was born and even my junior school in the small town of Whitnash, three miles from Warwick, was built and endowed by Henry Eyres Landor, Landor's brother.

My following of the Landor trail is a subject in itself. The first I knew of him was when I went to the King's High School for Girls in Warwick in 1949 at the age of eleven. Above the door of the old house, which formed the original part of the school in 1879, was the notice 'Landor born 1775'. Who was this Landor? I had no idea.

From time to time, the school magazine "The Ilex" carried amusing articles or poems about him, usually dwelling on his bad temper. These I read with minimal interest. In the hall of Landor House there was a bust above a doorway, but the face depicted seemed remote and forbidding. For part of a term I enjoyed the famous old ilex tree, from which the school magazine took its name, but when I knew the tree, it was surrounded by tarmac in a playground and there were few other remnants left of the once large garden.

In the last few decades, Landor and his work seem to have gradually faded from view, although many of his contemporaries are still very well known. The National Portrait Gallery in London (in whose archives I conducted a great deal of my pictorial research) have placed Landor's bust by Gibson and his portrait by Fisher in store, like the rest of their drawings of him. It seems the general public is no longer interested in his life.

I must confess that when I first began to study him for a local history book I was writing in 1990, concerning the house in which he was born, I took the official line, as begun by John Forster in the original biography. I believed that Landor was a quarrelsome man whose works were largely irrelevant today. On 28th September 1990 (my diary confirms the date) I carefully explained to a friend that I thought Landor a bad-tempered man, who had wasted much of his inheritance. Later that day I returned to my studies.

That same evening, the penny suddenly dropped and by the following day I had completely changed my mind! I began to read Super's, Elwin's and Colvin's biographies and I realised how wrong I had been. I now realised Landor was a splendid character, the kind of person I admired. He rapidly became my hero and I loved him for his individuality above all else. As I read more I found beautiful sweet verses which brought tears to my eyes just as they had brought tears to Eliza Lynn. I discovered for myself just what a profound effect he had on kindred spirits and now I counted myself amongst these.

I began to collect books on Landor and soon I was hot on the

Landor trail! I determined to write a biography of him and as the years passed, I grew more passionate in my endeavour. I soon realised that I was not the only one who had fallen under Landor's spell, in fact many of the people who met him during his life time felt the same and his biographers in the twentieth century have also done so.

After I had become pro-Landor in 1990, many other coincidences seemed to crop up. Amongst my numerous books, I found I had inherited from my late father several books which he had collected about Landor, plus various notes which he had made on his works. Quite unwittingly, was I following in my late father's footsteps and had he too fallen under the Landor spell? The more I thought about it, the more I could see similarities between my father and Landor, albeit a century apart. My father used old Warwickshire words like "cowcumber" and so did Landor, and both men loved nature and art and were extremely courteous to all women.

My entire life began to be Landor-orientated and I bought all the books I could which described his life or even mentioned his name. In this I was helped considerably by a local book dealer, Martyn Davies, of Portland Books in Leamington Spa. The young, enthusiastic, knowledgeable Martyn began to share my delight when he managed to find book after book for me at my request and by 1998 I had put together quite a sizeable collection.

A massive stroke of luck came in 1999 when the Antique Map and Bookshop of Puddletown, Dorset, sent Martyn details of a collection of books which had once belonged to the Landor family. I was overjoyed to be able to buy such items as the copy of "The Life of John Stirling" which its author, Thomas Carlyle, inscribed and gave to Landor in 1852, an 1803 copy of "Gebir" which had belonged to a relation of Landor in Rugeley and the tiny leather-bound prayer-book which Maria Landor had given to Robert Eyres Landor, her godson, on the occasion of his christening. Martyn Davies also helped me to acquire two original letters by Landor, plus a page of a manuscript and finally in 1999 he found me an original photograph, signed by Landor in 1855.

It is hardly surprising that the friend to whom this book is dedicated began to feel that Landor himself was by my side! An old school friend who had moved to North Wales rang to tell me of the important Dylan Thomas article she had discovered in a library book. I have good reason to be very grateful to Margaret Leech and to Penygroes Library. I visited Swansea and was lucky enough to talk to an old man who had been taught by Dylan Thomas's father and I came to realise that Dylan Thomas's house in Cwmdonkin Drive was but a few streets away from Ryddings House where Landor stayed in Swansea. I visited as many of the other places in Landor's life as I could. I walked on the nearly deserted beaches near Tenby in winter and stood and measured barnacle marks in caves which might have been known to Landor and Nancy Jones. Port Eynon, Laugharne, Carmarthen, Clifton Hill, Bristol, all followed in quick succession and for a few heady days in 1998 I actually rented a flat in Rivers Street, not far from Landor's lodgings in Bath in the 1850s. I leant on the parapet of a bridge over the Tach Brook near Savage's House in Bishop's Tachbrook and I viewed the exterior of the house itself. Did I find the real Landor in all these wanderings? I thought I did, when gazing at the view from Lansdown Crescent above Bath. A poem sprang readily into my mind – hardly a work of art, but I was pleased in that it showed I was on the right track.

Perhaps most strangely and emotive of all, I visited Llanthony late in 1997 with a friend who kindly offered to walk round the site of Landor's house, as the distance involved was too great for me. When the photographs of the walk arrived some weeks later, I suffered! The very walls in the photograph seemed to move and I was left with a shivery feeling down my spine that the trees were trying to push out the remains of Landor's building. This feeling still remains today.

Had I begun to look at life through Landor's eyes? I dipped into other biographies and I came to the conclusion that it was more than possible. Why had I chosen to write about Landor in the first place? Had I indeed been chosen for some reason or another?

It was only a few months ago in 1999 that I realised that my search for the real Landor was going to be a life-long quest. His life had rapidly become the most important thing in my life, after my family and first grandchild, and on 30th January 2000, the 225th anniversary of Landor's birth, I invited a group of friends to join me outside the house of his birth and together we agreed to form an informal LANDOR SOCIETY. Ownership of most of the original items which I acquired have been transferred to the society in the hope that after my death, the collection will live on to encourage the study of Landor and his works.

(Anyone who feels they wish to help or join the Landor Society can seek out details on the Internet, or contact the local history librarians at Warwick or Leamington Libraries who will probably be able to point them in the right direction.)

And what of Landor's works? For myself I would still be passionately interested in him as a person if he had never written a word – in other words it is his character which I find fascinating. However, I do not think one can ever divorce a person from their works and I realise that a man like Landor would have considered his works all-important. Like his friend Dickens, Landor would have been content to be judged by his works alone.

Are his works important? If one picks up any anthology of verse or any book about poetry, there are usually one or two offerings from Landor included in the collection. However, as the years go on, these contributions grow fewer and one is left with the distinct impression that Landor's star is on the wane. Yet why is this? I admit to being biased, but I believe that some of Landor's miscellaneous verse and little known short poems are some of the most emotive and pleasing items I have ever read. I can only conclude that his work has become obscure and difficult to find, hence I felt a new introduction to his life and works was necessary.

As regards Landor's work I think there is a simple question to be answered. Does the man who wrote the following delicate verse and thought-provoking, prose extract (both my own personal favourites from Landor's work) deserve to be remembered?

> It often comes into my head
> That we may dream when we are dead,
> But I am far from sure we do.
> O that it were so! then my rest
> Would be indeed among the blest;
> I should for ever dream of you.

****

"Sad is the day, and worse must follow, when we hear the blackbird in the garden and do not throb with joy."
(From the Imaginary Conversation between Leofric and Godiva)

****

I feel sure Landor would be content to be judged on his works – I rest my case!

As a final summary, the last two paragraphs in this book should, I feel, go to two people who knew Landor very well. Both of the writers of the following quotations were women and both were successful writers, albeit in different genres.

The first passage from a letter by Elizabeth Barrett Browning to her sister in 1859 tells us a huge amount about Landor and is amazingly perceptive.

"He has never led a dissipated life, never taken wine over much, & with regard to women, he has always had numerous flirtations & lovemakings, but always in the spiritual and sentimental way – Never but once in his life he told Robert had he sinned otherwise – I am afraid this is very peculiar among men of his time and stamp – The consequence is a sort of healthfulness of the senses & of the mind – innocent tastes, as for the society of young children, and for animals, & a power of enjoying life in quiet & solitude."

The second passage is my personal favourite and if I tried for the rest of my life, I do not think I could write such a marvellous description of such a wonderful man. It comes from a book of reminiscences entitled "My Literary Life" by Mrs Lynn Linton and seems to capture the essential vitality of Landor in a few sentences.

"… Walter Savage Landor was essentially heroic in both his virtues and his faults. No shabby, underhand insinuations for him, no skinflint meannesses, no slimy insincerity – fair to your face and foul behind your back – no treacherous letting you down when your foes assailed you, and a little kudos might be had by joining the cry. No! Faithful, upright, tender to the loving, loyal to the true, uncompromising as an enemy, and staunch to the death as a friend, he stands in the past of my life as one of the most honoured of all those I loved and honoured – as a very splendour of intellect and a rock of manly virtue combined."

13. A PERSONAL SELECTION OF SHORTER POEMS BY WALTER SAVAGE LANDOR
Twenty five Complete Poems with a Linking Explanation

Amazingly Landor's poetical career spanned nearly seventy-five years. He began in his mid-teens around 1790, yet his last lines were written only months before his death in 1864.

The first love of Landor's life was a girl named Nancy Jones whom he met in Tenby in 1793, when he was eighteen years old. In this poem, written after Nancy's death a few years later, Landor summarises his love-affair with "Ione" and he includes an emotive description of an embrace in a cave near Tenby.

> And thou too, Nancy! – why should Heaven remove
> Each tender object of mine early love?
> Why was I happy? O ye conscious rocks!
> Was I not happy? when Ione's locks
> Claspt round her neck and mine their golden chain,
> Ambition, fame, and fortune, smiled in vain.
> While warring winds with deaf'ning fury blew,
> Near and more near, our cheeks, our bosoms, grew.
> Wave after wave the lashing ocean chased,
> She smiled and prest me closer to her waist.
> "Suppose this cave should crush us," once I cried;
> "It cannot fall," the loving maid replied.
> "You, who are shorter, might be safe," I said;
> "O let us fly!" exclaim'd the simple maid.
> Springing, she drew me forward by the hand
> Upon the sunny and the solid sand,
> And then lookt round, with fearful doubt, to see
> If, what I spoke so seriously, could be.
> Ah memory, memory! thou alone canst save
> Angelic beauty from the grasping grave.
> And shall she perish? by yon stars I swear,

Here she shall live, though fate hath placed her there.
The sigh of soft surrender, and the kiss
For absence, doubt, obedience, merit this.
Let fears, let fame, the cancel'd vow suggest,
Love, to whose voice she listen'd, veils the rest.
Though Nancy's name for ever dwell unknown
Beyond her briar-bound sod and upright stone;
Yet, in the lover's, in the poet's eye,
The gentle young Ione ne'er shall die.

****

Between 1793 and 1804, Landor often stayed for lengthy periods in Swansea and other parts of South Wales, such as St Clears and Laugharne. He became very fond of this stretch of the coast and once declared that unspoilt Swansea Bay, before industrialisation, was the part of the world he liked better than any. The next three poems describe the coast near Swansea.

I wander o'er the sandy heath
Where the white rush waves high;
Where adders close before me wreath
And tawny kites sail screaming by.

Alone I wander! I alone
Could love to wander there!
"But wherefor?" – let my church-yard stone
Look toward Tawey and declare.

****

Along this coast I led the vacant Hours
To the lone sunshine on the uneven strand,
And nipt the stubborn grass and juicier flowers
With one unconscious inobservant hand,
While crept the other by degrees more near
Until it rose the cherisht form around,
And prest it closer, only that the ear
Might lean, and deeper drink some half-heard sound.

****

INTERLUDE

My guest! I have not led you thro'
The old footpath of swamp and sedges;
But … mind your step … you're coming to
Shingle and shells with sharpish edges.

Here a squash jelly-fish, and here
An old shark's head with open jaw
We hap may hit on: never fear
Scent rather rank and crooked saw.

Step forward: we shall pass them soon,
And then before you will arise
A fertile scene; a placid moon
Above, and star-besprinkled skies.

And we shall reach at last (where ends
The field of thistles, sharp and light)
A dozen brave and honest friends,
And there wish one and all good-night.

****

Landor wrote many poems to friends but some of his finest love poems were addressed to Ianthe, in reality an Irish girl named Jane Sophia Swift whom he met in Bath in 1803. Sadly Ianthe was not free to love him as she was already betrothed to a distant cousin and she returned to Ireland not long afterwards and was married. From time to time their paths crossed in later life and for over fifty years, Landor remained deeply in love with the amusing, dark-haired, violet-eyed Ianthe, even when she was a grandmother. The following group of poems tell this rather sad love story for Ianthe died thirteen years before Landor.

IANTHE'S TROUBLES

From you, Ianthe, little troubles pass
Like little ripples down a sunny river;
Your pleasures spring like daisies in the grass,
Cut down, and up again as blithe as ever.

****

Thou hast not rais'd, Ianthe, such desire
   In any breast as thou has rais'd in mine.
No wandering meteor now, no marshy fire,
   Leads on my steps, but lofty, but divine:
And, if thou chillest me, as chill thou dost
   When I approach too near, too boldly gaze,
So chills the blushing morn, so chills the host
   Of vernal stars, with light more chaste than day's.

****

She I love (alas in vain!)
Floats before my slumbering eyes:
When she comes she lulls my pain,
When she goes what pangs arise!
Thou whom love, whom memory flies,
Gentle Sleep! prolong thy reign!
If even thus she soothe my sighs,
Never let me wake again!

****

Soon , O Ianthe! life is o'er,
And sooner beauty's heavenly smile:
Grant only (and I ask no more)
Let love remain that little while.

****

Twenty years hence my eyes may grow
If not quite dim, yet rather so,
Still yours from others they shall know
      Twenty years hence.
Twenty years hence tho' it may hap
That I be call'd to take a nap
In a cool cell where thunder-clap
      Was never heard.
There breathe but o'er my arch of grass
A not too sadly sigh'd *Alas*,
And I shall catch, ere you can pass,
      That winged word.

****

Well I remember how you smiled
  To see me write your name upon
The soft sea sand … "Oh! what a child!
  You think you're writing upon stone!"
I have since written what no tide
  Shall ever wash away, what men
Unborn shall read o'er ocean wide
  And find Ianthe's name agen.

****

ON THE DEATH OF IANTHE

I dare not trust my pen it trembles so;
It seems to feel a portion of my woe,
And makes me credulous that trees and stones
At mournful fates have uttered mournful tones.
While I look back again on days long past,
How gladly would I yours might be my last.
Sad our first severence was, but sadder this,
When death forbids one hour of mutual bliss.

****

Although outwardly a very positive person, much given to loud laughter, a deep vein of melancholy often seems to underly some of Landor's poems. This next poem was written at Clifton on his sixty-second birthday in 1837. He had not long turned his back on his deeply-unhappy marriage, left his wife and children in Italy and returned to England to live alone in lodgings. He missed his daughter Julia in particular.

The day returns, my natal day,
  Borne on the storm and pale with snow,
And seems to ask me why I stay,
  Stricken by Time and bowed by Woe.

Many were once the friends who came
  To wish me joy; and there are some
Who wish it now; but not the same;
  They are whence friend can never come;

178

Nor are they you my love watcht o'er
Cradled in innocence and sleep;
You smile into my eyes no more,
Nor see the bitter tears they weep.

****

Many of Landor's poems sprang from past incidents in his own life
and this next poem describes how on a visit to Studley Church,
Warwickshire, he was reminded of his early friendship with the
beautiful Warwickshire heiress Dorothy Lyttelton. Sadly Dorothy
married someone else and died in 1811, when only thirty-six and
Landor is looking at her memorial tablet as he writes. However,the
picture which Landor paints of the two of them when teenagers,
sitting alone in the chancel playing silly games when reciting the
responses, is quite amusing.

ON THE DEAD

Yes, in this chancel once we sat alone,
O Dorothea! thou wert bright with youth,
Freshness like Morning's dwelt upon thy cheek,
While here and there above the level pews,
Above the housings of the village dames,
The musky fan its groves and zephyrs waved.
I know not why, since we had each our book
And lookt upon it steadfastly, first one
Outran the learned labourer from the desk,
Then tript the other, and limpt far behind,
And smiles gave blushes birth, and blushes smiles.
Ah me! where are they flown, my lovely friend!
Two seasons like that season thou hast lain
Cold as the dark-blue stone beneath my feet,
While my heart beats as then ... but not with joy!

O my lost friends! why were ye once so dear!
And why were ye not fewer, O ye few!
Must winter, spring, and summer, thus return,
Commemorating some one torne away,
Till half the months at last shall take, with me,
Their names from those upon your scatter'd graves!

****

For many years Landor was friendly with Mrs Paynter (the half sister of Rose Aylmer, commemorated in the famous poem on page 59) and he often used to write to her and her daughters Rose and Sophy. The next two brief verses come from Rose's album.

> Ah what happy days were those,
> When I walkt alone with Rose;
> They were days of purest gold,
> Days when mortals grow not old.

****

IGNORANCE OF BOTANY

> I hardly know one flower that grows
> On my small garden plot;
> Perhaps I may have seen a *Rose*
> And said, *Forget-me-not.*

****

This next poem remained unpublished until it was included in Forster's biography of Landor in 1869. Landor had many ideas about the reform of spelling and some words in this verse remind us of this.

AN OLD MAN AND A CHILD

> A child pickt up a pebble, of the least
> Among a myriad on a flat sea-shore;
> And tost it back again.
>   "What hast thou done?"
> Said mildy an old man.
>   "Nothing at all,"
> Replied the child; "it only was a pebble,
> And not worth carrying home, or looking at,
> Or wetting, tho' I did it, with my tongue:
> Tho' it was smooth, it was not large enough
> To copy on when I begin to write,
> Nor proper in the winter to strike fire from,
> Or puss to pat and roll along the floor."
>   Then said the elder:
>   "Thoughtful child art thou,
> And mightest have learnt from it some years hence
> What prouder wise ones never have attain'd.
> The wisest know not yet how many suns

Have bleacht that stone, how many waves have roll'd
Above it when upon its mountain's breast;
How once it was no stone nor hard, but lapt
Amid the tender herbage of the field."
   The child stared up, frighten'd; then ran away.
Before she had run far she turn'd her face
To look at that strange man.
              "He seem'd so calm,
He may not be quite mad nor mischievous.
I shall not mind him much another time;
But, O, what random stories old men tell!"

****

Let it not be thought that all Landor's poems are sad or solemn. All his life he had a keen sense of humour and he often collapsed into loud, infectious laughter. From his schooldays he was well known for writing witty epigrams similar to this well-known one about the hated Hanoverian kings.

THE GEORGES

George the First was always reckoned
Vile, but viler George the Second;
And what mortal ever heard
Any good of George the Third?
When from earth the Fourth descended
(God be praised!) the Georges ended!

****

Another amusing poem concerned the infamous Judge Page "the hanging judge" who died in 1741. Landor took great pleasure from finding exact words and rhythms and here he is clearly enjoying himself.

(JUDGE AND THIEF)

O'erfoaming with rage
The foul-mouth'd Judge Page
Thus question'd a thief in the dock:
"Didst never hear read
In the church, lump of lead!
Loose chip from the devil's own block!
'Thou shalt not steal?' " "Yea,"

181

The white chap did say,
" '*Thou* shalt not:' but *thou* was the word.
Had he piped out 'Jem Hewitt!
Be sure you don't do it,'
I'd ha' thought of it twice ere I did it, my lord."

****

In complete contrast Landor wrote a beautiful poem admiring John Keats and his poetry which was inserted in the Imaginary Conversation "Landor, English Visitor and Florentine Visitor".

Fair and free soul of poesy, O Keats!
O how my temples throb, my heart-blood beats,
    At every image, every word of thine!
Thy bosom, pierced by Envy, drops to rest;
Nor hearest thou the friendlier voice, nor seest
    The sun of fancy climb along thy line.

But under it, altho a viperous brood
That stung an Orpheus (in a clime more rude
    Than Rhodope and Hemus frown upon)
Still writhes and hisses, and peers out for more
Whose buoyant blood they leave concreted gore,
    Thy flowers root deep, and split the creviced stone.

Ill may I speculate on scenes to come,
Yet I would dream to meet thee at our home
    With Spenser's quiet, Chaucer's livelier ghost,
Cognate to thine … not higher, and less fair …
And Madalene and Isabella there
    Shall say, *without thee half our loves were lost.*

****

Landor was very proud that he hailed from the same county as Shakespeare and this little-known poem may have been written around 1847 when the restoration of Shakespeare's birthplace was under discussion. A keen fisherman, Landor loved the rivers of his native county, so perhaps it was natural that he wrote a poem about the birthplace of Shakespeare's river, instead of the half-timbered building in Henley Street, Stratford-upon-Avon.

TO THE RIVER AVON

Avon! why runnest thou away so fast?
Rest thee before that Chancel where repose
The bones of him whose spirit moves the world.
I have beheld thy birthplace, I have seen
Thy tiny ripples where they played amid
The golden cups and ever-waving blades.
I have seen mighty rivers, I have seen
Padus, recovered from his firy wound,
And Tiber, prouder than them all to bear
Upon his tawny bosom men who crusht
The world they trod on, heeding not the cries
Of culprit kings and nations many-tongued.
What are to me these rivers, once adorn'd
With crowns they would not wear but swept away?
Worthier art thou of worship, and I bend
My knees upon thy bank, and call thy name,
And hear, or think I hear, thy voice reply.

****

In many ways Landor was an ecologist years ahead of his time. He loved all animals and trees and thought that wherever possible plants should be allowed to grow undisturbed. A deep vein of Celtic-like spirituality seems to underly his work and a reverence for rivers, sunsets and other natural phenomena is often apparent.

Boastfully call we all the world our own:
What are we who should call it so? The form
Erect, the eye that pierces stars and suns,
Droop and decay; no beast so piteously.
More mutable than wind-worn leaves are we;
Yea, lower are we than the dust's estate;
The very dust is as it was before;
Dissever'd from ourselves, aliens and outcasts
From what our pride dared call inheritance,
We only live to feel our fall and die.

****

In the 1840s, Landor often stayed with Lady Blessington and Count Alfred D'Orsay in Gore House, Kensington. The house had a beautiful garden and Landor had his own favourite seat on the terrace, near two lilac trees. In this next very sad poem, he is saying that never again will they be able to meet for in early 1849 the house had to be sold to meet Lady Blessington's debts. The captive referred to here may be Prince Louis Napoleon who came straight to Gore House after escaping in 1846.

GORE HOUSE LEFT FOR PARIS

Under the lilacs we shall meet no more,
Nor Alfred's welcome hail me at the door,
Nor the brave guardian of the hall contend
In harsher voice to greet his trusty friend,
Nor on the banks of Arno or of Seine
Sure is my hope to bend my steps again;
But be it surer, Margarite, that Power
May stil remember many a festive hour,
More festive when we saw the captive free,
And clasp afresh the hand held forth by thee.

****

Sometimes Landor used one of his poems to convey public support for someone he admired. When the following literary compliment addressed to the relatively-unknown Robert Browning appeared in the Morning Chronicle newspaper on November 22nd 1845, it caused quite a stir. Both Browning and his future wife Elizabeth Barrett were delighted and it is said that Browning's father was so impressed with Landor's poem that he had it reprinted on a leaflet some weeks later.

TO ROBERT BROWNING

There is delight in singing, though none hear
Beside the singer; and there is delight
In praising, though the praiser sit alone
And see the prais'd far off him, far above.
Shakespeare is not our poet, but the world's,
Therefore on him no speech; and short for thee,
Browning! Since Chaucer was alive and hale,
No man hath walk'd along our roads with step

So active, so inquiring eye, or tongue
So varied in discourse. But warmer climes
Give brighter plumage, stronger wing; the breeze
Of Alpine heights thou playest with, borne on
Beyond Sorrento and Amalfi, where
The Siren waits thee, singing song for song.

****

Unlike many of his contemporaries, all his life Landor was an ardent republican and he greatly admired Oliver Cromwell and the rule of the Commonwealth. He also admired foreign republics and he felt that he had much in common with Americans. Even during his life-time, Landor's works were said to be more popular in America than in Britain and in this poem (unpublished until well after his death) he summarises his support for Garibaldi in Italy and republicanism in general.

TO AMERICA, ON ITALY

My eyes first saw the light upon the day
It dawn'd on thee, but shone not brightly yet,
America! and the first shout I heard
Of a mad crowd, around a madder king,
Was shout for glorious victory, for blood
Of brethren shed by brethren.
                   Few the years
Before I threw my cricket bat along
The beaten turf to catch the song of France
For freedom – ah poor slave! free one short hour.
Glorious her women: will she ever bear
A man, whom God shall raise so near Himself
As Roland, Corday, and the Maid of Arc,
Deliverer of her country, vanquisher
Of her most valient chiefs, enraged to see
The captive lilies droop above the Seine?
   America! proud as thou well mayst be
Both of thy deeds and thy progenitors,
Thy hero, Washington, stands not alone;
Cromwell was his precurser, he led forth
Our sires from bondage, Truth's evangelist,
And trod down, right and left, two hostile creeds.

185

Brothers of thine are we, America!
Now comes a sister, too long held apart.
Lo! Italy hath snapt her double chain,
And Garibaldi sounds from shore to shore.

****

In 1858, at the age of eighty three, Landor was forced to flee to Italy because of a libel action and he returned again to the family villa near Florence. He had hoped that his wife and family would welcome him, but instead his eldest son Arnold, to whom much of the family property had already been transferred, treated his father very shabbily. Landor felt himself to be in a similar situation to King Lear.

INGRATITUDE

Can this be he whom in his infancy,
Hour after hour, I carried in my arms,
When neither nurse nor mother could appease
The froward wailing?
                Thus went on two years;
I laid the burden softly in its crib,
And hardly dared to kiss it lest it wake.
  For whom were planted on thy grassy slopes
Lantony, larch and oak, mile after mile,
Guarded from rapine and now lifting high
These their stout arms, and those their slender spires?
By whom, ancestral Ipsley, were thy groves
Held sacred? at whose hand rose cypresses
Beyond the solitary cedar twins,
(Now fifty winters old) and spreading wide
Their hospitable arms.
  Tender are aged feet; in vain I plead
For one smooth walk, where gravel stones are sharp
Aside the villa by my care adorn'd,
With ancient marbles, and with Salvator's scenes
And Raffael's and Correggio's forms divine
I plead in vain even for the books I wrote,
And for those dearer given me by my friends,
Some distant, and some dead: beloved the more,
Nor undervalued those from men whose names
I hope my own may live with, years to come.

All, all I gave; and what is the return?
Not even a bell-rope at my sick-bed-side.
   O thou of largest, wisest, tenderest heart,
Truly thou sayest that a serpent's tooth
Wounds not so sharply as a thankless child.

****

This small collection of Landor's poems could not end without the quatrain which today is most famous of all. It was written in the evening of his 74th birthday January 30th 1849, not long after Charles Dickens and John Forster had left for London on the night train. The following morning Landor sent this note and poem to John Forster.

"My thanks were not spoken to you and Dickens for your journey of two hundred miles on my birthday. Here they are – not visible on the surface of the paper, nor on any surface whatever, but in the heart that is dictating this letter. On the night you left me I wrote the following, which you may insert or not in the Examiner."

DYING SPEECH OF AN OLD PHILOSOPHER

I strove with none, for none was worth my strife:
   Nature I loved, and next to Nature, Art:
I warm'd both hands before the fire of Life;
   It sinks; and I am ready to depart.

****

(Other complete poems can be found on pages 33, 50, 52, 59, 91, 112, 172)

14. SELECTIONS FROM THE PROSE OF WALTER SAVAGE LANDOR

1) THE IMAGINARY CONVERSATIONS

Athough many consider Walter Savage Landor's poetry to be more worthy of praise, it was his prose, in particular the five volumes of "Imaginary Conversations" which first brought him to the notice of the general public. He considered his prose to be of greater value for he wrote "*Poetry was always my amusement; prose my study and business*".

The following Imaginary Conversation was said to be Landor's own favourite. At the end of it, he attached an emotive note concerning his boyhood, which makes it doubly interesting.

Landor was fascinated by the old legend of Leofric and his young wife Lady Godiva who allegedly rode naked through the streets of Coventry in an effort to persuade her medieval lord to relieve the poor people of the unreasonable taxes to which they were subjected. As he often did, Landor chooses to describe the day before a great event took place and here Lady Godiva knows exactly what she must do the following day.

LEOFRIC AND GODIVA
(Imaginary Conversations 1829)

GODIVA. There is a dearth in the land, my sweet Leofric! Remember how many weeks of drought we have had, even in the deep pastures of Leicestershire; and how many Sundays we have heard the same prayers for rain, and supplications that it would please the Lord in his mercy to turn aside his anger from the poor pining cattle. You, my dear husband, have imprisoned more than one malefactor for leaving his dead ox in the public way; and other hinds have fled before you out of the traces, in which they and their sons and daughters, and haply their old fathers and mothers, were dragging the abandoned wain homeward. Although we were accompanied by many brave spearmen and skilful archers, it was perilous to pass the creatures which the farm-yard dogs, driven from

188

the hearth by the poverty of their masters, were tearing and devouring; while others, bitten and lamed, filled the air either with long and deep howls or sharp and quick barkings, as they struggled with hunger and feebleness or were exasperated by heat and pain. Nor could the thyme from the heath, nor the bruised branches of the fir-tree, extinquish or abate the foul odour.

LEOFRIC. And now, Godiva, my darling, thou art afraid we should be eaten up before we enter the gates of Coventry; or perchance that in the gardens there are no roses to greet thee, no sweet herbs for thy mat and pillow.

GODIVA. Leofric, I have no such fears. This is the month of roses: I find them everywhere since my blessed marriage: they, and all other sweet herbs, I know not why, seem to greet me wherever I look at them as though they knew and expected me. Surely they can not feel that I am fond of them.

LEOFRIC. O light laughing simpleton! But what wouldst thou? I came not hither to pray; and yet if praying would satisfy thee, or remove the drought, I would ride up straightway to St Michael's and pray until morning.

GODIVA. I would do the same, O Leofric! but God hath turned away his ear from holier lips than mine. Would my own dear husband hear me, if I implored him for what is easier to accomplish? what he can do like God.

LEOFRIC. How! what is it?

GODIVA. I would not, in the first hurry of your wrath, appeal to you, my loving lord, in behalf of these unhappy men who have offended you.

LEOFRIC. Unhappy! is that all?

GODIVA. Unhappy they must surely be, to have offended you so grievously. What a soft air breathes over us! how quiet and serene and still an evening! how calm are the heavens and the earth! shall none enjoy them? not even we, my Leofric! The sun is ready to set: let it never set O Leofric, on your anger. These are not my words; they are better than mine; should they lose their virtue from my unworthiness in uttering them!

LEOFRIC. Godiva, wouldst thou plead to me for rebels?

GODIVA. They have then drawn the sword against you! Indeed I knew it not.

LEOFRIC. They have omitted to send me my dues, established by my ancestors, well knowing of our nuptials, and of the charges and festivities they require, and that in a season of such scarcity my own lands are insufficient.

GODIVA. If they were starving as they said they were ...

LEOFRIC. Must I starve too? Is it not enough to lose my vassals?

GODIVA. Enough! O God! too much! too much! may you never lose them! Give them life, peace, comfort, contentment. There are those among them who kissed me in my infancy, and who blessed me at the baptismal font. Leofric, Leofric! the first old man I meet I shall think is one of those; and I shall think on the blessing he gave, and (ah me!) on the blessing I bring back to him. My heart will bleed, will burst ... and he will weep at it! he will weep, poor soul! for the wife of a cruel lord who denounces vengeance on him, who carries death into his family.

LEOFRIC. We must hold solemn festivals.

GODIVA. We must indeed.

LEOFRIC. Well then.

GODIVA. Is the clamorousness that succeeds the death of God's dumb creatures, are crowded halls, are slaughtered cattle, festivals? are maddening songs and giddy dances, and hireling praises from parti-coloured coats? Can the voice of a minstrel tell us better things of ourselves than our internal one might tell us; or can his breath make our breath softer in sleep? O my beloved! let everything be a joyance to us: it will, if we will. Sad is the day, and worse must follow, when we hear the blackbird in the garden and do not throb with joy. But, Leofric, the high festival is strown by the servant of God upon the heart of man. It is gladness, it is thanksgiving; it is the orphan, the starveling, pressed to the bosom, and bidden as its first commandment to remember its benefactor. We will hold this festival; the guests are ready: we may keep it up for weeks, and months, and years together and always be the happier and the richer for it. The beverage of this feast, O Leofric, is sweeter than bee or flower or vine can give us: it flows from heaven; and in heaven will it abundantly be poured out again, to him who pours it out here unsparingly.

LEOFRIC. Thou art wild.

GODIVA. I have indeed lost myself. Some Power, some good kind Power, melts me (body and soul and voice) into tenderness and love. O my husband, we must obey it. Look upon me! look upon me! lift your sweet eyes from the ground! I will not cease to supplicate; I dare not.

LEOFRIC. We may think upon it.

GODIVA. Never say that! What! think upon goodness when you can be good ? Let not the infants cry for sustenance! The mother of our blessed Lord will hear them; us never, never afterward.

LEOFRIC. Here comes the bishop: we are but one mile from the walls. Why dismountest thou? no bishop can expect it. Godiva! my honour and rank among men are humbled by this: Earl Godwin will hear of it: up! up! the bishop hath seen it: he urgeth his horse onward: dost thou not hear him now upon the solid turf behind thee?

GODIVA. Never, no, never will I rise, O Leofric, until you remit this most impious tax, this tax on hard labour, on hard life.

LEOFRIC. Turn round: look how the fat nag canters, as to the tune of a sinner's psalm, slow and hard breathing. What reason or right can the people have to complain, while their bishop's steed is so sleek and well caparisoned? Inclination to change, desire to abolish old usages ... Up! up! for shame! They shall smart for it, idlers! Sir bishop, I must blush for my young bride.

GODIVA. My husband, my husband! will you pardon the city?

LEOFRIC. Sir bishop! I could not think you would have seen her in this plight. Will I pardon? yea, Godiva, by the holy rood, will I pardon the city, when thou ridest naked at noontide through the streets.

GODIVA. O my dear cruel Leofric, where is the heart you gave me! It was not so! can mine have hardened it?

BISHOP. Earl, thou abashest thy spouse; she turneth pale and weepeth. Lady Godiva, peace be with thee.

GODIVA. Thanks, holy man! peace will be with me when peace is with your city. Did you hear my lord's cruel word?

BISHOP. I did, lady.

GODIVA. Will you remember it, and pray against it?

BISHOP. Wilt thou forget it, daughter?

GODIVA. I am not offended.

BISHOP. Angel of peace and purity!

GODIVA. But treasure it up in your heart: deem it an incense, good only when it is consumed and spent, ascending with prayer and sacrifice. And now what was it?

BISHOP. Christ save us! that he will pardon the city when thou ridest naked through the streets at noon.

GODIVA. Did he not swear an oath?

BISHOP. He sware by the holy rood.

GODIVA. My Redeemer! thou hast heard it! save the city!

LEOFRIC. We are now upon the beginning of the pavement: these are the suburbs: let us think of feasting: we may pray afterward: tomorrow we shall rest.

GODIVA. No judgements then tomorrow, Leofric?

LEOFRIC. None: we will carouse.

GODIVA. The saints of heaven have given me strength and confidence: my prayers are heard: the heart of my beloved is now softened.

LEOFRIC. (aside) Ay, ay ... they shall smart though.

GODIVA. Say, dearest Leofric, is there indeed no other hope, no other meditation?

LEOFRIC. I have sworn: beside, thou hast made me redden and turn my face way from thee, and all the knaves have seen it: this adds to the city's crime.

GODIVA. I have blushed too, Leofric, and was not rash nor obdurate.

LEOFRIC. But thou, my sweetest, art given to blushing; there is no conquering it in thee. I wish thou hadst not alighted so hastily and roughly: it hath shaken down a sheaf of thy hair: take heed thou sit not upon it, lest it anguish thee. Well done! it mingleth now sweetly with the cloth of gold upon the saddle, running here and there, as if it had life and faculties and business, and were working thereupon some newer and cunninger device. O my beauteous Eve! there is a Paradise about thee! the world is refreshed as thou movest and breathest on it. I cannot see or think of evil where thou art. I could throw my arms even here about thee. No signs for me! no shaking of sunbeams! no reproof or frown or wonderment ... I will say it... now then for worse ... I could close with my kisses thy half-open lips, ay, and those lovely and loving eyes, before the people.

GODIVA. Tomorrow you shall kiss me, and they shall bless you for it. I shall be very pale, for tonight I must fast and pray.

LEOFRIC. I do not hear thee; the voices of the folk are so loud under this archway.

GODIVA. (to herself) God help them! good kind souls! I hope they will not crowd about me so tomorrow. O Leofric! could my name be forgotten! and yours alone remembered! But perhaps my innocence may save me from reproach! and how many as innocent are in fear and famine! No eye will open on me but fresh from tears. What a young mother for so large a family! Shall my youth harm me! Under

God's hand it gives me courage. Ah, when will the morning come! ah, when will the noon be over!

Note by Landor

The story of Godiva, at one of whose festivals or fairs I was present in my boyhood, has always much interested me; and I wrote a poem on it, sitting I remember, by the square pool at Rugby. When I showed it to the friend in whom I had most confidence, he began to scoff at the subject; and on his reaching the last line his laughter was loud and immoderate. This conversation has brought both laughter and stanza back to me, and the earnestness with which I entreated and implored my friend not to tell the lads; so heart-strickenly and desperately was I ashamed. The verses are these, if any one else should wish another laugh at me:

> *In every hour, in every mood,*
> *O lady, it is sweet and good*
> *To bathe the soul in prayer,*
> *And, at the close of such a day,*
> *When we have ceased to bless and pray,*
> *To dream on thy long hair.*

May the peppermint be still growing on the bank in that place!

2) BRIEF QUOTATIONS

Many of Landor's longer prose works contain short, memorable sentences which convey a universal truth or philosophical idea. The following selection is from "A Day-Book of Walter Savage Landor", chosen by John Bailey and published in 1919 by Oxford University Press.

... old trees in their living state are the only things that money cannot command."

Imaginary Conversation between Marchese Pallavicini and Walter Landor

****

Clear writers, like clear fountains, do not seem so deep as they are: the turbid look the most profound.

Imaginary Conversation between Southey and Porson.

****

Love always makes us better, Religion sometimes, Power never.
Pericles and Aspasia

****

Study is the bane of boyhood, the aliment of youth, the indulgence of manhood, and the restorative of old age.
Pericles and Aspasia

****

North America may one day be very rich and powerful; she cannot be otherwise: but she never will gratify the imagination as Europe does.
Imaginary Conversation between William Penn and Lord Peterborough

****

Man is a hater of truth, a lover of fiction.
Imaginary Conversation between Epicurus, Leontion, and Ternissa.

****

There are folks who, when they read my criticism, say, 'I do not think so.' It is because they do not think so, that I write.
Imaginary Conversation between Southey and Porson

****

Of the future we know nothing, of the past little, of the present less; the mirror is too close to our eyes, and our own breath dims it.
Pericles and Aspasia

****

(speaking of Chaucer) *Among the English poets, both on this side and the other side of Milton, I place him next to Shakespeare; but the word 'next' must have nothing to do with the word 'near'.*
Imaginary Conversation between Southey and Porson

****

We fancy we suffer from ingratitude, while in reality we suffer from self-love.
Imaginary Conversation between Epicurus, Leontion and Ternissa

****

194

I hate false words, and seek with care, difficulty and moroseness, those that fit the thing.

Note to Imaginary Conversation between Bishop Burnet and Humphrey Hardcastle.

3) QUOTATIONS FROM PUBLIC LETTERS

As one might expect, Landor wrote numerous public letters, many of which appeared in 'The Examiner' newspaper, which was edited from 1847 to 1856 by John Forster, a great friend.

In mid 1847 the house in which Shakespeare was born was offered for sale and two interesting letters by Landor dealt with this subject.

SHAKESPEARE'S HOUSE

I am now writing to you on the very day and in the very town in which the Archaeological Society is assembled. My habits of life withhold me from crowded parties and from long speeches; therefore I would rather make my solitary and silent appeal through the Examiner. The report has long been prevalent, and uncontradicted, that the house in which Shakespeare was born is offered for sale. A letter of Lord Morpath has avowed the fact, and that government has declined to be the purchaser. Are our rulers aware of the ignominy that will pursue them for their indifference to the best poet and wisest man, whom not only England but God's whole world has produced? Are they aware that the reign of Victoria will thus be rendered by them inglorious and disgraceful in our annals? While many thousands of pounds are expended in the installation of a royal chancellor at Cambridge, two thousand are refused by the learned and the royal to preserve the most memorable edifice that exists on earth. This edifice contained that illustrious cradle near which all human learning shines faintly, and where lay that infant who was destined to glorify and exalt our greatest kings. And this was among the least of his labors ...

The impassioned letter ends,

... If the crown and parliament are so insensible to disgrace, if the English people at large are so ungrateful to the teacher of whom they have been boasting all their lives, let me exhort and implore his more immediate neighbours to protect his deserted mansion.

Landor's second letter on this subject to the Examiner a short time later is in many ways a classic for in it he gives a superb answer to the perennial question. The last sentence might still serve, over 150 years later to silence the numerous critics who still refer to Shakespeare's "Alleged" Birth-place!

In the Examiner of August 7th I find an interesting letter, and personally to me a very courteous one, from the Rev. Geo. Wilkins, of Wix, near Manningtree. It gives me the information that the house in which Shakespeare was born is no better known than Homer's. Mr Wilkins is so obliging as to promise that he will "look up" a publication of his, in which the proofs of deception on this subject are manifest. It appears, that the house in question was occupied by Shakespeare's father, in the poet's boyhood. The fact is curious, that, in all countries, the birth-place of of an illustrious man is more sought after than the country of his education, or of his writings, or of his exploits. If this in reality is not the house in which the unbaptised infant uttered his first cries, nevertheless it appears to be the very place in which his first ideas germinated: if it was not the birth-place of the child, it was the birth-place of the poet ...

****

In 1853 when it was proposed to build a new National Gallery, Landor wrote to 'The Examiner' with an unusual suggestion.

We are about to build another national picture gallery; to expend nearly a hundred thousand pounds in purchasing the land around it; and perhaps the double of that amount in the edifice itself. The situation is not such as will very long exempt it from the effect of smoke and many other annoyances. We may be sure that houses of all descriptions will cluster and inclose it. For a tenth of the money the palace of Kensington, obnoxious to no such inconvenience, might be converted to the same purpose. Little more would be necessary than to replace the roof by one similar to that of the Louvre; to remove the partitions and floors; to divide it into seven or eight compartments, and to decorate the exterior with pilasters ...

The letter ended with a handsome tribute to Gladstone.

Integrity is for once united with sagacity in a Chancellor of the Exchequer; and we may confidently hope from Mr Gladstone what we should vainly have expected from any of his predecessors.

****

A letter of Landor's entitled "European Revolutions" appearing in 'The Examiner' of November 18th 1848 began with a statement which might serve as a summary of his political views. It is a truly majestic piece of prose.

In my views on politics I have given offence to many good and sensible men. Perhaps I may be erroneous in some of my opinions, but is it quite certain that they themselves are exempt from fallibility in all of theirs? Permit me to ask whether they have given proofs to the world of more research, more intellect, more information, more independence. I come forward not to offend, but to conduct; not to quarrel, but to teach; and I would rather make one man wiser than ten thousand friendly to me; yet I profess no indifference to the favourable opinion of those writers who influence the public judgment ...

... Dependent on no party, influenced by none, abstaining from the society and conversation of the few public men I happen to be acquainted with, for no other reason than because they are in power and office, I shall continue, so long as I live, to notice the politics and politicians which may promote or impede the public welfare ...

4) QUOTATIONS FROM PRIVATE LETTERS

During his long life, Landor wrote thousands of private letters, yet these were also carefully constructed and bore the unmistakeable Landor talent for clear expression.

A letter Landor wrote to Miss Rose Paynter in 1843 puts forward a classic case against shoooting and blood sports.

... You did right in not killing the grouse. Let men do these things if they will. Perhaps there is no harm in it – perhaps it makes them no crueller than they would be otherwise. But it is hard to take away what we cannot give – and life is a pleasant thing – at least to birds. No doubt the young ones say tender things to one another, and even the old ones do not dream of death ...

****

Landor loved dogs but in this letter to Miss Rose Paynter in 1839 he describes how he was attacked by one. However he still defended the animal and as always spoke of the dog as if he was human.

... In the courtyard was a magnificent black Newfoundland dog. No sooner had I entered the gate than, before I could deliver my credentials, or make the sign of dog-freemasonary, he seized my leg. A swinging box on the ear was opposed to this manoeuvre. My Newfoundlander had what the boxers (not very elegantly) call 'pluck'. He renewed the attack, despite some severe appellations and admirable parasol-thrusts of Miss Boyle. However she conquered him – for neither my box on the ear, nor a kick at the second round, which sent him upon his back, made him give in. We were pretty good friends at last, although I told him I should trouble him, at his leisure, just to look over a certain article in my tailor's bill, which might as well be transferred to his account ..."

****

A second passage concerning dogs came from a letter to the journalist Henry Crabb Robinson in 1836.

… Somebody told me that your illustrious friend Goethe hated dogs. God forgive him, if he did. I never can believe it of him. They too are half poets; they are dreamers. Do any other animals dream? For my part as you know I love them heartily. They are grateful, they are brave, they are communicative, and they never play at cards …

****

In a letter to Rose Paynter (by now Mrs Graves Sawle) Landor gives a description of a perfomance of Jenny Lind, the legendary Swedish opera singer. Landor, who was passionately fond of opera wrote on July 5th 1847,

… How often, or rather how perpetually I asked for your presence at the opera when Jenny Lind was singing … Her acting was infinitely beyond any I conceived to be possible. One night when she performed in Sonambula, I had the good fortune to occupy a front seat in the Russsian Minister's box just over the stage. Sometimes Jenny Lind came within four paces of me ….

****

Many of Landor's letters contain lively descriptions of his visits to friends. On January 15th 1839 Landor sent a letter to Lady Blessington describing a visit to Francis Hare.

… I have been in Berkshire for four days on a visit to Hare, who insisted on my keeping his birthday. He is residing at West Woodhay House, built by Inigo Jones. It would do passably well for Naples, better for Timbuctoo. All but my victuals were congealed. I almost envied the bed of Procrustes, so enormous was mine, such a frozen sea. A company of comedians might have acted in it any piece they chose, and there would have been ample room for prompter and orchestra. I was ready to say my prayers when I was delivered from it.

****

In 1998 I was lucky enough to purchase two original letters by Landor and since both are very short, I thought readers would like to be made aware of them. The first letter is undated, but it contains a marvellous comment concerning poetry. (A photograph of this letter appears on page XXVII.)

> *Bath*
> *Sunday Eve*
>
> *Dear Sir,*
>   *Altho I never lost a child, I could not read without tears the beautiful lines on yours. Never did purer poetry spring from the human heart and it is in the heart that lies the deep well of poetry.*
>   *To be thought worthy of such a sympathy is the highest honor that can be conferred on*
>
>   *W.S. Landor*

The second note is more prosaic but nevertheless tells quite a lot about Landor and his habits.

> *My dear Sir,*
>   *Knowing the value and importance of whatever Mrs Hal(ron?) writes, I deeply regret that I did not return the note in question. Most unhappily I replaced it in your letter, which with all the others of the week, was committed to the fire.*
>
>   *Very truly yours*
>   *W.S. Landor*
>   *Bath Jan 8.57*

****

Apart from the two short letters, in July 1999 I was delighted to be able to acquire an undated fragment of a manuscript by Landor. It mentions Warwick and Birmingham besides referring to Shakespeare and readers who like a puzzle, may well find it interesting.

   … James Graham: but fourscore in that quarter are less wonderful than a single one in Sir J. Packington. The town of Birmingham, where so many zealous and intelligent men have come forward on this momentous occasion, feels its present force but has hardly any notion of its future importance. The time must come (God grant that it may be distant) when England once more will be invaded. Engineers however late, will discover that Warwick an outwork of Birmingham may be rendered as strong as Lisle or Ales-sandria. Two rivers and two works are ready. Birmingham must be the great arsenal of the Empire and Warwickshire will not for ever be contented with her one great genius, altho' the greatest that the universe has produced. The industrial Arts will work together with the intellectual and the patriot will lift up his hand even in presence of the poet.

199

I believe this manuscript may date from around 1851. Landor supported the revolutionary movement in Hungary in 1848 and wrote much in praise of Kossuth, the revolution's leader. Kossuth visited England in the autumn of 1851 and a banquet was given in his honour in Birmingham on November 12th 1851. Landor became an increasingly frequent correspondent with the leaders of the workingmen's movement in Birmingham and the fragment quoted here may be a portion of such a letter.

****

The final example is from a letter written when Landor was 83, not long after he had arrived back in Fiesole in 1858. Landor felt that his old friend Lord Normanby who lived nearby had slighted him and being hurt and angry he dashed off a note. The trivial circumstances of the misunderstanding soon became forgotten, but the last three sentences of the superbly worded-letter linger in the memory and illustrate Landor's prose at its best.

... *We are both of us old men, my Lord, and verging on decrepitude and imbecility, else my note might be more energetic. Do not imagine I am unobservant of distinctions. You, by the favour of a Minister, are Marquis of Normanby; I by the grace of God am Walter Savage Landor.*

BIBLIOGRAPHY

Documents
The bulk of my research was conducted in Warwickshire County Record Office, Warwick where I consulted numerous documents from the Landor Papers (ref CR931 and CR1908).

Published Sources
I owe a great debt to the late R.H. Super for "WALTER SAVAGE LANDOR" (London: John Calder, 1957). Time and time again R.H. Super's thorough notes have pointed me in the right direction. "LANDOR A REPLEVIN" by Malcolm Elwin (London: Macdonald & Co, 1958) has also been invaluable.

It would be impossible for me to list all the printed material I have used in my research. The books listed here are those which other readers who desire to know more about Landor and his period might find useful. They do not appear in any particular order, but instead are grouped together according to the subject.

THE COMPLETE WORKS OF WALTER SAVAGE LANDOR, ed. T. Earle Welby (Prose, Vols 1 to 12) and Stephen Wheeler (Poems, Vols 13 to 16). 16 volumes, London: Chapman and Hall Ltd, 1927–1936. (I used the 1969 edition by Barnes and Noble, Inc., New York which was manufactured in the United States of America.)
WALTER SAVAGE LANDOR A biography by John Forster. 2 vols, London: Chapman and Hall 1869.
THE WORKS AND LIFE OF WALTER SAVAGE LANDOR by John Forster. 1876.
LANDOR by Sidney Colvin. London: Macmillan and Co, 1881.
LETTERS AND OTHER UNPUBLISHED WRITINGS OF WALTER SAVAGE LANDOR ed. Stephen Wheeler, London 1897
LETTERS OF WALTER SAVAGE LANDOR, PRIVATE AND PUBLIC ed. Stephen Wheeler. London: Duckworth and Company 1899
LANDOR, POETRY AND PROSE. Introduced by E.K. Chambers. Clarendon Press: Oxford University Press 1946.

WALTER SAVAGE LANDOR, LAST DAYS, LETTERS AND CONVERSATIONS by H.C. Minchin. London: Methuen and Company 1934.
MY LITERARY LIFE by Eliza Lynn Linton. London, Hodder and Stoughton. 1899.
MRS LYNN LINTON, HER LIFE, LETTERS, AND OPINIONS by George Somes Layard. London: Methuen and Company 1901.
THE LITERARY LIFE AND CORRESPONDENCE OF THE COUNTESS OF BLESSINGTON by Richard Robert Madden. 3 vols, 2nd edition. London 1855.
THE LETTERS OF ELIZABETH BARRETT BROWNING Edited F.G. Kenyon 2 vols. London 1897.
ROBERT EYRES LANDOR, A BIOGRAPHICAL AND CRITICAL SKETCH by Eric Partidge. London: The Franfolico Press 1927.(Also Books for Libraries Press, Freeport, New York 1970)
HISTORIC HOUSES IN BATH AND THEIR ASSOCIATIONS by R.E. Peach. 2 vols, London and Bath 1883–1884.
EVERYWHERE, AN AUTOBIOGRAPHY by A.H.Savage Landor. London: T. Fisher Unwin Ltd, 1924.
RUGBY, THE SCHOOL AND NEIGHBOURHOOD by M. H. Bloxham. London: Whittaker and Co. 1889.
A HISTORY OF RUGBY SCHOOL by W. H. D. Rouse. London: Duckworth and Co. 1898.
BATH CELEBRITIES AND FRAGMENTS OF LOCAL HISTORY by Jerom Murch. London (Isaac Pitman and Sons) Bath (William Lewis and Son) 1893.
THE ANTIQUITIES OF LAUGHARNE by Mary Curtis. London 1880.
THE BRIGHTON OF WALES by David Boorman. Swansea Little Theatre Company 1986.
SWANSEA BEFORE INDUSTRY Vol 1 by Gerald Gabb. Swansea Museums Service 1991.
THE STORY OF THE VILLAGE OF MUMBLES by Gerald Gabb. D. Browne and Sons & the Ostreme Community Association, Mumbles 1986.
THOMAS ROTHWELL, VIEWS OF SWANSEA IN THE 1790s by Michael Gibbs and Bernard Morris. Glamorgan Archives 1991.
EARLY PROSE WRITINGS by Dylan Thomas. London: J.M. Dent and Sons Ltd. 1971.

FAIR AND FASHIONABLE TENBY by John Tipton. Tenby Museum 1987.
CHARLES NORRIS AND HIS LEGACY TO TENBY by John Tipton. 1997.
OLD LONDON (BELGRAVIA, CHELSEA AND KENSINGTON) by Edward Walford. Published pre 1897 (Reprinted London: The Village Press Ltd 1989)
THE HISTORY OF KNOWLE by Eva Wootton. The Roundwood Press 1972.
DR WILLIAM LAMBE by H. Saxe Wydham. London Vegetarian Soc. 1941.
VICTORIA COUNTY HISTORY OF WARWICKSHIRE Volumes 3,4,5,6 and 8.
DR PARR, A PORTRAIT OF THE WHIG DR JOHNSON by Warren Derry. Clarendon Press: Oxford University Press 1966.

Local Newspapers.
Warwick (County Record Office) THE WARWICK ADVERTISER, LEAMINGTON SPA COURIER
Swansea (Reference Library) THE CAMBRIAN
Bath(Reference Library) BATH CHRONICLE, BATH EXPRESS, BATH HERALD

Whilst I felt it inappropriate to burden this book with notes, fully annotated copies are deposited with Warwickshire County Record Office, Priory Park, Warwick CV34 4JS and also with Warwick Library, Barrack Street, Warwick CV34 4TH

INDEX

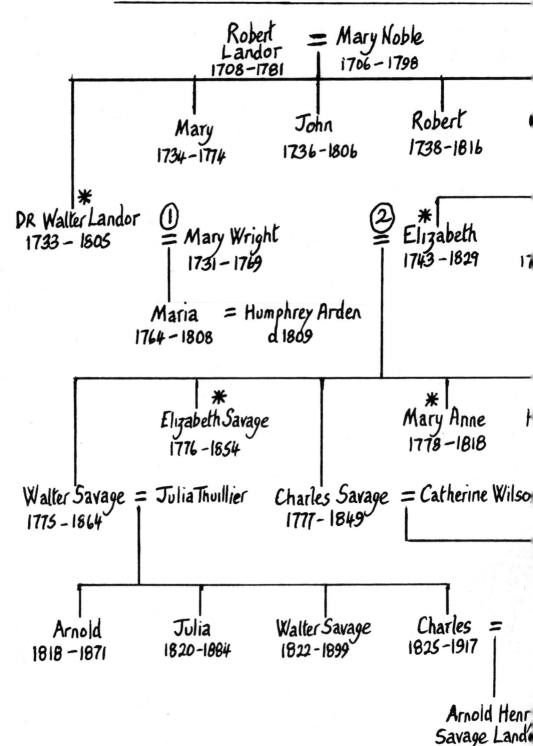

THE LANDOR FAM.

Robert Landor 1708–1781 = Mary Noble 1706–1798

Mary 1734–1774

John 1736–1806

Robert 1738–1816

＊ DR Walter Landor 1733–1805

① = Mary Wright 1731–1769

② ＊ Elizabeth 1743–1829

Maria 1764–1808 = Humphrey Arden d 1809

＊ Elizabeth Savage 1776–1854

＊ Mary Anne 1778–1818

Walter Savage 1775–1864 = Julia Thuillier

Charles Savage 1777–1849 = Catherine Wilso

Arnold 1818–1871

Julia 1820–1884

Walter Savage 1822–1899

Charles 1825–1917 =

Arnold Henr Savage Land 1865–1924